SOMETHING TO CELEBRATE

VALUING FAMILIES
IN CHURCH AND SOCIETY

SOMETHING TO CELEBRATE

VALUING FAMILIES
IN CHURCH AND SOCIETY

The report of a Working Party

of the

Board for Social Responsibility

CHURCH HOUSE PUBLISHING
Church House, Great Smith Street, London SW1P 3NZ

ISBN 0 7151 6579 8
GS 1153

Published 1995 for the General Synod Board for Social Responsibility by Church House Publishing

The publishers wish to express their thanks to the following for permission to reproduce copyright material:
pp. 32, 33, 36, 37: Source: *Social Trends 1995*. Central Statistical Office. Crown Copyright 1995. Reproduced by permission of the Controller of HMSO and the Central Statistical Office.
p. 38: Source: *Population Trends 78* 'Estimated numbers of one-parent families and their prevalence in Great Britain'. Crown Copyright. Reproduced by permission of the Office of Population Censuses and Surveys.

This report has only the authority of the Board by which it was prepared

Cover design by Leigh Hurlock
Printed in England by The Cromwell Press, Melksham, Wiltshire

Contents

Acknowledgements

Our warm thanks go to the many individuals and groups who responded with such openness to our consultation document on the future of the family. All their views were carefully considered. To respect their privacy we have not listed them by name.

We also wish to acknowledge the people who generously gave their time with expert advice or comments on drafts as our work progressed. Particular thanks go to members of the Board for Social Responsibility's Social Policy Committee, Canon David Atkinson from Southwark Cathedral, Richard Best from the Joseph Rowntree Foundation, Joan Brown, Revd David Gamble from the Methodist Church Division of Education and Youth, Ceridwen Roberts from the Family Policy Studies Centre, Hannah Ward and Jennifer Wild. They are not, however, responsible for the way in which we may have made use of the advice which they kindly offered.

A summary of this report is available from the Board for Social Responsibility, Church House, Great Smith Street, London SW1P 3NZ. A study guide will be available in autumn 1995 and further details of this can be obtained from Church House.

Members of the Working Party

The Rt. Revd Alan Morgan (chairman)

Bishop of Sherwood

The Revd Dr Stephen Barton

Lecturer in New Testament Studies, Department of Theology, University of Durham

Dr Anne Borrowdale

Freelance trainer and writer, former Oxford Diocesan Officer for Social Responsibility

Professor Jonathan Bradshaw

Professor of Social Policy and Social Work, University of York

Ms Elisabeth Dodds

Principal Training Officer, the Nugent Care Society, Liverpool

Mrs Jennifer Jenkins

Solicitor, former Manager of the Family Law Team, the Law Commission

The Revd Ermal Kirby (serving as ecumenical consultant)

Co-ordinating Secretary for Public Affairs, the Council of Churches for Britain and Ireland

Ms Christine McMullen

National Co-ordinator of the Family Life and Marriage Education Network, Member of General Synod and former Central Vice-President of the Mothers' Union

The Revd Canon George Nairn-Briggs

Social Responsibility Adviser, Wakefield Diocese, Member of General Synod, the Board for Social Responsibility and the Social Policy Committee

Dr Alan Storkey (until April 1995)	Lecturer in Sociology, Oak Hill Theological College
The Revd Sue Walrond-Skinner	Family therapist and Adviser in Pastoral Care and Counselling, Southwark Diocese
Ms Alison E. Webster (secretary)	Secretary of the Social Policy Committee, Board for Social Responsibility
Mrs Deborah Cunningham	Administrative Assistant

With part-time assistance from the Revd Antony Hurst

Foreword

Something to Celebrate brings good news about the variety and strength of many families. Everyone hopes to experience happiness, fulfilment and security in their families. Yet there is much damaging breakdown and conflict which gives rise to widespread anxiety in society about the effects of this turbulence now and for the future.

The Working Party set up by the Board was asked to address four questions:

- What is happening to families at the present time?
- What do Scripture and tradition say about the family?
- What can the Church contribute to the current debate?
- What are the implications of current changes in family life for public policy and for the Church?

As in any group of people, members of the Working Party had experienced very different family patterns. Working together challenged their assumptions. There were those who wanted the report to focus on the scriptural ideals and the moral tradition of the Church. Others wanted to concentrate on how the Church should be responding to the reality of people's lives, marked as they are by disadvantage, deprivation and shifting patterns of relationships.

This recurring tension has been familiar to the Church throughout its history – how far should its practices reflect the received tradition or be changed in the light of new experience and knowledge? What the Working Party has tried to do is identify the good things which have resulted from changes in attitude and behaviour, and what should be resisted as wrong or unhelpful. So, for example, the vision of the Report is to affirm marriage as the basic framework and to emphasise the quality of relationships, whatever legal arrangements may be in place.

The Board is very grateful to all those involved in the preparation of this report, especially the Bishop of Sherwood and Working Party members. We also give profound thanks for the work of Alison Webster and her secretary Deborah Cunningham for the monumental task they have undertaken. They in turn are grateful for the support they have been given by other members of staff in Church House.

It is vital that discussions of family life should be clearly based both on an understanding of the Christian tradition and reliable information about what is happening to families today. The report brings together a great deal of research and Christian thinking on these matters.

The Board commends the report of its Working Party, confident that it will prove to be a rich resource for debate across the country. In an area as complex as that of family life, many different views are held both within the Church and outside it. Not every member of the Board would want to support every specific approach that appears here, but all agree that this is a positive contribution to the debate which will encourage widespread reflection and action.

Something to Celebrate is a resource for Church and society, for debate by the General Synod, community organisations, local churches, schools, colleges and people young and old.

+ David Liverpool
Chairman, Board for Social Responsibility

+ James Bath and Wells
Chairman, Social Policy Committee of the
Board for Social Responsibility

April 1995

Introduction

Everyone has belonged to a family of some kind. Everyone can talk about families with the authority of first-hand experience. Most people have strong views on the matter. Their deepest hopes and fears are likely to be bound up with the people they know most intimately, who share their home, whom in different ways they love and care for, and by whom also they can be most deeply hurt. It is difficult for anyone to stand aloof from the often passionate debate about changes in family life at the end of the twentieth century.

However debate about families is not new. Families are so fundamental to society that they easily become a focus for anxiety whenever society is anxious about itself. During the last half century, phenomena such as the increase in female employment in the 1970s, the questioning of authority and new experiences of affluence and freedom in the 1960s, the emergence of a teenage culture in the 1950s, and wartime displacement in the 1940s have all been accompanied by fears for the future of families. So what, if anything, is special about the present? Earlier concerns focused on new pressures to which families were subject; today's concern is more usually about the speed and scale of change.

The questions involved are complex. What is the truth of claims about a breakdown of family life? Is such talk too alarmist? What is staying the same and what is changing? What new opportunities are opening up and how does one judge which changes are for the better and which for the worse?

The Churches have always had a deep concern for families and have tried to support and strengthen them within a changing social framework. What might Christians have to offer to family life in the 1990s, both in support and in critical evaluation? What can they learn from others? These are the questions which are addressed in this report.

Our report draws attention to the complexity and diversity of family experiences in this country and the range of views within the Church. Our task is also to discern what families hold *in common,* and what the Church can affirm to be true for all people in their family relationships.

Christianity is not the only religion which influences family life. Britain is a diverse society to which people of all faiths and people who have no faith contribute richly. Those who hold views which differ from the Christian tradition deserve respect and need to be taken seriously. A Christian view of family life needs to take account of the fact that there are other religious viewpoints, with some similarities and differences. Nevertheless, many people in this country look to the Church of England to speak with authority and vision, and this report aims to communicate with a wide audience. Our calling as Christians is to draw on the gifts we have received – Scripture, the Christian tradition, and our living experience and knowledge of God – in order, in the words of our terms of reference, to 'perceive the will of God for the human family within contemporary English society'. Though our traditions may be unfamiliar or not accepted by everyone, we hope that this report will also contain meaning and encouragement for people who do not call themselves Christians.

Establishing the Working Party

Twenty years have passed since the Church of England last grappled with these issues at a national level. *Marriage and the Family in Britain Today,* the brief study of the family which the Board for Social Responsibility prepared in 1974,[1] hinted at many of the family trends which are now well established, and reflected on the dilemmas they raise for individuals, public policy and the ministry of the Church. The earlier Lambeth Conference report, *The Family in Contemporary Society* (1958),[2] also makes fascinating reading now, and there is more discussion of both reports in Chapter 2.

Recognising that the world of the 1990s is significantly different from either the 1950s or the 1970s, the Board for Social Responsibility decided to commission a new study. In 1992, a Working Party was set up, chaired by the Bishop of Sherwood, with the following terms of reference:

- to perceive the will of God for the human family within contemporary English society, and in particular:

- to review the teaching and insights of Scripture and the Christian tradition about the nature of the family;

- to examine the range of experience of the family unit and the individuals within it against its wider background and likely future;

- to offer a Christian contribution to the debate by reflecting critically and theologically on these developments;
- to make recommendations for action in public policy and in the life of the Church.

The General Synod of the Church of England has considered related matters on several occasions during the past few years, and we have not therefore done this work again:

- In 1985 issues of human fertilisation and embryology were explored in the Board for Social Responsibility's report, *Personal Origins*[3] and the subsequent Synod debate.
- In 1987 General Synod discussed the Board for Social Responsibility's reports on the welfare state, *Not Just for the Poor,*[4] on homelessness,[5] and on women and work, *All That is Unseen.*[6]
- In 1990 General Synod discussed the Board for Social Responsibility's report *Ageing* and its accompanying study guide *Happy Birthday Anyway?*[7] These drew attention to the changing age structure of our society, and emphasised the needs and contributions of older people. The General Synod welcomed the report and in particular urged churches to take action to support carers.
- In 1991 General Synod debated family breakdown and its causes. In 1992 it debated cohabitation. On both occasions it seemed wise, rather than initiating separate pieces of work, to ask the present Working Party to consider these important topics. This report therefore includes reflections on both issues.
- In 1994 General Synod debated the Lord Chancellor's proposals for Divorce Law Reform contained in the Government's Consultation Paper and gave guidance for the Board for Social Responsibility's response.[8]
- There have also been Private Members' or Diocesan Motions on sexual morality (1987),[9] child abuse and neglect (1988),[10] the effect of violence on children (1990),[11] community care and mental health (1992),[12] abortion (1993),[13] clergy marriage breakdown (1993),[14] and the further marriage of divorced people in church (1994).[15]
- In 1988 and 1991 the General Synod debated the Board of Education's reports, *Children in the Way*[16] and *All God's Children?*[17]

Other important discussions have been initiated by reports from the House of Bishops, notably on issues relating to sexuality, in 1991.[18]

How the Working Party set about its task

When we first met as a Working Party, it was obvious that we held very different views on the family. Each of us had a perspective that was influenced by our age, gender, class, culture and faith commitment and, in particular, our own family experiences. In our small way we reflected some of the diversity that exists within society. This required us to respect the personal perspectives of other people and to try to discern what we could say in common. It also required of us the discipline of being faithful to our own experiences without generalising from them or assuming them to be true for everyone.

It became clear at an early stage that our work was taking place in a context of vigorous political and social debate about the family. The Working Party had its first meeting in September 1992. In January 1993, James Bulger was murdered in Liverpool and the newspapers were filled with analysis and speculation. Later in the same year came high-profile debates about lone-parent families initiated at a party political conference, the 'back to basics' campaign, the publication of the Lord Chancellor's consultation document on Divorce Law Reform, discussion about the ethics of certain forms of infertility treatment, and so on. If anything, the debates became even keener in 1994, which had been designated the United Nations International Year of the Family. To members of the Working Party, it sometimes seemed impossible to open a newspaper or turn on a television or radio without some aspect of the family being discussed.

The consultation process

The Board for Social Responsibility recognised that, if our reflections were to have real meaning for the audience we were addressing, the Working Party would need to consult widely. We were therefore asked to seek views from relevant voluntary organisations, from the main political parties, and from a number of Government Departments. These groups are listed in Appendix B. We also co-operated closely with research bodies and drew on the multitude of events organised for the International Year of the Family. Working Party papers were sent out for comment or published in the Board's journal *Crucible*. Three special consultations were arranged on the family and education, the history of the family, and moral theology. We are very grateful for all the information, advice and help which we were given. The report is a collaborative effort, drawing on a wealth of experience and wisdom up and down the country.

We were also keen to canvass views about families from within the Church of England and to find out what local churches felt was most likely to offer family stability and happiness. A questionnaire was devised (see Appendix A), and this was circulated widely. At first we printed 5,000 copies and sent them to the dioceses. Demand rapidly outstripped supply and by the end of 1993 we had circulated 25,000 copies. It was clear that the respondents were concerned about families and their future, and that they were keen to talk with others about this issue. Responses came from far and wide, ranging from ecumenical house groups in urban priority areas to Mothers' Union branches and rural churches. In many churches the questionnaire was photocopied and used as a basis for group reflection. Some groups and churches sent individual replies from each member, while others sent a single reply summarising all the views. Over a thousand written responses were sent back and many thousands of people took part in discussions.

Many people writing to the Working Party told us of the good things that they had experienced in their own and other people's families and the happiness that their relationships with their parents and children and other relatives had brought them. They spoke of the sense they had of their families helping them to become more fully themselves, and of how they had challenged them to change and to grow. But they also spoke of their disquiet about the breakdown of marriages and the difficulties that many children were having, whether in broken, lone-parent or two-parent families. They described the challenges involved in bringing up children, the economic pressures on many family units, the violence and destructiveness in some families, and the breakdown of love. They also described the pressures on families caused by crime, the persistence of racism, and the continuing high levels of long-term unemployment, poverty and deprivation.

We did not set out to make a representative survey of the whole country. The responses have formed an important background to our thinking, but we have not attempted a quantitative analysis of them or drawn conclusions about the extent to which particular viewpoints are held nationally or in different parts of the country or different kinds of parish. We are grateful to everyone who took the trouble to complete the questionnaire and we quote extensively from the replies. In our view this consultation was very valuable, both to us and to the participants, and we recommend it as a model for future working parties.

Three themes

A number of themes are important in this report. The first is that of *diversity and respect*. One aspect of society at the end of the twentieth century is the wide variety of family forms. The two-parent family with children, a breadwinning husband and a wife who stays at home with the children now makes up only a small minority of all the households in the UK at any one time,[19] though in the course of their lives many people will be part of that kind of family. It has become a cliché to say that the family typically portrayed on the front of a cereal packet in the 1950s now barely exists. Most of us know from experience of our own and other people's families that there are many ways of bringing up children, maintaining relationships and building friendships. An honest discussion about families today must start by recognising this fact.

Diversity is also apparent in the multi-ethnic nature of our society. We have tried to take account of this in our report. We recognise however that several reports could be written on families from an African, African-Caribbean or Asian perspective, and that such reports are undoubtedly needed. As Herman Ouseley, Chairman of the Commission for Racial Equality has put it:

> We need to keep pushing the fact of life that British society is now rich with a diversity of cultures, beliefs, backgrounds. We must be aware that family traditions operate in different ways for different people at different times, socially, economically and culturally. In relation to black and ethnic minority families, cultural traditions which have been transferred from different countries over the years are the 'bedrock' upon which many of these families operate. It is therefore imperative to recognise the legitimacy of different cultural traditions and different ways in which families operate.[20]

This diversity can be richly creative. During our survey, we have reflected on the ethnic diversity of this country and considered patterns of life of other times and in different parts of the world. In the process it has seemed increasingly clear that we cannot assume that a particular shape of family, to the exclusion of all others, is God-given. To suggest, say, that belonging to a nuclear family is the only real way in which human beings can find fulfilment, and then to compare every other kind of family with that, seems to us unhelpful. It denies the evidence of our eyes and ears. Diversity, like uniformity, should not, however, be accepted uncritically. We should be aware of the disadvantages, as well as the advantages, that may be associated with any family form. There also therefore needs to be a much greater understanding of what helps families thrive.

Welcoming diversity implies a respect for differences. It is important to be open to how God is working in people's lives as they are. We offer challenging ways forward for families but we do not give easy answers. There is a value in suggesting to families the directions in which they might travel, but there is no value in telling them that they ought to start from somewhere other than where they are. Indeed reflecting on family life today seems to require us to put aside some of our desire for certainty.

This is important because discussions about the family often swing between two extremes. On the one hand there are those who utter apocalyptic statements and predictions of disaster and who find it hard to see anything good at all in the current scene; on the other there are those who are easily optimistic, refuse to be troubled by contemporary changes, or to acknowledge pain and distress. Neither approach has much to offer people in the daily demands of their lives.

Our second theme is that of *community*. People are both individuals in their own right, and also dependent on their relationships with other people for their development and growth. There is inevitably tension between a person as an individual and a person as a member of a group, but at various points in our report we express regret about the extent to which the pendulum has swung too far towards the extreme of individualism. The most intimate form of community to which we belong is our family, and families have a special importance in offering us opportunities to give and receive from others. Families are where we learn to love.

Families too cannot survive as islands. Concern is often expressed about the 'privatisation' of the family, and we stress in our report the need for families to have strong links with neighbours and friends. There will be many times when families need special help from others, for example when a new baby is born or when a family member is ill or at particular times of family tension. Help is much easier to ask for and receive if good relationships have already been established.

The theme of community is also apparent in our report when we talk about families' needs for outside support. Society has a vested interest in the well-being of families, because families are where most people live and are cared for. But families cannot be expected to do everything for themselves, and society needs to ensure that there is a framework within which families have access to appropriate employment, housing, education, specialist health services and so on.

The third theme is that of *Christian vision*. Many people said to us that they hoped we would set out a clear Christian vision of the family. This is an expectation which is easy to express, but difficult to meet. There are those who say that through the Bible, tradition and Christian experience there are clear and distinctive Christian teachings which amount to an overall vision of what family life should be. There are others who believe that it is impossible to derive a single vision from Christian sources, and indeed that this might be harmful because it would imply a judgement on people whose families or households do not match up to the vision.

This is an understandable but quite misleading polarisation. The Christian vision is a vision of the truth. It is not about escaping from reality but about discovering reality and becoming more real in the way we live. It is about the change that is possible when we learn to die and rise again in our daily lives and everyday relationships. For that is the way to life revealed by Christ, and it holds good for everyone. How this works out in practice is a matter of spiritual discernment, practical wisdom and community co-operation. It is not a matter of being idealistic, in the sense of having high-minded notions which are forever unattainable and only make us feel inadequate. Rather, it is a matter of simply acknowledging that the truth about life together is made known to us in the death and resurrection of Christ and that the power to live together truthfully comes from becoming united to Christ.

As a consequence of this, we recognise that there are a variety of family patterns which work well and that it is important to earth any discussion in contemporary realities. We believe that the Christian faith is determinedly about the world as it is in all its messiness and ordinariness. It is about recognising God's activity here and now in the world as God brings in the Kingdom. However our conviction is that simply accepting the world as it is is not the Christian way. The Christian faith builds on the old to create *new* ways of understanding our relationship with God and with other people. It is about men, women and children discovering a more just ordering of human community. It is a message of hope, which has the power to lift much contemporary secular thinking from its disillusion and despair.

The structure of the report

Introductions to reports often contain warnings, and this one is no exception. One of our hardest tasks was to decide where we should draw the boundaries of our work. What should we include and what should we leave out? With a subject as all-embracing as 'the family', difficult choices had to be made; some readers will be disappointed that a matter of great concern to them is only considered briefly or not at all. We hope however that the broad principles we explore will have wide application.

We also decided not to look in detail at issues connected with family life where work has recently been done by General Synod and other Christian bodies. So for example on matters to do with assisted conception, abortion, divorce law reform, ageing and clergy marriage breakdown, we refer the reader to the relevant studies.

We emphasise that this report is primarily a Christian reflection on *families*. This necessarily involves a consideration of *marriage*. But while marriage has a clear legal definition, the notion of 'family' is much more elastic. It is used of a wide range of relationships, with varying degrees of affinity and responsibility, where ties may be based on kinship, adoption, custom or consent. Families exist where marriage may not (or cannot) and we should not treat them as if they were one and the same thing.

This report falls into three parts. Part I seeks to explore what is happening to families by describing their cultural and historical context (Chapter 1), and some important facts, figures and research (Chapter 2).

Part II moves on to try to understand families by considering some different ways of looking at families (Chapter 3) and reflecting on what families are (Chapter 4). It draws on Scripture and the Christian tradition to develop a Christian perspective on families (Chapter 5). Chapter 6 considers how the insights offered by our faith connect with current trends. What do the vision and the values which we wish to proclaim mean in practical terms?

Part III looks at the kinds of support and resources which families need in our complex society. Families are more than individual units: they depend for their survival and well-being on social structures. So we ask what families need from social policy in order to thrive (Chapter 7). Finally (in Chapters 8 and 9), the report considers the many ways in which families can be helped both by the Church's ministry and by the wider community.

Part IV (Chapter 10) sets out our conclusions and summarises our main recommendations.

PART ONE

What is happening to families?

Chapter 1

The cultural context

In the 1990s many of us are living with a new uncertainty . . . about our jobs, our future, about how to live our lives.

(from a submission by a man in Guildford)

On the street where you live

Take a walk down a street. It need not be a real street but it need not be entirely fictitious either. Who lives there?

Perhaps in the first house are a mother, father and their two children, a group which is often called an 'average family'. But there are all sorts of other households in the street as well, of various ages and ethnic origins: a married couple whose two children have grown up and moved away; a single mother with one child; a stepfamily with three children from previous relationships; two gay men who have lived together for many years; a cohabiting couple with two children; a couple who have not been able to have children of their own but who take a keen interest in their several godchildren; a family with three children, an uncle and a widowed grandmother; some young people sharing a flat for a few years, who spend occasional weekends with their parents; a couple with two foster children; an elderly man living on his own, whose children live in other parts of the country; a woman in her forties who has never married, but who is in touch with her two sisters and their children . . .

The list could go on. Most streets in Britain today reflect at least some of this variety. Which of these households should be called families and on what grounds? There is such diversity that generalisations are difficult to make. Yet behind the differences what do these relationships have in common? And what will best support these people in the stages of their lives and enable them to be happy and fulfilled?

In every age, family forms and underlying values are influenced by the prevailing culture – its political, social and religious beliefs and its economic necessities. Any attempt to understand the changes taking place within families today and the expectations and pressures they are experiencing, has to take into account what is actually happening in

13

society. This chapter starts by exploring some of the factors which seem to be shaping present-day society. It then looks very briefly at families in history. It concludes with some reflection on the role of the Church and on some of the attitudes which currently exist within the Churches.

A changing society

In the last few decades society in Britain has changed radically, profoundly affecting attitudes towards families, and how roles within families are perceived. All societies develop, but present-day society has been changing so rapidly that the common perception is of one change overtaking another before the first has begun to be understood or absorbed.

This is particularly true in the field of communications and computer technology. Television has made a dramatic difference to the home and to our perspectives on the world. Some of our respondents argued that TV and the media were to blame for children's attitudes to sex and violence, and for a general breakdown of society's values. Clearly television can be a negative influence. The pictures of family life it gives may either be idealised in advertisements, or concentrate overmuch on the negative or dramatic – adultery, incest, murder. But television can also be an influence for good. It can increase our knowledge of the world, and unite people and families around a common interest. The exploration of family dilemmas in popular soap operas, for example, may provide a useful focus for discussion of moral issues – and it may be that the Church should draw more on them.

It is outside the scope of this report to look in detail at all the social and economic changes which affect families today. We are aware of fundamental changes in health and welfare, in the education system, in housing provision, and in employment. In addition to their direct effect, they have an impact because of the uncertainty they create about how life is to be managed. Even change which is felt to be positive can create stress.

The roles of women and men

One of the most significant trends in our culture in the last century has been the gradual emancipation of women. Attitudes towards, and opportunities for, women have changed substantially during this period. Many argue that the advent of reliable contraception in the 1950s is the single most important medical and social advance of the twentieth century. In allowing women more control over their fertility, it opened the

14

way for them to play a much greater role in society outside the home. Since the Second World War, women, and especially married women, have entered the workplace in steadily greater numbers, and there have been marked changes in women's expectations.

At a deeper level, there has been a detailed exploration of what it means to be male and female. We are much more aware of the masculine and the feminine as dimensions of human personality, as well as being much less certain about how these terms should be defined. More is known about the role that sexuality plays in childhood and in all adult relationships, and about how power is expressed in male-female relationships.

Much of the early energy in this debate came from the Women's Movement during the 1960s and 1970s. Its critique of the family raised serious issues and was at times harsh. The view was expressed that family roles prevented women from achieving personal, economic and social autonomy, and made them vulnerable to domestic violence. The struggle focused on the desire to achieve parity between women and men in the home and at work. Although there is disagreement about exactly how much has been achieved, and how positive every aspect of these changes has been, there is certainly greater awareness of issues of gender. The different responsibilities of women and men in the home and the workplace are still being worked out, and there is tension in many families in this area. In particular, there is growing debate about the role of men as partners and fathers; this was emphasised by a number of the organisations which responded to us.

Like women, men are facing new challenges as the nature of work changes. Many of them face long-term unemployment, and many young men lack any clear route into the adult community. Meanwhile there has been much debate about what it means to be a man in contemporary society. Two of our submissions raised this point:

The historic role of the father has broken down and the model of the home-father is not yet in place. A good deal of work needs to be done here, not least by the churches, to enhance the vision.

(from a submission by Bristol Council for Voluntary Service)

The whole of the twentieth century has been a journey for women and children out of being the property in law of men within the family into having substantial rights. The changes in family law that reflect this run parallel with women's entry into education, the professions and the workforce. Their aspirations have changed without a consequent change on the part of men to accommodate new partnerships for the effective upbringing of children . . .

If men can no longer bring a wage to the family, their role within it is put in question . . . fewer men are coping with the responsibilities of working and family life. There is little to make them grow up and as they bring relatively little with them, refusal to cooperate usefully as a parent makes it a logical choice for young women to elect to do without one in the home. There is thus a real crisis for what it means to be a father.

(from a submission by the National Council for One Parent Families)

As our report will show, people's hopes are still high that they will be able to find lifelong happiness, despite the unresolved tensions in relationships between the sexes. People want to live in a humane, caring society. But the high expectations placed on relationships can lead to disappointment and breakdown. While most couples aspire to the ideal of mutually fulfilling, equal relationships, they may not always appreciate the difficulties of working these out in practice, particularly if they have children.

Individualism

One of the influences behind the pursuit of equality for women has been what has become known as individualism, a belief in the value of people as individuals and in their right to personal freedom, self-fulfilment and self-expression. Belief in individualism has underpinned many recent developments in social policy. Personal responsibility, the value of 'standing on your own two feet', and the dangers of dependency have been emphasised. Within families, it has encouraged the perception that family members, particularly children, are people in their own right. Individualism has therefore been an impurtant strand in twentieth-century thinking though its roots extend further back than that. It has been responsible for initiating creative changes in the way we value other people.

However, human beings need to recognise their proper dependence on other people. Family relationships provide the most obvious opportunities for learning about the subtle balance between being individuals and being members of society. Family life also forces people to recognise their need for interaction with others for mutual inspiration and support, and their need to make use of services which can only be provided on a communal basis. Emphasising the moral behaviour of the individual, and the

16

individual's responsibility for distinguishing right from wrong must be accompanied by an emphasis on creating social circumstances in which individual morality is best nurtured. Individual morality matters, but the growth of individualism is damaging if it undermines the interdependence of individuals in families and wider communities.

Pluralism and relativism

All disciplines, whether in the social or physical sciences, are now characterised by much greater uncertainty than in the past. They offer new perspectives on truth, an invitation to explore questions rather than to claim that the answers have all been found. The post-modernist approach insists, for example, on taking into account who is doing the research and what values they are bringing to it. Contradictory viewpoints may be held to be equally valid when examined within this more complex understanding of how truth is reached.

Alongside this uncertainty, there is a clear desire for a unifying vision which might bring together spiritual, rational, political, psychological and ecological dimensions. Many people are beginning to question the split between the private and the public which is described in the submission below:

> *In the west, we stand in a modern tradition which divides the public world of politics and work, from the private realm of personal moral values, religious beliefs and practices, and sexual behaviour. The private realm is taken to be a secret and untouchable space for the free expression of each individual, outside the rule of public law unless that law is explicitly transgressed in interfering with the freedom of others, and untouched by considerations of justice which are the measure of the moral in the wider sphere. The family tends to be the symbolic and functional focus of this privacy, being the space within which it is learned and protected.*
>
> *(from a submission by Dr Susan Parsons, published in* Crucible, *July-September 1993)*

Where a large variety of views are seen to be equally valid, it is inevitable that traditional sources of authority and guidance, such as the Church, Law, and Government, should be called into question. The private lives of public figures are now paraded for critical scrutiny rather than presented as exemplary role models. A survey of young people in January 1995 found that few looked to the Church for guidance, or to politicians for inspiration.[1] Many assert that we should instead look within ourselves to discover what to do, and there are large numbers of self-help manuals giving advice on practical and emotional difficulties, as well as a growth in the number of self-help groups. At the same time, there is often a longing for guidance from others and for clear rules which can be followed.

Christianity is caught up in all these movements and the dilemmas they pose. Does Christianity possess absolute and ultimate truth, so that it can stand in judgement upon other beliefs and provide clear moral guidelines? The debate between 'absolutes' and 'possibles' is a tension which runs through this report. We have tried to be true to the nature of the Christian revelation, to be honest about the insights of our tradition and to listen to the voice and experience of people today.

A glance at history in Church and society

Many of the people who wrote to the Working Party said they felt bewildered by these contemporary trends. They looked back with yearning to what they thought had been a golden age of moral certainty and family stability, when roles and rules were clear and everybody knew his or her place. Though there have always been different cultural attitudes towards the family within our society, originating for example in regional differences and in differences in social class, a generation ago it was possible to disregard these differences and to assume that there was a cultural consensus on family life. Yet a longer-term perspective shows that many of the family phenomena which cause anxiety now, such as cohabitation, births outside marriage, lone-parent families and stepfamilies, were as common in earlier centuries as they are today, even if the causes and consequences were somewhat different. The history of the family is a history of diversity of form, of function and of attitudes to family relationships. It is an important and remarkable fact that the changes that have taken place during the past 20 years have been changes in a pattern of family life that became established only during the earlier part of the present century.

One difficulty in looking at families in the past is that the idea of the family has been used, not just as a description of how people actually live, but also as a metaphor for how people wished their lives had been. The idea of the family has a powerful grip on people's imaginations and represents something over and above their actual experience. The family is invested with significance because it expresses, perhaps more vividly than any other idea, a sense of collective well-being.

The Bible

Starting this brief sketch of the history of the family in biblical times, the first thing to note is the meaning behind words describing the family. The Bible uses Hebrew and Greek words, not English ones; these words denote either 'houses' in the sense of dwellings, or 'households' in the sense of quite wide networks of people related either by kinship, marriage and shared territory or by duty, obligation and economic necessity. The main social groupings, especially in Old Testament times, were tribes, clans and extended households. Slave-owning within households was taken for granted. Although monogamy was the ideal, polygamy was accepted and household authority rested with the senior male, who was the household head. A typical household might consist of four generations related by kinship, along with all the non-related dependants. Thus, the total number of persons could be between 50 and 100, all residing in a cluster of dwellings and presided over by the male head. Within that grouping the Old Testament witnesses again and again to the strength of the bonds which linked together, for good or ill, husbands and wives, parents and children, brothers and sisters.

In New Testament times, the household or extended family (Greek *oikos;* Latin *familia*) continued to be the basic unit of society. It included blood relatives over several generations, plus other dependants – slaves, employees and 'clients'. From Judaism, Christianity inherited sacred writings and customs in which genealogies, family relations and family law bulked large. From the Graeco-Roman world, Christianity inherited political ideals and social patterns which accorded the patriarchal household a central role as the city-state in microcosm. It is not surprising then that questions to do with marriage and household life have been Christian concerns from the beginning. The New Testament and other early Christian writings show that there was a lively debate over precisely how the new faith ought to be embodied in man–woman and parent–child relations and the ordering of the household generally. For some, conversion even meant the radical subordination of household ties for the sake of a higher allegiance to Christ, expressed in the single life and celibacy.

The Early Fathers and beyond

Against this background, it is not surprising that many of the Christian writers of the patristic age from the second century to the fifth were strongly ascetic. Many of the Early Fathers showed little appreciation of the family and often reminded their readers of the trials of pregnancy and the pain of childbirth. They adopted a pessimistic view of matrimony, reserving their highest praise for those who remained virgins. Gregory of Nyssa wrote of marriage as a 'sad tragedy', and Tertullian believed in the superiority of a higher sanctity: 'How far better it is neither to marry nor to burn.'[2]

Augustine was more sympathetic to marriage and family life, but was nevertheless very ambivalent about sex, speaking in his *Confessions* of his 'struggles as a prisoner of lust'.[3] In *The City of God* he speaks of the three 'goods' of marriage – children, fidelity and the sacramental bond. He paints an orderly picture of family life in which everyone has their proper place, but one in which the oppression of one person by another is ruled out.

> For this is the foundation of domestic peace, which is an orderly rule and subjection in the parts of the family, wherein the provisors are the commanders, as the husband over his wife; parents over their children, and masters over their servants, and they that are provided for obey, as the wives do their husbands, children their parents, and servants their masters. But in the family of the faithful man, the heavenly pilgrim, there the commanders are indeed the servants of those they seem to command, ruling not in ambition but being bound by careful duty; not in proud sovereignty, but in nourishing pity.[4]

Such views were developed by Aquinas, who saw sexuality and family life as a lesser calling than a wholly spiritual vocation. In his view, procreation was the only natural purpose of sexual intercourse, and his vision of the ordered family firmly placed women lower down the hierarchy than men.

In *Summa Theologicae* he speaks of the goal of family life and the place of families within society:

> Clearly the household comes midway between the individual person and the state or realm, for just as the individual is part of the family, so the family is part of the political community . . . the final purpose of domestic management is the good life as a whole within the terms of family intercourse.
>
> As a human being is part of a household, so a household is part of a state which, according to Aristotle, is the complete community. And as one individual's good is not an ultimate end, since it is subordinate to the common good, so the good of the household is subordinate to the good of a political community.[5]

The Middle Ages and beyond

Moving rapidly through history we find that, in our own country, slavery and the higher but still unfree status of villein (a feudal tenant subject to a lord or attached to a manor) persisted through to the beginning of the Middle Ages. Marriage determined status – whether slave, villein or free – and remained substantially a transaction based on property. In the relatively closed and stable rural communities, the extended family network continued to play an important role, a role which survived greater urbanisation to a marked extent.

It used to be thought that the nuclear family as we know it today was a product of the Industrial Revolution, but it now seems more likely that the pattern of children and parents living in the same household was common as early as the fourteenth century. War, poverty, illness and early death were constant features of family life, and children were expected to become self-sufficient at a very early age. Amongst even the smallest landowners, marriage remained essentially a property deal and marriages were normally arranged by the spouses' parents. Though love could and did flourish in many marriages, romantic love existed primarily in the courtly tradition where it was associated with a chaste commitment outside the marriage bond. Nevertheless, the earliest forms of the Christian marriage service describe marriage as having three purposes: the begetting of children, the provision of a remedy for sexual incontinence with the option of a vow of continence within the marriage, and the giving of a sign to the world of the marriage of Christ and the Church. The husband remained the head of the family, with the wife and children obedient to his will.

The Reformation

Significant changes in attitudes towards the family began to develop at the time of the Reformation, not least because clergy in the new Protestant churches were allowed to marry. Luther saw the family as the starting-point for all social development, emphasising the importance of religious fellowship and prayer within the home. For him the family was an expression of the natural law regarding the ordered union of the sexes and the ordered procreation of children; the household was both an economic unit and a focus of relationships and the religious exercise of love. Rather than seeing children merely as needing to be obedient to their parents' wishes, he regarded the family as a place of education, recognising parents as the first missionaries in communicating the

21

Christian message. Luther's thinking represented a major shift away from a low estimation of the family and the denigration of sexuality; his was a key statement about the freedom of the individual before God.

In England, the Reformers' teachings were further developed by the seventeenth-century Puritans. They saw marriage and family life as a calling: the domestic calling of the husband and father, and the entire calling of the wife and mother. They believed that humane family life, in which Christian love and joy would find full and free expression, could not be achieved until the ordered pattern of a structured routine and discipline had been firmly established. They called for:

> a well thought-out flow of activities in which all obligations were recognised and met, and time found for everything that mattered: for personal devotion, for family worship, for household tasks, for wage-earning and employment, for intimacy with spouse and children, for Sabbath rest and for whatever else one's calling required.[6]

Richard Baxter, writing in 1656, commented:

> Family is the seminary of Church and State, and if children be not well principled there, all miscarrieth . . . Keep up the Government of God in your families; holy families must be the chief preservers of the interest of religion in the world.[7]

The eighteenth and nineteenth centuries

Marriage in England was not defined by legislation until Lord Hardwicke's Act of 1753. The main purpose of the Act was to protect property and patriarchy by imposing residency requirements, parental consent, and either the calling of banns or the purchase of a wedding licence. However, the Act's main effect was to regularise the great variety of common-law forms of marriage which till then had taken place 'without the benefit of clergy'; these included jumping over a broom in front of witnesses, and having smoke come out of the chimney in the morning![8]

The social change which accompanied the Industrial Revolution encouraged the development of nuclear families rather than extended family households. What is known about family life then makes interesting comparison with today's statistics:[9]

- At the beginning of the nineteenth century, about 60 per cent of first births in England were conceived outside marriage, a figure which suggests levels of premarital sexual activity not markedly lower than at the present day.

- In 1800, about two-fifths of children had lost one of their parents by the age of 15 and 4 per cent had lost both. In 1851, 12 per cent of children lived in lone-parent families. If these are added to the numbers of orphaned and deserted children living in institutional care and the large numbers, particularly those born outside marriage, living with grandparents and other relatives, it matches the proportion of children living outside the 'traditional' two-parent family of today.

- In the 1820s, 36 per cent of all marriages ended within 20 years because of the death of one of the partners. Today 33 per cent of all marriages last less than 20 years, though through divorce as well as death.

- The proportion of elderly people living in Poor Law institutions in 1906 is similar to the proportion of elderly people living in residential care homes today.

Reaction against the misery and disruption which these figures represent formed part of both the Evangelical and the Anglo-Catholic revivals. The Victorian Church was in the forefront of the campaigns to restore public morality and end the exploitation of children and women. It made its own contribution through the development of Sunday Schools, the founding of orphanages, the rehabilitation of prostitutes, the provision of family housing, and the promotion of teetotalism. The Victorian Church, high, low and reformed, put a great deal of effort into the promotion of family values and the strengthening of family life.

The twentieth century

The history of the family during the first half of the twentieth century in the UK has been one of a steady rise in the standard of living. Improvements in public health in the late nineteenth century (such as better housing, drainage and cleaner water) led to a slow improvement in family health up until and beyond the 1950s. This was assisted and supported by legislation, in particular by the implementation of the great reforms of the Welfare State in the 1940s with their promise of cradle-to-grave support.

The main reason why the family demography of today is very different from that of previous generations is that the pattern of deaths and births has changed so much. People live longer, fewer die in childhood and children can expect their parents to live into their own middle age. Marriages last much longer (typically more than doubling in length since the late nineteenth century) and a much larger proportion of people in their 60s have elderly parents to care for. At the same time the decline in the number of births means that families have smaller networks of living kin and thus the burden of care has increased. The cycle of family life has also changed. In the eighteenth and nineteenth century and indeed well into the twentieth century a period of post-childhood dependence in the parental home under the control of parents was unusual – most boys and girls left home to become servants or lodgers. Today's society, by contrast, lays on parents much more demanding expectations for supervision and control of teenage children than did almost any earlier generation.

Statements by the Church of England during the twentieth century display a tension between those who seek to affirm its past orthodoxies and those who seek to adapt its teaching to changing circumstances. The tension is apparent, for example, in the debate which followed the appointment in 1909 of a Royal Commission on Matrimonial Law set up to look at the grounds for divorce. Hensley Henson, then a Canon of Westminster and later Bishop of Durham, said in his evidence:

> The absolute and uncompromising language (about the indissolubility of marriage) now common in Anglican circles is not really warranted either by the scriptures by which it is commonly justified, or by ecclesiastical history which is assumed to require it.[10]

The Commission eventually concluded:

> In view of the conflict of opinion which has existed in all ages and in all branches of the Christian Church and the fact that the State must deal with all its citizens, whether nominally Christian or non-Christian, our conclusion is that we must proceed to recommend the legislature to act upon an unfettered consideration of what is best for the interest of the State, society and morality.[11]

However, Cosmo Lang, then Archbishop of York and a member of the Royal Commission, took an uncompromising line. He helped to draft a minority report which argued that the Commission's proposals to widen the grounds for divorce would threaten the institution of family life and that the State should strengthen and not relax the strictness of its marriage law.

During and after the Second World War many church publications interpreted social change as moral decay, pointing to the Church's role in conserving the family by Christian teaching and understanding of family life, and especially by its opposition to any extension of the grounds for divorce. A typical example was the British Council of Churches' pamphlet

Home and Family Life, published during the Second World War, which referred to the escalation of social and economic changes. It argued that individualism was threatening the stability of the family. A constant theme in these years was the centrality of the family and of the pressures it was facing. A speaker from the Mothers' Union argued in 1952, to another Commission on Marriage and Divorce:

> The family itself is being squeezed out in our national set up by two great influences, the one collectivism and the other the exact opposite, individualism. Members of families are caught up into great groupings – trade unions, educational groups, youth movements and women's movements and these groupings demand a loyalty which very often conflicts with the loyalty to the family as a whole.
>
> We believe that that is having a detrimental effect on family life to a very marked extent. At the same time there is individualism. Each member of the family is treated very much as an individual and claims individual attention and relief and thereby loses a great deal of that corporate sense of unity and responsibility which used to be such a great feature of family life.[12]

By the end of the 1950s a different tone is to be discovered in church statements. One of the most important is the pre-Lambeth Conference report *The Family in Contemporary Society.*[13] This maintained that the family 'far from disintegrating is in some ways in a stronger position than it has been at any period of our history of which we have knowledge'. Although some aspects of its style and tone seem old-fashioned today, the analysis of family issues is broad and generous and there is a remarkable anticipation of and wrestling with many of the trends that are now commonplace. Already in 1930 the Lambeth Conference had made a major shift in the Anglican position on contraception. This was then more precisely defined in 1958 and the use of contraception by married couples was fully accepted.

As the century has progressed, Anglican statements have increasingly recognised the changes and stresses facing the family. The report of one group at the Lambeth Conference in 1978, 'What is the Church For?', chaired by the then Bishop Desmond Tutu started by setting out firmly some ideals for the Christian family. These included the sacredness of marriage 'instituted by God and blessed by our Lord Jesus Christ', the need for faithfulness within marriage and the ways in which prayer, Bible reading and corporate sacramental worship and other resources of the Christian faith can nourish families. But the report also highlighted some particular pressures: the smallness of modern western families, for example; the marginalising of elderly people; and the particular economic policies of certain governments which forced long separations of married persons in migratory work camps and mining communities. Indeed all recent reports to the Lambeth Conference (such as *Transforming Families and Communities*[14]) have shown themselves well aware of the varying contexts in which families live.

In recent years other documents have addressed issues related to family life. The House of Bishops' report, *Issues in Human Sexuality*,[15] offered as part of an educational process within the Church of England, argued that lifelong heterosexual marriage is the biblical norm but emphasised that 'homosexual people are in every way as valuable to and as valued by God as heterosexual people'. It urged that the homophobia experienced by gay and lesbian people and their families be tackled and overcome. *Life in Christ: Morals, Communion and the Church*[16] includes a section on the family which seeks to show the areas of agreement between the Anglican and the Roman Catholic Churches. All denominations have grappled with what God is calling them to affirm and to live out about families, and have suggested both theological and practical approaches to family life. Significant documents have been prepared by the Roman Catholic Church, the Methodists, the Baptists, the Society of Friends, the United Reformed Church and the Church of Scotland.[17] In this report we can do no more than refer from time to time to the major discussion on sexuality that has been taking place in all the Churches during the past decade, the fruits of which are partly represented in these reports.

In concluding this section we must remember that official statements of the Churches, though important, are only a tiny part of their witness. Far away from Lambeth and Whitehall, Christian men and women have always organised themselves to meet the needs of disadvantaged families and communities, and to create the social and economic conditions that would help families. In the nineteenth century, for example, universities founded missions and settlements in inner-city areas, doughty moral welfare workers in dioceses set up mother-and-baby homes and placed children for adoption, the Waifs and Strays Society (now The Children's Society), Barnardo's, and National Children's Home (now NCH Action For Children) started to help young people in need across the country and the Church Army worked with prostitutes. The Girls' Friendly Society set up pioneering hostels for young women in service living away from home and the Mothers' Union was founded by Mary Sumner and rapidly spread across the country. The language used by these organisations then may seem old-fashioned to us now, with their talk of 'penitentiaries', 'girls in moral danger' and the 'deserving poor'. But it was the language of people who showed a robust determination to help those in poverty and in need. The deeply-held Christian convictions of William Wilberforce, Lord Shaftesbury, Josephine Butler and others, changed many people's lives, as did the major charity work for children and families undertaken by the Roman Catholic Church and the Anglican Church through their religious orders.[18]

The role of the Church

When people ask for a voice of authority, it is common to find the Church of England, as the established church of the nation, called on to provide a strong moral lead. During the period in 1993 which followed the murder of James Bulger and the trial of the boys who killed him, there was intense debate about the family, crime and morality. The Church of England was criticised for its failure to promote a robust view of the family. Yet it has to be remembered that only a minority of the population are worshipping church members. Moreover, it is scarcely possible to teach people to be moral simply by issuing statements about what they should and should not do – 'thou shalt' and 'thou shalt not'? Pope John Paul II's encyclical letter *Veritatis Splendor* received mixed reactions, but was welcomed by many because it was uncompromising in its moral stance.[19] We have been aware of those who would like this report to be equally clear and uncompromising about right and wrong in family relationships. Yet we also recognise a constant tension in the Church between the desire for a firm moral line, and the wish to care for people and offer them fresh starts in the messy, complex situations of actual life.

The responses to our questionnaire revealed a wide range of attitudes towards the Church's role in supporting family life. Some wanted the Church to reassert what were perceived as being its traditional values – faithfulness, caring and a respect for authority:

'The Church should be accepting and loving, but not at the expense of compromising the highest teaching on marriage and the family.'

'Christian teaching is bound to fail if it gives in to the spirit of the age.'

'Those in authority in the Church should counter secular standards by firm repetition of the true teaching of Christ. They should resist the temptation to win cheap approval by accommodating their teaching to what is likely to be acceptable.'

27

'The Gospel imperative to love does not remove the need for the law; surely the Ten Commandments still apply.'

'The Church should be true to her Master, and advocate clear biblical principles in its moral teaching. Acceptance of the whole Bible should be a minimum requirement for ordination.'

'We do not want a changing Church, we want responsive families.'

Others were keen that the Church should adapt to changing cultural circumstances:

'Teaching which relates my situation to the Bible is more useful than taking the Bible and fitting me into it.'

'The Church needs to address the fact that it alienates a great many people by the way it puts across its views on the family.'

'Christian teaching can seem very inflexible, and often doesn't explain the reasons for its teachings, for example, on pre-marital sex.'

'The Church's teaching on women is spectacularly out of step with the contemporary world.'

'Children are required to honour their parents, but as parents we should remember that respect has to be earned.'

Clearly, we live not only in a diverse society, but in a diverse Church. It is difficult for the Church to speak with one voice when much of the change and uncertainty which permeates society is mirrored in the Church's own membership. Christians like everyone else have to respond to social change and cope with its pressures, and it is not surprising that there should be disagreements on how Scripture and tradition are to be interpreted, and on how God's purposes for family life are to be perceived.

One of the problems that the Church has to face is that it so often sounds judgemental when drawing attention to human failings. Perhaps one way round this is to acknowledge more openly that whatever is said of people generally is also true of Christians. Christians are affected by the changes and chances of life, their marriages can break up and their children get into trouble. Christians too can be dishonest and unloving. We are reminded of Jesus' parable of the wheat and the tares, which grow together till the end of time. We cannot always distinguish which is which; good and evil are intertwined in our individual lives and in our society's development. One of the contributions we can make as Christians is to recognise that sin is present even in our best endeavours, but that God is also present. For this reason, a Christian analysis must be realistic about the problems society faces, as well as holding out hope for the future.

The context in which we must examine families is complex. The many strengths in families enable them to flourish and raise children despite the changes which society is going through. Yet there are pressures on families which can be immensely destructive to those who are already vulnerable. As Christians, we believe we have important certainties to uphold – God's loving presence in the world, God's mercy and forgiveness, God's intention that people should live in right relations with one another and with God. Families are where much of human love is expressed, and we believe that this love is rooted in God's love for all people, not just for Christians. What is more difficult is to translate such general beliefs into specific statements about family life. Our theology must draw on a proper understanding of human nature and the society in which we live, as well as on revelation and tradition. In the rest of this report, we consider both these dimensions.

Chapter 2

Families today

Despite its critics and prophets of doom, family life continues to adapt and adjust. It is likely that the process of change will continue in forms we cannot yet foresee.

(from a submission by Barnardo's)

Concern about the speed and scale of change in the landscape of families has been expressed by political leaders, by the media and by community groups and organisations. It was one reason for the establishment of the Working Party and the nature of these changes has formed a background to our work. This chapter sets out some facts and figures and findings of some of the key research. The figures describe what has happened, not why it has happened. They do not tell us what these changes mean in people's lives, nor whether they are for the better or for the worse. The facts and figures are needed as the basis for our discussion of family change; commentary and reflection will come later.

The figures used in this chapter are mainly drawn from official sources, in particular the regular collection and analysis of population statistics undertaken by the Office of Population Censuses and Surveys (OPCS) and by the General Household Survey, much of which is summarised in Social Trends. Other references will be found at the end of the report.

The birth-rate

Each year the OPCS calculates a 'total period fertility rate', that is, the average number of children per woman during her child-bearing life if current birth rates remain the same. The interest is twofold: whether enough children are being born to maintain the population at its present level through births alone (called the replacement rate); and what will be the average size of families with dependent children. The replacement rate is at least 2.1. The post-war UK fertility rate fluctuated sharply, remaining above replacement level until 1977. Since then it has been fairly stable, but it has stayed below the replacement rate. In 1993, it stood at 1.76.

Some of this decline in the number of children being born has been due to women starting to have their babies at older ages. Birth control and abortion have undoubtedly had an impact on family size and also enabled women to postpone child-bearing. There is also some evidence that levels of male fertility may have deteriorated, probably due to environmental agents.[1]

The increased participation of married women in the workforce is also likely to affect the birth-rate because of the difficulties, at least in the UK, of combining child-rearing with working. Added to the considerable direct costs of child-rearing are the indirect costs of a loss of a second income if a woman gives up work (often called the opportunity costs). Other factors, such as unemployment and changes in the housing market, may also affect decisions to have children.

The overall effect of this decline in family size is that the average number of dependent children (under 16 or aged 16 to 18 and still in full-time education) in families is now 1.8 children. Large families – three or more children – are now a minority of the family population.

All of this can affect the ways families function. For example, the birth of a child may be postponed until the family feels able to manage financially without the woman's earnings or until the woman feels established in her career. The fewer the number of dependent children under five years old, the more likely the woman is to return to the labour market. Much later in life, smaller families may mean that fewer people are available to care for elderly parents.

People living alone

One of the main changes in household structure is the growth in the proportion of people living alone. As shown in the chart on the next page, in 1993, more than a quarter of the households in Great Britain were one person households, almost double the proportion in 1961. Elderly women are the largest group living alone but they have formed a relatively stable proportion of the total since 1971. The main area of growth has been among people under pensionable age living alone, particularly men. By 2001, nearly one in ten households in Great Britain are projected to consist of a man under pensionable age living alone.

Household size 1961

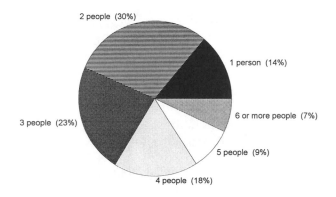

2 people (30%)

1 person (14%)

6 or more people (7%)

3 people (23%)

5 people (9%)

4 people (18%)

Household size 1993

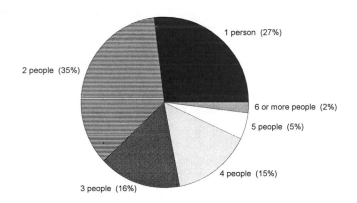

1 person (27%)

2 people (35%)

6 or more people (2%)

5 people (5%)

4 people (15%)

3 people (16%)

Source: Social Trends, HMSO 1995

32

Marriage

Until the 1960s, marriage had never been more popular. Now marriage is taking place later in life and the number of marriages per year in the UK is falling.

- The marriage rate for first marriages in England and Wales fell from 82 per thousand bachelors aged 16 and over in 1971 to 37 per thousand in 1992.

- Although there is a high marital breakdown rate, a majority of people still choose marriage. Nearly two-thirds of marriages are still ended by death of a partner rather than divorce. As the chart below shows, four out of five families with dependent children are headed by a married or cohabiting couple.

- Perhaps the most notable change is the fall in marriages occurring after conception. At the beginning of the 1970s, a young woman under 20 who became pregnant usually opted for marriage. Now marriage is the third choice: the first choice is a birth outside marriage and the second choice is an abortion.

- The most common age for first marriages is 26 for women and 28 for men.

- Remarriages are a growing proportion of all marriages. Over a third of marriages involves a partner who has previously been married. Three-quarters of all divorcees eventually remarry. However the rate of remarriage has also been declining.

Families with dependent children: by family type, 1991

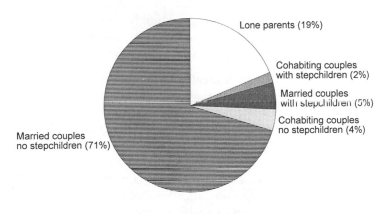

Source: Social Trends, HMSO 1995

Cohabitation

Cohabitation (that is, living together as husband and wife outside marriage) is becoming an increasingly common stage in many people's lives. There are few official statistical surveys to draw on and many gaps in our knowledge. Enough, however, is known to give a broad picture of what is happening.

Since 1979 women respondents aged 18 to 49 in the General Household Survey have been asked whether they were living with a man 'within a union that has not been formalised with either a civil or religious ceremony'. Since 1987 the data has been collected also for both men and women aged 16 to 59 and there is some data from the 1991 census. In the past few years research studies have also added much useful detail.[2]

- The percentage of women aged 18 to 49 cohabiting outside marriage increased from 3 per cent in 1979 to 9 per cent in 1992. During the same period the percentage of never-married women aged 18 to 49 cohabiting increased from 11 per cent to 21 per cent.

- The peak age of cohabitation is 25 to 34, though in general cohabiting women tend to be younger than men. Teenage cohabitation and cohabitation beyond age 45 are rare at the moment.

- Two-thirds of cohabitees have never been married and the third that have been married are mainly divorced. The rate of cohabitation among the divorced and separated is higher than for the unmarried and has been growing faster. Thus in 1979 one in five divorced women was cohabiting and by 1992 this had increased to one in four.

- The period of cohabitation tends to be short-lived. One-third of couples cohabit for less than a year and only 16 per cent live with their partner for more than five years. A cohabiting relationship lasts two years on average and then the couple either separate or marry.

Thus the statistical evidence indicates that there has been a rising trend towards cohabitation before marriage. To illustrate this, of those women marrying for the first time in the late 1960s, only 6 per cent had cohabited. By the late 1970s it was 33 per cent and for those marrying between 1985 and 1988 it was 58 per cent. If this rate of increase has been sustained into the 1990s we can expect about 80 per cent of all women marrying in the 1990s to have cohabited before their first marriage. Therefore we can conclude that cohabitation is now common behaviour before marriage and usual behaviour between marriages.

Researchers have identified three groups of cohabitees:[3]

- young, never-married childless couples (about half of the total);
- those who had previously been married (about a third of the total);
- never-married couples with children (about a sixth of the total).

People clearly enter cohabiting relationships with different expectations of permanence and commitment, and there is further discussion of this in Chapter 6.

The UK is not alone in the trend towards cohabitation. There have been increases in cohabitation and extra-marital child-bearing in many other industrialised countries. Sweden, Denmark and Iceland have the highest levels of cohabitation. Over half of all children in Sweden are born outside marriage, though 95 per cent of them within an established partnership. In Norway, former West Germany and the Benelux countries cohabitation is slightly more prevalent than in the UK, but France's rate is similar to ours. The southern European countries and Ireland still have very low rates.[4]

Divorce

There were bulges in the divorce statistics following the implementation of the Divorce Reform Act 1969 and the Matrimonial and Family Proceedings Act 1984, but the rise in the UK divorce rate over the long term has been continuous, increasing from 2.3 per thousand married men in 1961 to 13.7 per thousand in 1992. After 1986, when there were 168,000 divorces, the numbers appeared to be levelling off, but from 1991 the upward trend resumed, reaching a high of 175,000 in 1992.

One consequence of changing family forms may be that divorce is less useful on its own as an indicator of family breakdown. The breakdown in cohabiting relationships also needs to be taken into account. On divorce we know that:

- if present trends continue, four in ten new marriages will end in divorce;
- the chances of divorce are much higher for younger marriages, recent marriages and higher among the previously divorced and marriages that follow cohabitation;[5]
- nearly one-quarter of divorces occur within the first four years of marriage, and one half in the first ten years. Nearly one-third of divorces take place after 15 years of marriage;

- in 1992, 169,000 children under 16 years experienced the divorce of their parents, up by 9000 from the previous year;
- in 1992 the UK had the highest divorce rate in the then European Union but it was still lower than in the United States where half of all marriages end in divorce.

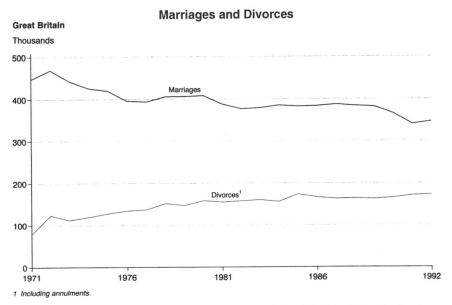

Marriages and Divorces

Great Britain

Thousands

1 Including annulments.

Source: Office of Population Censuses and Surveys; General Register Office (Scotland)

Births outside marriage

The decline in marriage and the increase in cohabitation has been associated with a rapid increase in births outside marriage. The proportion has risen from 6 per cent of all births in 1961 to 31 per cent of all births in 1992. In 1991 the number of never-married lone parents overtook the number of divorced lone parents for the first time. The percentage of total births outside marriage has increased for all ages of mother; for births to mothers under 20 it is now over 80 per cent of all births and nearly half of all births for those aged 20 to 24.

However, over three-quarters of births outside marriage were registered by both parents and three-quarters of these were living at the same address. So over half of births outside marriage appear to be to cohabiting couples.

Births outside marriage as a proportion of all births

United Kingdom

Percentages

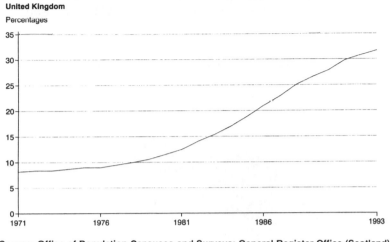

Source: Office of Population Censuses and Surveys; General Register Office (Scotland); General Register Office (Nothern Ireland)

Lone-parent families

The increase in births outside marriage and in divorce and separation has led to the number of lone-parent families more than doubling between 1971 and 1992.[6]

- In 1992 there were 1.4 million lone-parent families containing 2.3 million children, over 90 per cent headed by a woman.

- In 1992 lone-parent families constituted 21 per cent of all families with children. Nineteen per cent of households with children are headed by a lone mother, and two per cent by a lone father.

- In 1992 around one third (34 per cent) of lone mothers were divorced, 5 per cent widowed and 23 per cent separated. Thus 62 per cent of lone mothers had previously been married.

- Over one-third of lone mothers (37 per cent) are single, never-married women. However a proportion of these will have conceived and/or borne the child within a cohabiting relationship which later broke down.

- Lone parents are not a static group. Within six years of the beginning of lone parenthood, around two-thirds of lone parents will have married, remarried, or entered into a cohabiting relationship. They will in turn be replaced by new lone parents.

37

The chart below looks at lone-parent families in a different way, in that it includes lone fathers. As a result, the percentages are naturally slightly different.

Lone parent families with dependent children, 1992

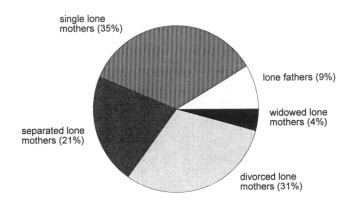

single lone mothers (35%)

lone fathers (9%)

widowed lone mothers (4%)

separated lone mothers (21%)

divorced lone mothers (31%)

Source: Population Trends 78, OPCS 1994

The material consequences of lone parenthood can be severe. A national study found that for the parent who has the daily care of the child (90 per cent of whom are women), poverty is the normal experience: over 70 per cent of lone mothers have to rely on Income Support and over 80 per cent claim benefits of one sort or another.[7]

For both parents, moving home is a common consequence. Usually it involves moving down the housing market, often, in the case of the parent with care, to local authority rented housing. The absent or non-resident parent (who is usually the father) often loses contact with his children. Just over half of absent parents have any contact with their children and for about a quarter of these the contact is less than once a month.[8]

It is not surprising therefore that few people enter lone parenthood casually or deliberately. The same national study found that only 12 per cent of single lone parents planned to have their baby outside marriage and many of these were cohabiting before they became lone parents. Taking all lone parents, in 47 per cent of cases lone parents themselves made the decision to end the relationship. The most common reason (31 per cent) was that they or their partner had found someone else with whom they wanted to live. However, violence was a factor in relationship breakdown in 20 per cent of cases. Only a minority of lone parents wish to remain on their own.

Stepfamilies

The cumulative result of the trends outlined above is that there is now a variety of step- and other family relationships.[9] Stepfamilies are created when one or both partners with children marry or cohabit after bereavement, divorce, separation, cohabitation breakdown, or lone parenthood.

- There are currently over one million children growing up in a stepfamily where one or both partners has a child or children from a previous relationship.

- It is likely that half of the 2.3 million children growing up in a lone-parent family will have a birth parent living elsewhere who has repartnered or remarried, creating a stepfamily which the child may visit occasionally.

- Children are seven times more likely to live with a stepfather than a stepmother.

Stepfamilies are not new family forms. In the past most of them would have been created after the death of a parent. If a mother died a widower felt it quite appropriate to seek another wife to run the household and care for his children. If a father died, a widow might want to remarry for economic reasons as well as to provide a figurehead for the household and to discipline the children. Now most stepfamilies are the result of separation or divorce rather than death.

There are a variety of types of stepfamily. The most common form is where the woman's children are resident (86 per cent) but in six per cent the man's children are resident and in another six per cent children of both parents from former partnerships are present. In over half of all re-partnerships a new child is born. Sometimes the birth parent and his or her new marriage partner will adopt a child from the parent's previous relationship, severing the child's legal relationship with the other birth parent and that 'side' of the family. These complex families affect the relationships of children, parents, grandparents and other family members now and throughout life.

Minority ethnic families

According to the 1991 Census, there are now three million people from minority ethnic groups living in Great Britain, representing 5.5 per cent of the total population. The census divides them into three groups:

- South Asian (Indian, Pakistani and Bangladeshi) – 2.7 per cent;
- Black (African and Caribbean) – 1.6 per cent;
- Chinese and other – 1.2 per cent.

Most minority ethnic families live in urban areas, in particular in Greater London and the West Midlands; relatively small numbers live in either Scotland or Wales.

There are large differences in family situations between the different ethnic groups. For example in Spring 1994, 29 per cent of white households were single person households; this compares with 31 per cent of black households but only 7 per cent of Pakistani/Bangladeshi households. Households headed by a Pakistani/Bangladeshi, on the other hand, were most likely to contain dependent children.

These differences are influenced by variations in the age structure of the various ethnic groups which make up the United Kingdom. The white population has an older age distribution than that of ethnic minority groups. Similarly the proportion of households with dependent children is related to the number of women of child-bearing age. There are also cultural differences. For example, over half African-Caribbean mothers were lone mothers in 1989-1991 compared with just over one in ten Pakistani/Bangladeshi mothers.[10]

Elderly people

No description of family trends would be complete without attention to elderly people and the contribution they make to family life. We live in an ageing society – that is, where both the absolute numbers and the proportion of older people in the population is increasing. The 1991 Census shows:

- The number of people aged 60 and over in Britain was 11.6 million, 8 per cent more than in 1981. This rise was due almost entirely to a large increase of people over 75.
- The number of people aged over 85 has doubled since 1981. There are now over 800,000 people aged over 85.

- There are more older women than men. In 1992, there were 2,390,000 women and 1,234,000 men over the age of 75.

Most people between the ages of 60 and 75 do not have any serious health problem or disability. The majority of people in what has been called the 'third age' continue to contribute usefully to society and to families. Younger retired people who are grandparents often make a vital contribution to the care of grandchildren. As the Board for Social Responsibility's 1990 report *Ageing* made clear, this group is fit and active, and plays a creative role in communities and churches.

After the age of 75, elderly people are likely to have some kind of physical disability or illness which limits what they can do. They may need substantial care. There are constraints however which limit the ability of families to fulfil these obligations. For example, most care of older people with disabilities is undertaken by women, who frequently have other roles as mothers and employees. Divorce among older people and in their children's families can complicate the question of who is responsible for their care. Smaller living accommodation or job insecurity may make it impracticable for a family to give or afford the care they would wish. Further, because people live longer, there are higher numbers suffering from illnesses such as dementia, which require more intensive help than a relative may be able to provide.[11] For a minority of families, the combination of pressures of caring and other problems can lead to a breakdown of relations between older people and their adult children. In some families, elderly people are abused. This is explored later in this chapter.

Nevertheless a large proportion of families keep some form of contact with their older relatives and provide support if it is needed: 69 per cent of elderly people are in contact with at least one of their children at least weekly, 32 per cent live less than an hour away from at least one of their children, and only 9 per cent more than five hours' away.[12]

What of the future?

All the evidence suggests that the trends described so far will continue. Almost every individual now has some experience in his or her immediate or extended family of births outside marriage, cohabitation, separation, divorce or lone parenthood. However facts and figures only tell us a small part of the family story. As part of our exploration of what is happening to families, the second half of this chapter moves on to look at research

41

on some current aspects of family life which cause concern. We look at couples in conflict, the effect of family breakdown on children, domestic violence, child abuse and elder abuse. Finally, we look at public attitudes to families.

Couples in conflict

All families experience conflict at times. Conflict is part of being alive, of relating to other people, of growing and changing. Indeed one of the functions of families is to be places where people can express anger safely, challenge and confront each other and experience both forgiving and being forgiven.

Many men and women today have different expectations about the nature of marriage and alternatives to marriage from those held by their parents and grandparents. Some argue that these changes in attitudes have been reinforced by changes in social institutions such as the law, social security, employment and the Church. Others would argue that any changes in these institutions have accompanied a change in behaviour rather than caused it. The question 'What has caused the increase in divorce, and the other changes in family form taking place at the present?' is therefore not easy to answer. Nevertheless, it is possible to point to profound cultural shifts which have taken place in the last 20 years, some of which were referred to in Chapter 1.

For example:

- Contemporary culture strongly affirms the value of self-fulfilment and this may make it harder for couples to ride out difficult periods in a relationship.

- Contraception has led to an increased emphasis on the quality of the relationship between the couple and on dimensions such as intimacy, companionship, sharing, and emotional and sexual fulfilment. Greater expectations are harder to fulfil and both partners can experience disappointment and become angry and withdrawn.

- Public attitudes to divorce have been transformed. Divorce is now greeted with much less disapproval and has come to be seen as an appropriate 'solution' to many marital problems.

- There has been a rapid expansion in the number of women working outside the home. This has resulted in an increase in the opportunity costs of child-bearing (i.e. what women lose financially by having children) while the need of women to be financially dependent on men has been reduced. It has been suggested that working women are more likely to divorce, perhaps both because they are more likely to be able to support themselves financially after divorce and because they are more likely to meet a new partner.[13]

- Social policies have become established to meet the basic needs of lone-parent families and thus have further reduced women's financial dependence on men and/or the necessity of putting up with a violent or unrewarding marriage.

- The roles of mother, wife and worker are not easy to reconcile. At the same time, women have developed much higher expectations of their role and relationships. Men have found it difficult to adjust to these changed expectations. At the most practical level some are taking a greater share in housework and child care but it is still the case that women, including many working full-time, have to carry the greater share of these.[14]

- There are growing pressures on families, such as high levels of unemployment, increasingly short term and mobile employment, low pay, poverty, increased housing costs, and homelessness. Some marriage relationships which might otherwise have survived may not be strong enough to withstand this additional stress.

The impact of relationship breakdown on adults

Divorce represents a major disruption to the family system at every level of its functioning. It makes more complex whatever issues the family is already tackling in its particular stage of the life cycle. It entails multiple losses and imposes severe stress upon family members. The mortality rates for separated and divorced people are higher than for the population at large and numerous studies have demonstrated that on every major indicator of health and emotional well-being, separated and divorced people score significantly lower than do the general population.[15]

It is known that men are more adversely affected by divorce than women. There may be several reasons for this. Marriage appears to be a healthier experience for men than for women; married women have a much higher incidence of illness and psychiatric disturbance than their unpartnered counterparts. Men are likely to experience the loss of the marriage more severely. They more often have to face several changes, usually moving out of the marital home and living apart from their children. Men are also usually less able to express their grief at their losses openly and are more likely therefore to experience depression and its consequences. They may, for the same reason, attract less sympathy from their wider social network. Men who are separated and divorced may need particular help. They more easily 'get lost' in overwork, or in unemployment, alcoholism and depression, or they may desperately try to move into a new marriage or other partnership prematurely. They may need special help in sustaining their contact with their children. None of this detracts from the pressures faced by women after divorce, who commonly face a marked drop in income and a new overall responsibility for their children.

The words and phrases most commonly used about the breakdown of a relationship in which many hopes were invested are pain, a sense of personal failure, a loss of confidence in oneself and others, depression, loneliness, grief and anger. Even where no children are involved, such individuals will need the help of family and friends, of the communities with which they have been involved – including the Church – and in some cases, professional help also. The goal may often be to try to resolve the couple's difficulties so that they can come together again and find new strengths in their marriage as a result of their difficult experience. But this is not always possible or even desirable – in the case of a violent or destructive relationship, for example. When the relationship has ended, the most useful goal will be to reduce the extent to which unresolved problems arising from the breakdown are carried into any new relationship, with destructive effects on the adults and possibly on future children.

The impact of divorce on children

One in four children is likely to experience their parents' divorce before they reach the age of 16.

There are disputes among researchers and policy makers about the long-term impact on children of being part of a divorce or relationship breakdown. No one doubts however that children suffer from conflict between their parents and between the adults in stepfamilies; their suffering can become acute when the adult relationships break down and separation follows. The pain of the children is increased by any conflict between their parents about residence and contact arrangements.

Research into the effects of divorce on children has been summarised in the UK.[16] It suggests that, arising from the breakdown of a family, the most active ingredient in damaging a child's future life chances is the impairment of that child's sense of self-worth. Other research combines to indicate that this is most likely to result from one or all of three conditions for children:

- their continuing insecurity caused by a succession of family and household changes after divorce;
- the loss of contact with a parent;
- their being drawn into the conflict between their parents both before, during and after divorce.

There is also recent evidence from Australia and the United States highlighting the fact that harm to children is more likely if they are living with one parent who does not adjust well to the new situation. Conversely, good loving care from the resident parent and conflict-free contact with the other and with the kinship network can do much to promote children's well-being.

What is clear from the research is that there is a need to prepare children for the departure of one parent from the family by explanations from both their mother and their father. Parents need to tell the children a coherent story about what is happening to the family in words and images they can understand. One recent study shows that sensible decisions about the children at the time of the separation were made less likely because of the stress being felt by the adults concerned, and because the parents themselves were undergoing a new and bewildering experience about which they knew little.[17] Access to information and advice, mediation, supportive relationships from family, friends, churches and others, and when necessary professional intervention, can all be useful at this stage.

Because most children whose parents divorce live for a time in a lone-parent household, it is these that we now consider. Taken at face value, the research tells us that some children growing up in a lone-parent household fare less well physically, psychologically, economically and socially than children who live with both their birth parents.[18] The list of problems includes poor health, behavioural difficulties, low achievement at school, delinquency, psychiatric illness and a greater likelihood that in later years, as young people and adults, they will have children outside marriage, that those married will be more likely to divorce, and that they will more often be involved in alcohol and drug abuse and in crime.

But others challenge the wisdom of taking these findings at face value. There are many kinds of lone-parent household: those with a widowed parent, those resulting from separation and divorce after first or subsequent marriages, those formed as a result of cohabitation breakdown and families where a single mother has brought up her child alone from birth. It is very difficult to make generalisations about such a varied group. Moreover, the quality of the research is uneven and it is difficult to make comparisons between the studies.

It is also argued that factors other than lone parenthood as such may be producing the adverse results. For example, most lone parents experience a period of reduced income and many spend periods – short or long – in poverty. Is it the financial stress or poverty that produces the poor outcomes for children or is it being in a lone-parent household itself? Where the lone-parent household is formed after severe conflict between birth parents, or within a stepfamily, are the children's problems due to this exposure to conflict, or to the experience of family breakdown, or do they arise from the later experience of growing up in a lone-parent household? The research findings are commonly expressed in terms of 'on average'. An average implies a range of outcomes – good as well as bad. But rarely, if ever, do the reports examine what factors contribute to a *good* lone-parent household and what *good* qualities are shown by children as well as parents in such situations. Are some of these children more socially competent, mature and independent than others in their age group? Are such families especially close-knit and loving? Are there rich and rewarding relationships to be made between each parent and their children after a divorce which allows children to learn something of the miracle of new, though changed, relationships developing out of failure and despair? All this is information that we badly need.

It would be foolish to ignore all the evidence of poor outcomes for children in lone-parent households. But it would be equally foolish to ignore the evidence from experience of the many parents doing an excellent job for their children and the many children from lone-parent households who have developed into mature, stable adults.

Domestic violence

In all families, tensions arise and relationships become strained and hurtful; in some families this spills over into occasional violence. There are also families where violence and habitual abuse are deliberate. The perpetration of violence is overwhelmingly a male problem, though a few women resort to violence and some women are involved with their partners in acts of violence and abuse against their children. Very few of our respondents named violence and abuse as serious problems for families; they were more likely to see the breakdown of families as the problem, rather than to denounce the destructive behaviour which pulls certain families apart.

The prevalence of domestic violence is difficult to establish. Home Office statistics suggest that it is rising, but reported incidents are only the tip of an iceberg, and the apparent increase represents a welcome erosion of the inhibitions which previously prevented people asking for help. A recent study shows that 100,000 women contact refuges by helpline each year, and 42,000 are admitted to them. At any given time more than half the residents in refuges are children accompanying their mothers in fleeing from the home.[19] Domestic violence is something which occurs in all classes of society, but middle-class women are more likely to have greater resources and more options open to them than working-class women and to be less visible at refuges and social services departments.

There are many related problems caused by domestic violence: the need for support for distressed women and children, increased housing needs where families break down and the cost of medical attention and police and court time. Women in minority ethnic groups often find it particularly difficult to take action when they suffer domestic violence. They may be more acutely aware of bringing disgrace on their wider community if they take the problem outside. There can in some cases be language difficulties. Women who have been in this country for less than 12 months cannot claim Income Support if they leave their partners, and they may fear they will be deported.

It is often asked why women tolerate domestic violence rather than leaving.[20] Many do in fact leave very quickly, perhaps giving their partners one warning and walking out after the second incident; others put up with it for years. They give a variety of explanations: that they love the man and believe that he will change; that they have nowhere to go and are afraid of what might happen to them should they leave; or that they have been so brutalised that they are incapable of taking any initiative.

A more significant question is why so many men should behave violently. Women in relationships are capable of being aggressive, domineering or manipulative; it is not only men who are at fault, but women's behaviour does not legitimise violence. Domestic violence seems to derive from patterns of patriarchal authority and the difficulty that certain men have in discovering how relationships can be based upon negotiation. Often family violence is inherited: boys whose parents inflicted violence on each other and on the children can grow up assuming that this is the normal way in which adults behave towards one another, and girls from violent families have a tendency to marry potentially violent men. There is a strong association between domestic violence and alcohol misuse, but it seems that this is because violent men drink heavily rather than that violence is due to intoxication.

Until comparatively recently a predominantly male police force was reluctant to intervene in 'domestics', women were reluctant to involve social services for fear that their children would be taken into care, and doctors did not ask questions about the causes of injuries because they did not have the resources that would have permitted an effective intervention. Police responses to domestic violence are now much more sympathetic to the predicament of women victims, perhaps as a consequence of the recruitment of more women officers, and detailed Home Office guidance issued in 1990 encouraged, among other things, the setting up of special domestic violence units.

Civil remedies prohibiting violence and sometimes even requiring the perpetrator to leave the family home can bring much added protection to victims. The Government has introduced a Bill to rationalise these remedies and make them more effective.[21]

Child abuse

The subject of child abuse is emotive and disturbing. It represents a profound disordering in the normal instinctive desire of the mature to protect the immature members of any species. It stands at the opposite end of the spectrum from the conditions for human flourishing which will be set out in Chapter 4. However its recognition as an event which happens to some people's children jerks all of us into realising some of our own propensities for violence towards even the vulnerable and the young.

There are four main kinds of abuse: physical abuse, neglect, sexual abuse and emotional abuse. As an example, at the end of March 1994 there were 34,900 names on the Child Protection Registers (which list all children considered to be suffering from or likely to suffer significant harm, and for whom a child protection plan has been drawn up by local professionals, involving the parents). Many of the names are only on the register for a matter of months and most children remain in their own homes without being subject to any court order. These are important points to emphasise because one of the main things which prevents parents, friends or relatives from seeking help in cases of suspected child abuse is the fear that the child may be removed from the home.

The recognition that some children are severely damaged in their families has been growing through the second half of the twentieth century. Serious abuse existed before this, but there was much less public acknowledgement of it. First came public concern at the physical abuse of children; then, in the 1980s, the issue of child sexual abuse also became prominent.

There have been many attempts to ensure that children are properly protected, for example through legislation such as the Children Act 1989, and through educational work in schools and youth groups. Such work is based on the idea that children have a right to say no to inappropriate behaviour, and to tell if an adult tries to abuse them. Those who deal with children who have been damaged by their families feel strongly that they must be better protected, even if there are occasional abuses of the system. In Chapter 9 we return to this issue to look at the responsibilities of the Church.

Elder abuse

Elder abuse first became a concern in the mid 1970s as a result of reports on 'granny battering' published in medical journals.[22] Since then there has been a growing recognition that some elderly people are being abused in their own homes, but the scale of abuse is not clear and it is only quite recently that the issue has been looked at 'as a social problem and in a systematic way'.[23] A lack of an agreed definition makes it hard to determine the number of instances of abuse. Some research studies are limited to physical abuse while others are wider and cover, for example, emotional, sexual, financial abuse and neglect. A definition from Action on Elder Abuse states:

> 'Elder abuse is a single or repeated act or lack of appropriate action occurring within any relationship where there is an expectation of trust, which causes harm or distress to an older person. [24]

There are probably many reasons why abuse occurs. Poor family relationships in the past, current drug or alcohol misuse, or long-standing mental health problems may be factors.[25] As we have said elsewhere in this report, the general population is ageing and carers, like those they are caring for, are growing older. These days a 70-year old may find herself caring for a parent in her nineties. As well as undertaking care at an older age, carers may be unprepared to care, and may have to provide care for a prolonged period at great personal cost.

For any elderly person being looked after at home, outside help may be vital. Such help may be available from local authorities who are required to carry out assessments of needs under the National Health Service and Community Care Act 1990, where they consider that people are in need of services.

In most cases, community care services will be welcomed by the elderly person. There are, however, cases where a third party blocks access to services or protection from harm, or where the elderly person refuses help. In these situations there is a particularly difficult balance to be struck between protection from harm and recognition of an adult individual's right to choose. Powers to intervene against the wishes of the person concerned already exist but these powers are rarely invoked, may be difficult to exercise and still leave some people unprotected. The Law Commission has recommended the repeal of existing powers and their replacement with new short-term protective powers providing for assessment and not simply removal from home.[26]

Public attitudes to the family

Finally, in the third part of this survey of what is happening to families, we look at attitudes to the family.

How has the general public reacted to the trends described in this chapter? Periodically, survey researchers take a 'snapshot' of attitudes at a particular time. In one such survey[27] people were asked what advice they would give to a young woman or young man thinking about a future partner. There was not much difference in the advice suggested to women and men. The following relates to young women:

- Only 4 per cent of those surveyed in the UK said she should live with a steady partner without marrying (11 per cent in West Germany, one per cent in Ireland).

- Some 43 per cent said she should live with a steady partner and then marry (50 per cent in West Germany, 32 per cent in Ireland).

- Some 37 per cent said she should marry without living together first (19 per cent in West Germany, 59 per cent in Ireland).

In the same survey, around 70 per cent in the UK, 73 per cent in West Germany but over 80 per cent in Ireland, said they believed that people who want children ought to get married. But in the UK, in particular, the older age groups were the most likely to take this view. Younger people were evenly split on whether there is a moral imperative to marry for those who want children.

What do people consider are important factors in a good marriage? In 1982 and again in 1987 a UK survey[28] put faithfulness at the top of the list, and mutual respect and appreciation second. Understanding and tolerance were ranked third.

In 1993 in a European Union (EU) survey[29] on the question of factors contributing to a couple's happiness, 'respecting one another' came top of the list, with a European average of nearly 87 per cent and a UK response of 91 per cent. 'Loving one another deeply' rated 78 per cent Europe-wide and 77 per cent in the UK. Asked what they thought were the implications of a decision to marry, 62 per cent Europe-wide, but 79 per cent in the UK said it was 'to commit yourself to being faithful to your partner'.

We can see the converse of some of these statements in the reasons believed to be sufficient for divorce. In the UK survey in 1987, 94 per cent named consistent unfaithfulness, 92 per cent violence and 75 per cent believed that 'ceasing to love one another' was sufficient. In the EU survey in 1993, violence topped the reasons in the EU countries (81 per cent) and in the UK (86 per cent). Lack of communication between the partners came second (65 per cent Europe, 68 per cent UK alone) and the fact that one or both partners was unfaithful came third, (60 per cent in Europe, 56 per cent in the UK). There may be a difference here between the 'consistent' unfaithfulness in 1987 and the simpler 'one or both unfaithful' in 1993. But there can be no mistaking the feeling about the unacceptability of violence in marriage.

Asked whether the consequences for the children of living with one parent only were positive or negative, the European average was only 15 per cent for positive consequences. The three countries with the most positive view of the potential of one-parent families were Denmark (29 per cent), Ireland (25 per cent) and the UK (24 per cent).

We can note that views about women working outside the home are still traditional – at least while the child is very young. Some 73 per cent in the UK and 76 per cent in the Europe-wide surveys thought the mother should stay at home with a young child. But there were interesting responses in relation to the father's role – 87 per cent in both the UK and Europe-wide surveys thought it was better if the father was closely involved in bringing the child up.

In this chapter we have outlined the major changes taking place in family forms. We have reviewed some of the consequences of these changes for the adults and children involved, as well as some aspects of family life which cause concern. By no means all these changes are for the worse, but even beneficial changes can call for painful readjustments on the part of those affected by them. In later chapters we will be discussing how families are successfully adapting to change and how many people are reaching out to those in difficulty to help them find new stability.

PART TWO

Understanding families

Chapter 3

Windows on the family

A group from my church met last night to talk about your questionnaire. As we talked, I felt as if we were opening windows on the family, one by one, and seeing something new through each.

(from a submission by a church in Bradford)

Few people have thought hard about why they feel as they do about families. To understand the nature of the family and why individuals feel as they do we need to explore the rich variety of perspectives that exist.

Go into any reference library and it will be clear that people approach family issues in dramatically different ways. Social scientists, politicians, psychologists, economists and theologians draw on different theoretical perspectives, which produce different *theories* of the family.

Below are set out a number of different perspectives on the family, and ways of making sense of it. All are based on particular values, beliefs and assumptions. That is what gives them their particular focus, and the ability to illuminate sharply particular facets of the family. Taken alone, none of them is adequate; no one perspective can make sense of an institution as complex as the family. But they can help us to understand the unstated and often unexamined assumptions which people bring to their thinking about the family. So let us wander into different sections of the library and dip into different books about families. We start by looking under 'sociology'.

Functionalism

Within sociology, a current very influential theory of the family is the one that asks the question 'What are families for?' This perspective sees the family as performing certain functions crucial to society: procreation, bringing up children, regulating sex, and providing workers needed for the wider society. It describes a close fit between society and families. Society helps families thrive and vice versa. As society changes, so does the family.

Functionalism argues that in modern societies the family's functions have narrowed as traditional functions – for example, the provision of health care and education – have passed to the public sector. But the family's role remains important in relation to the socialising of the next generation and the provision of emotional and psychological support for adult members.

This perspective also gives attention to who does what within families, that is, to family roles. Until recently it assumed that families would be based on marriage for life, the automatic obedience of children, family loyalty, a father who earned a wage and a mother who looked after the children. All this was set within a network of relatives from whom the business of family was learned. For example, during the era of ration books, the wireless and free orange juice, people looked to the continuity of family life, even while it was being disrupted by the war.

Functionalists point out how families adapt to change in order to meet the needs of wider society. For example, as women have increasingly gone out to work, so roles and responsibilities have evolved from a clear separation between the tasks of mothers and fathers, towards a pattern of a rather more equal sharing of family responsibilities.

Politics

A second window on the family is offered by those who see families primarily in political terms. Here there are sharply opposing views. We pick out two extremes but there are many positions in between. One such perspective – also currently very influential – is that held by a group of thinkers sometimes called the New Right. The New Right sees the family – mother, father and children, with a periphery of other members – as the key institution of civil society: 'The family is the matrix within which the citizen is well formed or misshapen. No institution is so important yet so easily overlooked'.[1]

The New Right emphasises the family's role in socialising its members, especially through teaching and enforcing responsibility. Mutual responsibility helps to maintain the family, helps individuals to grow, and contributes to social stability. The New Right is wary of state intervention, because it sees such intervention as weakening rather than supporting the family, and acting as an incentive to irresponsible behaviour. Responsibilities within the family are seen as a bonding force. So it is good for family stability to have to care for the elderly generation and to support young people.

The New Right also sees the family as having an economic importance; improving the family's circumstances is a spur to economic effort, since it gives people a future orientation and an incentive to invest. The family becomes central to political democracy in that it creates economic independence and self-confidence in its members, and acts as a barrier against state activity and interference.

A quite different political perspective is the Marxist view. Marxism argues that the family can only be understood within its context; in western societies, that means as part of a capitalist economic and social system. Marxists see capitalism as shaping the form and ideology of the family, so what we have in contemporary Britain is one form of the family – the capitalist family.

Marxists see the family as a bulwark supporting a system of private property and they see a preoccupation with property, consumption and inheritance as shaping the family. The family ensures continuity. It becomes 'an institution [which] ensures the continuity of the havenots as well as entrenching the power and privilege of the haves'.[2]

Marxists stress, too, how women's work within the family also services capitalism. It helps in the replenishment of the labour force – what aspects of other theories of the family call socialisation. It is an important site of consumption; every family feels the need to own for itself a range of consumer goods and this stimulates production. In their economically dependent position in the family, women can be seen as a reserve army of labour, waiting in the wings till their economy needs them and returning meekly to domestic labour and dependency when the need no longer exists. The family also locks men into the economic and political system which is capitalism. Once men take on family commitments, their primary concerns become private and domestic rather than public and political. The family becomes an emotional refuge from the alienation which is the fate of the worker in a capitalist economy.

Therapy

Because families and their members experience all sorts of difficulties at different periods of their life, another interesting window is to be found through looking at the many therapeutic approaches to the family. All the major schools of psychotherapy have something to say about the family and the profoundly important work of Sigmund Freud, Jung, Adler, Klein and Anna Freud in the first half of the twentieth century was all rooted in observations of the individual's earliest family relationships, primarily with the mother. In addition a huge body of literature has developed around behavioural and cognitive approaches to helping children and adults.

In Britain, the insights of psychoanalysis emphasised the importance of the relationship between mother and baby, and the emotional environment they created.[3] There was also great interest in the development of ideas about the importance of our early human experiences of bonding and attachment.[4] These need to occur between the baby and his or her primary care-giver, if the roots of the individual's personal identity and self-esteem are to be firmly fixed, which will in turn, help him or her to withstand the many experiences of separation and loss to be faced in later life.

Further work has continued to be done on what creates a 'good enough' emotional environment for the individual to flourish as a child and to be mature as an adult.[5] To be creative in the world and to form satisfying personal relationships are broad yardsticks against which to measure maturity. Further studies in this area have included ways of understanding the relationships that occur in families – between both parents and their children; between brothers and sisters and between sexual and marital partners, and the way in which the individual passes from the dependence of infancy to the relative independence of young adulthood to the interdependence of the mature person. If we look along the shelves in the therapy section of our mythical library, we will find a great many studies of marital interaction, of parent-child relationships, and of the individual's life cycle of development.

But we will probably find that the largest number of books written during the last forty years, will be devoted to trying to understand the family as a *whole*. From this came the idea of the family as a particular kind of social system, in which whatever happens to one family member inevitably affects each of the others and their relationships. Most crucially, when one member or part of a family is in trouble, we can often see the way in which their behaviour is expressing unhappiness or difficulties on behalf of the family as a whole. This metaphor of the family as a system has enabled us to understand the way in which a family behaves as an interacting group, made up of its individual members and the dynamic and complex relationships between them, and between the family and the outside world. Family members remain unique persons in themselves with all their own weaknesses and strengths but it is also true, this perspective argues, that they are fundamentally shaped by the emotional relationships within the family. Family therapists view the family in this way and this approach has influenced many professional and voluntary agencies who try to be helpful to families in difficulties.

Family therapists argue that there are many advantages in this approach. It enables everyone who is affected by the particular difficulty or crisis to get help, not only the one or two people most obviously in pain; it helps people to understand more fully the often complex roots of their difficulties and makes it more likely that any help given will be effective. By coming together as a whole family, family members can learn new ways of tackling difficulties when they next arise.

Viewing the family as a system, with its own history, has also led therapists to consider the way in which families move through a kind of life cycle, rather like the individual's developmental stages. Every family moves through periods of stability, when everything seems to go along in much the same way. But as each new stage in the family life cycle is reached, a marriage or new partnership for example, a birth or death, a young adult leaving home or after the breakdown of a relationship, the family enters a new period of rapid change. Often the family will change its structure, shape and size at this point, moving for example from a three to a two-generational system or from a 'nuclear' family unit to a lone-parent household. It is often at these crisis points and times of rapid change that the family needs some extra help and support.

Gender

The study of gender roles and relationships, and the many changes that have occurred over the last twenty years, will fill many shelves in our library. The women's movement, feminism and more recently, men's studies, have all looked at the meaning of masculinity and femininity and the degree to which they are biologically determined ways of being human, or are social constructions of reality. Since most families are made up of a mixture of men and women, girls and boys, this has led to a large body of literature which examines the ways in which family relationships are determined by the politics of gender and, on the other hand, the ways in which family life helps to shape the individual's understanding of what it means to be a man or a woman.

Feminist writers argue that the family is not so much a partnership as an institution of structured inequality. Housewives and mothers who have no outside employment are dependent on their partners and have little influence in the public world. Though women increasingly have jobs outside the home, feminists would still argue that their position in the public sphere is unequal. Further, women's traditional role in the family is seen as perpetuating an ideal of femininity as caring and nurturing to

59

the exclusion of other aspects. Feminists also argue that the family often oppresses women through the way it gives men physical control over them, making the family a dangerous place for women.

More recently, men's studies have opened up new challenges. Men have begun to ask new questions about their unanswered needs in response to the changed expectations of women. Whilst some of this material is defensive, there is much that promises the breaking down of old barriers and the liberation of men from the oppressive nature of old stereotypes and norms. In terms of family life, this movement is leading men to expect and desire a greater involvement as fathers with their children, as equal adults fully involved in the domestic sphere of family life and as persons who have a need and a right to express grief, tenderness and vulnerability.

The relationship of gender to family life is crucial. In most families there is a close network of relationships between the sexes – men and women, boys and girls. The challenge of coping with difference, ambiguity and power in gender relationships creates occasions both for growth and for potential conflict. In particular, these may affect the development of a satisfying and fulfilling sexual relationship between adult family members and the secure formation of sexual identity in the young.

Economics

Economists are interested in the family as an economic unit, involved in both production and consumption. Members of families may own property in common, work together, share the same food and housing. In this way they should be able to maintain a better standard of living than they could on their own.

Economists point out how fundamental are the changes which have affected family life in the last decades. Up until the Second World War, most people relied on their families for their financial security. Husband, wife, children and grandparents all had a vested financial interest in holding the family together. The husband needed someone to look after the children, do the housework and perhaps help in the business as well. The wife was often dependent on her husband as her only source of income. The children needed to be looked after until they were financially able to leave home, perhaps to set up a new family of their own, and in some cases they might also hope for an inheritance or help to follow in the family trade. Elderly people needed the support of their children and a roof over their heads. The various members of the family had different needs and abilities, which complemented one another to mutual benefit. Where family co-operation was successful, the family could be the source of prosperity for all its members. Most economic partnerships involve some sort of contract defining the rights and duties of the participating members, and provision for renegotiating the contract if circumstances change. Families, and more particularly marriages, were non-negotiable.

Within this scenario, an important rationale for permanent marriage rested on the economic position of the wife and mother. She needed a commitment from her husband, backed up by penalties for breaking it, that her husband would continue to support her and her children. Otherwise it would not be in her interest to get married in the first place. But this scenario has now changed, and the economics of family life become quite different when both husband and wife can have paid jobs. In setting out the changes that have happened during the past fifty years, economists argue, it is not easy to sort out what is cause and what is effect. It is possible to see the participation of women in the labour force as a consequence of feminism, or of changes in the character of family life, but it is at least as convincing to consider the changes in the economic environment as the cause, and the social revolutions of the late twentieth century as the result.

Technology has certainly favoured the participation of women in the labour force. The need for strength and stamina in manual work has diminished, and housework has been transformed so that it is much less demanding of effort and time; clothes are now often cheaper to buy than to make or repair, central heating has largely replaced dirty coal fires, washing machines and dishwashers are commonplace.

At the same time, the role of the family in providing social care has changed. Old people are now less likely to live with their grown-up children, sick and disabled people are less dependent on the care of their families, and children are encouraged to seek their own fortunes in the world. And perhaps most importantly, social security provides an economic safety-net for those who leave family life behind, whether they are unhappy wives or runaway children.

Economists argue that the family still has a very important economic role. There are considerable savings to be made from joint consumption and shared caring and housework. But the nature of the economic partnership has changed, especially in households where the wife is working full time. Individual members of the family can now get by, if need be, on their own. Looked at economically, if they stay together it is because they

61

see it as being to their advantage, not because there is no other reasonable alternative.

Theological perspectives

Finally, moving into the theological section of the library, we find that the Christian heritage also has many different perspectives on the family. Below are summarised several of these: first, Roman Catholic and Anglican perspectives; second, evangelical and liberal perspectives (two traditions which are found in a number of churches); third, the perspectives of two contemporary Christian movements – liberation theology and feminist theology. The positions inevitably overlap; and most people will find that they recognise themselves in more than one category.

Roman Catholic

In Roman Catholicism, marriage and the family have great practical and symbolic significance as part of the natural order given by God for the good of the marriage partners and for the procreation of children. According to Roman Catholic theology, marriage is a sacrament. It is a means through which a man and a woman become a blessing and source of divine grace to each other, and for the community of which they are a part. In order to preserve this sacramental understanding, there is a strict marriage discipline. Marriage is for life. Divorce and remarriage are not permitted, though a marriage may be annulled where there is an incapacity to enter into a true and mature marriage relationship. Sexual relations outside marriage are understood as going against the will of God because sexual love is seen as the language and expression of total and permanent commitment, and because the procreative potential of sexual intercourse presupposes the undergirding of the marriage bond. Central to Roman Catholic teaching on the family is the equal dignity of every member, children as well as husband and wife. The family is understood as the foundation of society. In its own right, it is a special kind of community where moral and religious formation takes place. The Christian family, in particular, is thought of as a 'domestic church'. Its common life expresses the communion within the life of the Trinity, and involves the practice of the faith and life that is characteristic of the Church as a whole.

Anglican

The understanding of marriage and the family in classical and contemporary Anglicanism is indistinguishable in many ways from developing Roman

Catholic doctrine. This is because there has always been a sense in which the Church of England does not have its own doctrine but seeks instead to be the English expression of 'the one holy catholic and apostolic church'. The prayer books of Anglicanism testify to the importance of marriage as a gift of God in creation, both for the enrichment of the lives of the marriage partners and for the procreation of children. The position set out in the Thirty-Nine Articles is that there are two 'dominical sacraments' (Baptism and Eucharist) and five 'commonly called sacraments'. Whether or not an Anglican holds that marriage is a sacrament in the strict sense, it is still regarded as 'a holy mystery' and a means of divine grace. On the question of divorce and remarriage, Anglican teaching and practice tends to give considerable weight to pastoral and practical considerations. This has meant that Anglican marriage discipline is flexible and pragmatic. What needs to be emphasised here, however, is that, as in Roman Catholicism, Anglican thought about the family is a corollary of the Anglican doctrine of marriage. For this reason, the way into a theology of the family is most likely to have a theology of marriage as its starting-point.

Evangelical

In the Evangelical movement, which cuts across the denominations, the family is also seen as part of the natural order, the will of God that is revealed in the Bible. For Evangelicals, as for Roman Catholics, the family is very important as the intimate community where parents and children are nurtured physically and spiritually. But the family also matters as a symbol of social stability and moral virtue. It is a divinely ordained guard against the ambiguities, individualism and experimentation of a modern world which has lost its way morally and religiously. Strong emphasis is placed on the responsible exercise of parental authority in the nurture of children. The family is seen, alongside the Church, as the basic institution for the induction of children into the beliefs, values and skills necessary for godly living. As in Roman Catholicism – but on biblical rather than sacramental grounds – marriage is understood as monogamous and lifelong, and sexual relations outside marriage are prohibited. Sexual fidelity within marriage is seen as one of the ways that Christians mark themselves off from a secular world gone morally astray. Family and marital ties are seen as particularly important because they reflect in human relationships the love relationship between Christ and the Church.

Liberal

Significantly different in certain respects is the approach of liberals within many of our churches. Liberalism is in part the heir of a Reformation theology which played down the sacramental interpretation of marriage and family in favour of a more civic interpretation. It brings the tradition of the Church into dialogue with contemporary ideas and experience and seeks to build on the tradition in the light of this. Here, the family is above all a focus for the development of human individuality, religious sensibility and mature personhood, and strong emphasis is placed on the rights of the individual, including and especially those of the child. In this tradition more than in the Roman Catholic and Evangelical traditions, there is flexibility in marriage discipline and relationships. This greater openness is due in part to a re-evaluation of Christian tradition and traditional notions of authority, including the respective authority of marriage partners. It is due also to a greater sympathy towards developments in modern knowledge, including developments in the social sciences and the various schools of psychotherapeutic thought and practice.

Liberation theology

Liberation theology is a more recent development in Christian thought and practice which has had a limited impact so far in Britain. It is a protest against what is perceived to be the denial of life, experienced by the poor, especially in developing countries but also in our own inner cities. Where liberal theology gives centre-stage to the individual, liberation theology focuses on the need for solidarity with oppressed classes and groups, not least impoverished families and exploited men, women and children. It challenges others to see how much family life and family values in the West are shaped by prior and often hidden commitments of race, class, property and political economics.

Liberation theology also claims that the patterns of household consumption in the West have a direct impact on the standards of living of families living in the 'Third World'. In the light of this approach, the Church has been helped to see more clearly that it is not possible to separate matters to do with personal spirituality from matters of social justice. A true understanding of the kind of justice God wants only comes by listening to the voices of the poor and identifying with them in their struggle to live. Furthermore, education in social justice and radical discipleship is a process of spiritual formation which has to begin in homes and families if it is to have lasting effect.

Feminist theology

Feminist theology shares with liberation theology the character of a theology of protest and a commitment to unmask injustice in Church, society and the family. But whereas liberation theology focuses on the experiences of the poor, feminist theology focuses on the experiences and oppression of women. In feminist theology, the traditional, bourgeois, nuclear family tends to be seen as an instrument of the patriarchal oppression of women. From this point of view the family is not a sacred haven from the 'macho' world of work and politics, but a context where issues of gender, work and politics have a major impact in quite profound – though usually unacknowledged – ways. Important as a starting-point for this type of theology is the experience of women, including women's experience of exclusion from the public domain and their history of oppression and sexual abuse. In feminist theology, the protest of the biblical prophets against social injustice becomes an example for the protest of women today. In relation to the family, this protest focuses on the unequal distribution of power in relations between the sexes and on the traditional confinement of women to the home and to the tasks of shopping, cooking and child-rearing.

Conclusion

This briefest of sketches of different theoretical perspectives on the family from the human sciences and from theology shows a number of ways of making sense of 'the family'. There is no single, simple approach which can explain everything once and for all: rather a rich variety of emphases, all with their limitations and all influencing contemporary attitudes to families. In the following chapter we move on to highlight some of the key purposes of family life as we see it.

Chapter 4

What are families?

The family, in its many forms, is the fabric of society . . .
(from a submission by Exploring Parenthood)

The opening of Chapter 1 described a street and imagined its residents. Behind each front door in this street lived people who were linked to each other in different ways – through a blood tie, marriage, a sexual relationship, or through friendship. A street of variety, and yet, we suggested, a street where the residents might have much in common.

We decided early on not to try to define the term 'family', nor to try to decide which groups in the street were families and which were not. We realised that some tasks – the presenting of the official statistics in Chapter 2, say, or the designing of social security benefits – require objective and precise definitions to do with adults and dependent children. But we felt that the most fruitful approach for this report was to start by accepting people's own, usually quite clear, sense of what was 'family' for them.

We took this step for two reasons. First, as Chapter 1 points out, even a brief historical survey shows how shifting a concept the family is. In different times and cultures the boundary has been drawn in different places – around a whole household, for example, including visitors, servants and others who were not necessarily kin. Second, we realised from the responses to the questionnaire that many people had all but abandoned the term 'family'. Though for many the word family was positive, for others the word brought to mind a rosy image which did not fit their experience. Some felt it represented a stifling institution; for others again it evoked a sense of failure.

We believe that it is important to hold on to the positive content of the term 'family', as outlined in this chapter, but to use it in a broader and more inclusive manner. The advantage is that we can then talk of families in an inclusive sense, without discussing at every turn whether this group or that can properly be thought of as 'a family'.

In order to discern the will of God in this matter we need to know what families are. Drawing on some of the perspectives outlined in Chapter 3, this chapter sets out briefly what the Working Party came to see as the main purposes of families, and suggests some questions by which healthy family life can be assessed.

Reproduction and the upbringing of children

Human beings are a reproductive success story and the biological function of families is fundamental to this. Families enable the survival of the human race through procreation, the passing on of genetic information from one generation to the next, and the nurture and protection of the young, the weak and the old. Families meet the needs of human beings for food, drink, warmth and shelter.

Studies of the organisation of the animal world give a fascinating insight into the complex process of conceiving and rearing the young. Often family-like structures are involved – for example, birds nesting and rearing their fledglings, and lions living in protective groups. The human infant is unusual in requiring around nine months from conception to birth, followed by months of complete dependency, and gradual separation over years from the adult. The subsequent development of the child requires careful nurture by adults. Patterns of behaviour, like those in adolescence for example, which at first sight seem purely cultural, may have a biological foundation.

Places of intimacy and commitment

As well as physical care and protection, human beings have strong needs for intimacy and commitment. When young they need to be cared for; as they grow up they need to be supported as they venture out into the world; as they embark upon their adult lives they need a memory of how things used to be. Throughout this period of childhood, adolescence and early adulthood, they depend on their families for all these things, and more. They need stability, so that they can be confident that their needs will be met; and they need continuity, so that there will be some consistency in the way that their expectations are met. Above all they need to know that they matter to other people, because only if they are valued as people in their own right will they end up valuing themselves. Every child needs an opportunity to establish bonds with one main care-giver with whom he or she can experience a secure attachment, especially during the very vulnerable period between six months and three years.

When human beings become adults, it is likely that they will want to establish families of their own. They will want companionship, they will want a firm base from which they can discover the worlds of employment and self-development, and they will want safety and continuity as they explore their sexual desires. Above all, they will want to love and be loved. Many of them will want to have children of their own, whom they can bring within the circle of their love.

Then when their own children leave home and perhaps start families of their own, humans have a new set of needs. They need to feel that they are still valued, that they can continue to love and be loved, and, as they get older and the wheel turns full circle, they need to be cared for once again. Families continue to be important in the later stages of life.

Creating identity

Families then are where human beings acquire their sense of self. The progress that has been made in knowledge about the emotional development of the human self has been advanced by psychology, medicine and the social sciences. A great deal more is now understood about the complex interaction between the individual child's sense of self and his or her need for others; about the child's inability to become who he or she is without a relationship with reliable, loving adults. It is clear that a child needs consistent loving care, as well as opportunities to discover his or her sexual identity through loving contact with both male and female carers. Learning to distinguish between the self and the other, between the inner world of subjective experience and the outer world of objective reality, between the realms of thought and feeling and between the experience of past and present, all require a continuing relationship with warm, dependable, trustworthy human beings.

Past, present and future

Families look backwards and forwards. The fascination that old family photographs hold shows the human need to have a sense of origin and roots. Families can preserve memory, history and that sense of tradition which help give people their sense of identity and belonging. This need to know about origins is particularly deep in many adopted people, even when their adoption has worked out well and they have a warm and loving relationship with their adoptive family. But families are also about the future. As new members join families – through partnerships made and babies born – future possibilities open up. Families have been the cradle of hopefulness for human beings in every generation.

Stability in the context of change

Families offer both continuity and change. They can meet human needs for stability over time, needs which are particularly clear in children but which remain part of being human throughout life. This function is probably particularly important in the late twentieth century, given its startling complexity and the anxiety this can create. Alongside the excitement of fast-moving imagery, the fantasy of limitless opportunity and of unpredictable change, come the intrusions of a world which can seem full of insoluble questions. These intrusions enter consciousness at every point, through the media and through a day-to-day awareness of redundancy, violence, crime, new viruses, collapsing markets, racial harassment, homeless street-dwellers, impossible traffic jams, and international unrest. Within this social environment families can provide a haven and a retreat. They may be seen as primary sources of strength, security and stability in an uncertain and frightening world.

Families cannot always bear the weight of such expectations. They are exposed to the same frightening forces within their boundaries as exist outside; the shadow side of family life is described in several places in this report. But the human longing for meaning and love is profound in its intensity. People go on longing for a safe place. It is part of human nature to search for networks of relationships, made up of different degrees of intimacy, that will go on meeting deep needs for security and acceptance. It is a hope and an expectation to which it is right to cling. The realistic acknowledgement of human vulnerability, more easily done within the context of close relationships, remains the best means for people to withstand the 'slings and arrows of outrageous fortune'.

Alongside the need for stability and a predictable environment is the contrary need for growth. The structures of families must change if they are to meet the changing demands imposed by their members' development over time, through their interconnected life cycles, and if they are to be responsive to the changing pressures that impinge from the wider social context. Thus, whilst structure is important, it must be flexible enough to adapt to the dynamic pressures that come from within and without. Two metaphors are helpful to Christians in emphasising the need for change alongside the important need for stability. The first is *exodus*, a going out, an image of freedom from slavery for the service of God which is central to Jewish and Christian thinking. Second is the concept of *pilgrimage*, an image about journeying with God's people to worship God at a holy place. We are all called out of the security of the present and on to an uncertain future; we place our faith in the fact that it is out of the riskiness of this change that new growth will occur. Christians can harness these two important strands from their faith story and place them alongside the knowledge that has been gained from developmental psychology and the other human sciences, namely that both we humans and the social structures to which we belong move through periods of transformation.

Places where people learn

Families are often talked about as the basic 'building blocks' of society. It is an apt image. There is a real though complex link between the resilience and well-being of families and the resilience of communities and society as a whole. Families, in partnership with others like neighbours, schools and churches, prepare young people to be citizens and members of the wider community, to contribute to it and respect the needs of others. They pass on values and skills and socialise members of the younger generation into the norms and expectations of society.

> Families are the most important providers of learning, setting a context of class, culture, religion and attitude which can empower and support education for and throughout life. People spend most of their waking time within their family environment, whether as adult partners, parents or grandparents with children, or the more extended connections of kith and kin, whether blood-related or not. The network of family and friends can encourage and guide learners, providing a social environment which crosses generational boundaries, and functions regardless of financial or material resources. Most early learning is stimulated within the family, and whilst it is not all positive and supportive, home background is still the most significant single conditioning factor in people's later learning achievements. We continue to grow through the encouragement and challenge of our families.[1]

On the other hand, families are also where individuals learn their prejudices and their most destructive stereotypes. Children are shaped by the beliefs and attitudes of adults in families towards people who are perceived as being different in terms of their race, class, sexual orientation, or physical and mental abilities. It is within the context of the family that a child may learn to become racially prejudiced or homophobic.

Questions about families

Families can provide structures within which a range of basic emotional needs can be met. They are also structures for providing for the developmental needs of children; role models for young people; arenas for negotiating ways of relating to the outside world, through school and peer group and church, and through the worlds of training and work; places where conflict can be faced and lived through; opportunities for adults to engage in sexual and procreative relationships and for elderly people to give of their wisdom and support and receive appropriate care. Using this developmental perspective, we can explore the healthy functioning of families by asking the following questions:

- Can this family help its members to form deep attachments to one another and also let each other go?
- Can this family develop a sense of identity with the outside world that gives its members an experience of belonging, but also allows interaction with the wider community?
- Can this family encourage in its members a belief in their own value and in the equal value of others, learning to tolerate differences between people of different ages and gender, race, temperament and style?
- Can this family enable its members to acquire the knowledge and skills that they need to move on to the next phase of their life cycle?
- Can this family handle conflict, deal with sins against each other and find forgiveness and reconciliation?
- Can this family provide 'good enough' role models that convey the way in which women and men flourish emotionally as individuals in relationship with others, and that are consistent with the family's cultural and religious norms?
- Can this family find its own ways of coping with the times of crisis which it is likely to encounter?
- Can this family enable its members to contribute to the well-being of society, through the creation of new members and/or new understanding of what the world is about?
- Can this family play its part in transmitting spiritual values that are generally agreed to be of importance to society, as well as the religious belief and faith commitments specific to the particular community to which the family belongs?

71

God's loving care for the people of God

We end this chapter with a statement which could equally well have been its starting-point. We believe that above all families are part of God's loving care for the well-being of humanity. Since God is love, the most fundamental response to the question 'What are families?' must be that they exist to receive and respond to God's love, to live out that love between and among their members, and to pass on that love to others. Marriage is one key to what families are about – a source of grace channelled through human love – and a context for intimacy. Children are another key, one of the ways in which God blesses the love relationship of a man and a woman, and an expression of hope in God for the future. But there are a myriad of other ways in which God's blessing is bestowed through the experiences of life in families.

Our faith story begins with God creating the world and creating a man and a woman in relationship together in the Garden of Eden. Much of the Jewish and Christian Scriptures describe God's revelation to his people through different kinds of family relationships. As Christians we understand the most fundamental purposes of family life to be the revelation of God's presence in the world and as providing occasions for experiencing God's justice, mercy, forgiveness and love. Our relationship with God lies at the heart of our faith, and the living out of the relationship between God and human beings lies at the heart of what families are. We turn now to a fuller discussion of this Christian perspective.

Chapter 5

Theological perspectives on families

*Nothing is more off-putting than a church which seems to have the motto:
'Come unto me, all ye that are heavy laden, but only if ye fit.'*

(from a submission by Mencap)

The previous chapter considered what families are, both for the individual and for society as a whole. It emphasised that families are one of the contexts where people have their most formative experiences, and often their most profound experiences of intimacy and love. Families are thus where most people's spirituality is grounded, and they provide the starting point for a person's awareness of God. At a time when family life is changing and being called into question, people are looking to religion for answers to the questions: what is ultimately important; what are the principles that can guide our lives and our relationships with other people? This chapter explores the resources of the Christian tradition and sets out some broad principles.

The theological task

The task we are undertaking in this chapter is a theological one. Christian theology tries to put into words the nature of Christian faith and life for today. As such, it has to engage, not only with the rich Christian heritage of Bible and tradition, but also with the range of human experience and scientific knowledge which go to make up life in the modern world. Failure to engage with the tradition will produce a theology which is unrecognisable as Christian. Failure to engage with the modern world will produce a theology which is either unintelligible or out of touch.

The kinds of questions Christian theology seeks to answer are questions like: what does it mean to say that we believe in God? How should we live today as followers of Jesus Christ? From the starting-point that God is the Creator of all and that Jesus Christ is Lord of all, Christians believe that the answer to these kinds of question are relevant, not just for members of the Church, but for all people everywhere. Christians also believe that there is nothing under the sun for which God does not care. So God cares how people live together in societies, communities and families. Christian tradition has great wisdom to offer as we try to discern what is for the best at a time when there are many pressures on families.

The task of theological reflection on the family is important. This is because the family, which is a basic building block of society, is widely regarded as facing tensions and problems. As has already been suggested in this report, the moral consensus on what constitutes good family life is less clear than it was. The principle of lifelong monogamy, the practice of women staying at home to look after the children, the discouragement of premarital sex, the unquestioned authority of parents over children – none of this is taken for granted any longer (if indeed it ever was) as the best way to foster happy family life and human flourishing.

At the socio-economic level, the family is caught between the contradictory pressures of ever higher expectations and ever greater demands. Increasingly, two salaries are needed in order to make ends meet. Many families are trapped in a downward spiral of poverty and unemployment. The divorce rate is high and the number of lone-parent families and of births outside marriage is increasing rapidly. A period of cohabitation, either as an alternative or precursor to marriage, is becoming common. Family life is changing as society as a whole changes; and the pressures which create fragmentation in our society come to be mirrored in the breakdown of families and households. But change can have its positive side as well, as new ways of living are called for and new opportunities open up. The theological task is to discern what is for the best.

But theological reflection on the family is also difficult. Insight into the truth about how people ought to live is not gained without struggle. Not only is the family a complex reality conceived of and experienced differently by different people, but Christian experience and the Christian tradition are complex and varied too, as was shown in Chapters 1 and 3. Further, recent developments in theology influenced by the experience of women and of oppressed peoples in developing countries have helped to show more clearly than before that a Christian theology of the family will only be true if it takes seriously the experience of families and individuals who are impoverished, marginalised, victimised or violated. There is a proper sense, then, in which theological reflection has to take sides. Otherwise, we are liable to be led astray by powerful hidden persuaders which present quite unrealistic, sentimentalised images of the family, suitable only for marketing washing powder or breakfast cereals and with no bearing on reality.

Part of this critical discernment involves acknowledging that, although the family is a God-given context for human nurture and blessing, it may also be life-destroying. Awareness of the full range of possibilities is important if we are to encourage the practice of good family life in the context of the building of a just and more godly society.

Help from the Biblc

Reading wisely

The biblical tradition provides much food for thought for a theology of the family. But we cannot take over the tradition without careful reflection. This is so for a number of reasons. Although its roots go back a long way, the nuclear family as we understand it is primarily a modern, urban development, whereas the biblical tradition has to do with tribes, clans and extended households (including slaves) in ancient rural civilizations. So what the Bible says about kinship, marriage and household ties has to be reinterpreted before we can begin to discern God's will for the sort of family life we have today.

The Bible does not offer a single, once-for-all model of the family. It offers what may best be thought of as 'prototypes' for us to work with as seems appropriate. It also contains lots of stories of kinsfolk and households which can feed our thinking and imagination in this area. Therefore, the onus is on us to use the biblical resources creatively and with Christian discrimination.

Another reason for caution is that the Bible presupposes a social order quite at odds with that which we have today. In the Bible, society is organised along lines which are both hierarchical and patriarchal: husbands, wives, children and slaves – in descending order of authority. In practice, this way of ordering society resulted in arrangements which are no longer morally acceptable: slave owning, for example, and the household head having life-and-death power over his dependants. The direction of Christian thinking and social changes has been towards a more egalitarian model, with significant attention being given to the rights both of women and of children, in the context of a deeper understanding of the importance of social justice under God.

Awareness of these kinds of issues is crucial if we are to take modern ways of thinking seriously and if we are to avoid the danger of too easy an appeal to what the Bible says. For what the Bible says and what the Bible means for us today are not necessarily the same. Wise interpretation of what the Bible says is always required. If we ignore this, the likely effect is that we will either bring the Bible into disrepute as out of date and therefore dispensable, or we will bring ourselves into disrepute for failing to engage with the modern world. Having said this, the Christian Church is able to affirm, with a confidence built up over years of experience, that the Bible remains the essential fount and wellspring for Christian theology and practice, including a practical theology of the family.

Stories

Christians reflecting on the nature and purpose of families can find a treasury of narratives in the Bible about tribes, clans, households and relationships. In the present day great store tends to be placed on the individual being able to fulfil his or her potential. While this is an important development in understanding what it means to be human, the individualist approach can diminish the sense that humans belong to one another and have mutual obligations. The social dimension of being human can fade from sight, and with it the value of those groups and communities, with their patterns of interdependence, that make human growth to maturity possible. Family life, neighbourliness, social concern, all suffer from diminished commitment.

The Bible points in a different direction. It presents God as caring for people as individuals, but makes it clear that the way individual people find their true identity is through their relations with God, with fellow human beings, with themselves and with the rest of creation. A good example is the story of creation in Genesis. God's desire here is for human beings to live in relationships. This is represented by the beautiful and intimate story of the man and woman, created of the same stuff, together in the garden of God and becoming 'one flesh' through sexual intercourse. The story expresses God's intention of mutual love and reciprocity between the man and the woman. The identity of the one is completed by the other. Together they bear the image of God. Together they are given the blessing of the power to procreate. Together they bear responsibility for each other's well-being, the propagation of the species and the care of the rest of creation. This is the biblical ideal which for Christians is embodied in family life and life in society. It offers a powerful challenge to modern individualism and libertarianism and to philosophies which deny or want to dispense with society. It also offers a challenge to interpretations of relations between men and women which see them only in terms of mutual antagonism and competition or in terms of domination and submission.

Many other stories in the Bible also point, in various ways and by examples which are both positive and negative, to the importance of the social dimension of being human and, within that, the importance of families for human nurture and flourishing. As well as Adam and Eve, there are the stories of Cain and Abel, Abraham and Isaac, Sarah and Hagar, Esau and Jacob, Joseph and his brothers, Naomi and Ruth, and so on. The list is very long. It continues into the New Testament, with the birth and infancy narratives of the gospels, stories of family members healed by Jesus or pulled apart by his call to follow, and stories in the Acts of the Apostles of the conversion of whole households. It is especially noteworthy that such biblical stories do not present a particularly 'rosy' picture of the family. There is fratricide, rape, incest, adultery and murder – as well as love, fidelity and self-sacrifice, both within households and beyond them. This intense realism challenges us not to be falsely sentimental about family life. If the family is a crucial context for human growth and mutual care, it is also a social pattern marred by sin and human frailty and – like all relationships – in need of God's redeeming grace.

Wisdom, poetry and laws

As well as stories, the Bible is full of law, custom, poetry and proverbial wisdom about kinship, marriage and household order. This includes the commandment to 'honour your father and your mother'. In the Old Testament, there are also the Books of Proverbs and Ecclesiastes with their traditional wisdom about good relationships; the celebration of sexual desire and human intimacy in the Song of Songs; in the New Testament there is Jesus' teaching on the good of marriage in the gospels; and the codes of behaviour for the ordering of Christian households in the epistles. Again, this rich biblical tradition has to be interpreted responsibly since it comes from places and times far distant from our own. But all of it points to God's care for people's growth and happiness in their common (including sexual and domestic) life. It also points to the importance of wholehearted obedience to God and love of neighbour.

The legal material, looked at in more detail, reveals that the universal vision of the creation story in Genesis is reinforced by the particularity of the story of God's dealings with the people of Israel. It is as if the vocation of Israel as God's special people was to become and to be what God intended for all humankind from the very beginning. Perhaps the most important expression of this vocation is the Ten Commandments, which stand today across the world as a classic statement of personal and social morality. According to the Book of Exodus, these were given directly by God to the whole people of Israel just after their liberation from slavery in Egypt. So the Commandments are a kind of founding constitution, providing the people with broad directions for their individual and common life in their covenant relationship with God. A number of points are of special relevance for the theology of the family.

The Commandments, like the creation and the liberation from slavery, are the gift of the God who is good. That is why they begin 'I am the Lord your God who brought you out of the land of Egypt, out of the house of bondage'. Their intention is not to restrict in an authoritarian, repressive style, but to show the way in which Israel in particular and human society in general needs to go. The Commandments are intended to function as norms. God has set his people free, not in order to do whatever they like, nor to be self-determining as some modern thought takes for granted, but to be the people God wants them to be in their relationship with him. Our libertarian age tends to view commands and prohibitions with suspicion, as infringements of individual rights. But within a biblical and Christian perspective, it is important to recognise that the legitimate rights of individuals can only be identified and protected if society as a whole orders its life in ways which are godly and just. The Ten Commandments provide basic parameters for doing precisely that.

Another important feature is that the Commandments give priority to right relations with God as the basis for a humane and just social and family order. Unless God alone is worshipped and obeyed, unless people turn away from the worship of anything that might take God's place, achieving a well-ordered society and happiness in family life will not be possible. Nevertheless worship of God which does not show itself in neighbourly love is not true worship. This is clear from the fact that, while the commandments begin with the 'vertical' dimension of the people's relations with God, they proceed to the 'horizontal' dimension of the people's relations with their fellow creatures. For it is in the ways we love and care for our families, neighbours and all of God's creation that we show in practice that we love and obey God.

When we look more closely at this 'horizontal' dimension, what is striking is how relevant the Commandments are to households and families. Thus, the command to 'remember the sabbath day' by observing it as a day of rest, is teaching directed to the whole extended household, including slaves and resident aliens. In this way, a barrier against exploitation and injustice is erected. All members of the household and society are to be given an opportunity to rest. This is of fundamental importance. It expresses the idea that the family or household is above all else a place of belonging, security and growth, ordained by God to share in the life of God in all God's goodness. The modern view of the family is sometimes dominated by economic concerns, according to which the home is either an escape from work or a base from which people do other work or go out to work. The Christian understanding is different. The role of the family is not, in the first instance, to produce workers. Rather, the role of the family is to produce healthy, mature and creative human beings who have learned that, in a quite profound sense, our true work as human beings is to love God with all our hearts and to love our neighbour as ourselves.

Then there is the command to 'honour your father and your mother', accompanied by the promise 'that your days may be long in the land which the Lord your God gives you'. Respect, obedience and trust across the generations are seen as vital for the preservation of a stable and humane social order. It is a summons to respect the wisdom of elders and to be grateful for what they have to give and teach. As well, it is a warning not to neglect or despise older people. What is prized is not fleeting novelty and capitulation to the demands of the moment, so characteristic of modern consumer culture, but respect for tradition and the bearers of tradition, and respect for stability and lines of continuity. The social vision implied is one in which personal identity is bound up with being a member of a household whose allegiances cross the generations, and in which the interests of individuals are served best by their contribution to the extended family group. Again this has relevance for modern societies where people are living longer and elderly people make up an increasing percentage of the population.

The last five Commandments are all prohibitions and begin 'You shall not . . .' What is prohibited is anything that destroys human relationships, anything that threatens to return the world God created to chaos: such actions as murder, adultery, theft, false testimony and covetousness. Of special relevance to family and household ties are the prohibitions on adultery and covetousness. Adultery destroys the bond of loyalty and trust upon which marriage is based. It fractures in a fundamental way the relationship of 'one flesh' intended for marriage partners from creation on. By undermining marriage it tears at the fabric of society, as the biblical story of King David's adultery and its calamitous consequences for his people makes plain. Covetousness, similarly, is a perverted, self-centred form of human desire which undermines the loyalty and

79

solidarity upon which households and society as a whole are based. It is no coincidence that it is the last and most elaborate of the prohibitions. In a sense it sums up all the others. Those who do not covet their neighbour's livelihood, property or spouse will not murder or steal or commit adultery.

These are the standards which God liberates his people to live by. They are standards given by God, but they reflect also what Israel as a people found to be true in their day-to-day experience. From a Christian viewpoint, their validity extends far beyond their role in guiding the life of Israel. They have a direct relevance to the present day. As fundamental teaching about the will of God, they provide important guidelines for the practice of just, humane and non-exploitative relations both in families and in wider society.

If we turn from the Old Testament to the New Testament, the lines of continuity are very strong. It is not a case of the one replacing the other, as is commonly suggested. Nor is it a case of moving from law to love, or from concern with the group to concern with the individual. On the contrary, both Testaments witness to the love of God for all creation. Both Testaments witness to God's desire for people to be fulfilled as individuals and in their common life, and give explicit teaching on how that fulfilment is to be attained in the context of the family.

Jesus

In the Bible as a whole, the covenant of marriage between a man and a woman is understood as a reflection and outworking of what it means to be in covenant relationship with God. So, when we turn to the teaching of Jesus in the gospels, it is not surprising to find that Jesus affirmed the importance of marriage within the purposes of God for human society. Jesus' opposition to divorce, for example, makes clear how highly he regarded the bond of marriage. Lifelong fidelity can provide the kind of context of loyalty and trust within which a relationship of sexual love can grow to maturity, and children and elderly people find care and nurture. At its best, marriage expresses the kind of love and faithful commitment which characterises life in relationship with God.

Nevertheless many Christians accept that divorce and subsequent remarriage can sometimes be the right way forward when a marriage has broken down irretrievably and in such a way that to stay married would be to do more harm than good. Christianity should not sanctify abusive and damaging relationships. On the other hand, the ideal of lifelong fidelity in marriage is an important protest against attitudes and behaviour which strip loving relationships of depth, commitment and sensitivity. The media, advertising and our consumerist society have made this approach all too prevalent. The consequences of it for children as well as for adults have been extremely costly in moral, emotional and economic terms. What Christians believe Jesus to be calling for is quite radical in terms of contemporary social mores. It is the practice in marriage and family relationships of the kind of love which comes from God, a love which demands fidelity and commitment strong enough both to make the successful raising of children a realistic possibility and to undergird mutual care and support through to old age.

Jesus also upheld the basic thrust of the Ten Commandments, including the command to 'honour your father and mother'. Such teaching is addressed primarily to adult children with respect to their elderly parents, although it is obviously relevant to younger children as well. It shows that Jesus took it for granted that responsibility in family relationships cannot be limited to parents and their children, as in the nuclear family, but that it involves a solidarity which crosses all the generations.

What, then, of those sayings of Jesus which speak of the necessity of 'hating' one's parents and kinsfolk for his sake or which prophesy that parents will turn against those of their own children who become his followers? None of this contradicts Jesus' teaching on the Commandments. What Jesus is doing is making the point, in a provocative and memorable way, that the Kingdom of God must have first place in his own life and the lives of his followers. If it comes to the moment of having to choose between allegiance to God and loyalty to one's family then God must come first. This does not make family ties less important, since the God of Jesus is the one who gave the command to 'honour your father and your mother'. It does however show that there are other ways of serving God than by marrying and raising a family, and that marriage and family life are no substitute for the life of faith. Christianity has always recognised the vocation to the single life – given classic expression in the development of the monastic movement.

But if Jesus taught about the marriage bond and about the respect due to parents, he did not neglect children. On the contrary, Jesus is shown blessing little children and teaching the surprising doctrine that anyone wanting to enter the Kingdom of God has to become 'like a child'. It is significant that Jesus here makes the very people sometimes seen by society as being of little importance a symbol of how to live in a godly way: his care for children expresses the universal scope of God's love. As such it is a rebuke to attitudes and practices in society today which give insufficient attention to people on the margins who have no say and therefore no power, including children. The command of Jesus, 'Let the children come to me', is a symbolic gesture whose true meaning has yet to be embodied in the life of Church and society. For we (and this is more true perhaps in Britain than in some other countries) have yet to learn how to give full welcome to our children in ways that protect them from abuse, allow their individual potential to develop, and induct them into the responsibilities of belonging to family and society.

Drawing attention to children in this way was highly unusual for the time. Jesus' attitude towards women was unusual also. The stories describing his encounters with women show that Jesus was willing to listen to women, to associate with them, to be supported by them, to heal them and learn from them. This kind of evidence testifies to the fact that the Gospel Jesus preached was for all humanity – men, women and children. In his presence women felt able to respond freely as God called them. They could make a wholehearted response even when this meant going beyond cultural norms. This helps to explain why women were among those who followed Jesus all the way to the cross, stayed with him to the bitter end, and became the first witnesses to the resurrection.

True freedom: the teaching of Paul and the Apostles

The biblical insistence that becoming fully human and truly free is a social process as well as an individual one also finds powerful expression in the other writings of the New Testament. Human beings are created and liberated by God not so that they can live in any way that suits them, but so that they can live as the people of God. Freedom, in Christian understanding, is freedom *from* all that inhibits growth as people made in God's image. But this freedom has a positive side as well. It is freedom *to* live for God in the service of our neighbour. This is because our highest good is to be found in surrendering sole claim on our lives out of love for God. This doctrine helps to explain the strong communal thrust of early Christian writings.

In the Acts of the Apostles, conversion to the Christian life is linked inextricably with transformation in the life of whole households and with the sharing of goods and property between richer households and poorer ones. Women held positions of responsibility along with men, children were baptised along with adults, hospitality was practised widely, and membership was open across the boundaries of race and colour. St Paul invites single people to interpret their singleness as a call from God to serve God free from the anxieties of family ties. The family for Paul is not the be-all-and-end-all of existence. At the same time, the Pauline writings insist that family relations and household ties become transformed according to the pattern of life in Christ. Now, husbands were to love their wives, not abuse them, parents were to treat their children fairly, and masters were to rule over their slaves with justice. Paul is concerned for reciprocity in household relations. All the members of the household are responsible for loving and just relations, both for their own well-being and for the good of the local churches and wider society.

Finally, there is the teaching about marriage in the Epistle to the Ephesians which has been influential down the ages in the Church's thinking. Especially striking is the claim that the love relation between a man and a woman in marriage expresses the love relation between Christ and the Church. Here, the marital imagery used in the Old Testament to portray the covenant relation between God and his people Israel is transferred to the new covenant relation between Christ and the Church. In Christian theology, this has contributed to a very high view of marriage and provided the basis for interpreting marriage as a sacrament. Human love in marriage is not to be taken for granted or demeaned, therefore. At its highest, it symbolises that greater love that unites heaven and earth, Christ and the Church.

Some Christians today feel uncomfortable about such biblical teaching on the grounds, for example, that it takes patriarchal and hierarchical social patterns for granted and appears to have little place for the rights. of the individual. As a result, some argue that we should leave early Christian teaching respectfully behind and progress to a higher, more enlightened ethic; others that we should get back behind Paul and the Apostles to the 'true religion' of Jesus. Although both of these options are understandable, neither of them is without its problems. The first runs the risk of leaving us in the precarious position of cutting off the scriptural branch on which we are sitting and on which we depend for reliable testimony to Christ and the Christian way. The second drives a wedge between Jesus and the apostolic testimony to what faith in Jesus is all about. The most responsible way to take seriously the kinds of criticism made of scriptural ideas and images is not to cut out the offending texts. Rather it is to interpret them with historical sensitivity and spiritual maturity in order to allow Scripture's witness to the love of God to be heard in every generation.

Help from the Church's tradition

The Christian heritage has many strands and the Church exists in many institutional forms, each with its own identity, tradition and doctrine. Because of this it is impossible to set out one single and definitive theology of family life. Rather it is wiser to recognise the rich variety of emphases within the main denominations. These were described briefly in Chapters 1 and 3 as part of our discussion of perspectives on family life.

In spite of the differences between the various traditions, they also have a lot in common. They suggest that a Christian theology of family life needs to include the following significant points.

The Christian understanding of God

The human story does not begin with the man and the woman in the garden. It begins with God: 'In the beginning God created the heavens and the earth.' This means that how we think about and experience God will affect how we think about families and every other aspect of human existence. In the belief of Christians, God is the One to whom the Scriptures, the Church and all creation bear witness, and who is revealed uniquely in Christ through the Holy Spirit. The God so revealed is the God who is love: in the Trinity of God's own personal being, in creation and providence, in the incarnation of the Son of God, in the redemption of the world through God's self-giving in death, and in the coming of the Kingdom of God.

In this light, life together in marriage, families and society is a gift of God for the giving and receiving of love, whose ultimate source is God. It is one of God's ways of enabling humankind to share in the love within the Trinity, and to pass that love on to the other orders of creation. Just as the love within the Trinity overflows in the act of creation, so it is God's will that his love overflows within creation, uniting male and female, making the procreation of children possible, and building family, church and social structures which protect love and help it grow.

When Christians pray to God as Father, and sometimes too as Mother (as seen in the writings of Clement of Alexandria, St Anselm and Julian of Norwich), they are acknowledging that God is the ultimate source of true love and nurture. They are showing that it is the high calling of parents and others in positions of responsibility to show to those in their care the kind of love which comes from God. When parents bring children into the world, not only are they procreating, they are also co-creating with the

God whose love is so strong that children can be brought into the world with confidence that their future is in God's good hands. When partners are taught to love each other 'as Christ loved the Church and gave himself for her', they are being encouraged to practise a love which shows itself in truthfulness, a willingness to forgive, and acts of self-sacrifice for the good of the other. When Christians practise hospitality to family members, neighbours and strangers, they are bearing witness to the loving welcome they themselves have received from God in Christ. Finally, when Christians work for greater justice and reconciliation in family life, the Church and society, they are testifying to that in-breaking of divine love which Jesus called 'the Kingdom of God'.

In short, a Christian theology of the family must begin with a Christian understanding of God. That God is Love. In the faith of Christians, life together in family and society is made possible by that love and is ordained by God to enable a sharing in that love.

Mature personhood

The Kingdom of God is not just about the personal, spiritual life of the individual. It is also about what God wants for people in their lives together, including their sexual relationships, family life, and life in the wider society. Seen in this context, the family or household group has an important role to play. Theologically speaking, it is a primary community, a set of love relationships based on kinship and mutual commitment, where God's grace may be experienced, and where people are nurtured in every aspect of their lives and can grow into the wisdom and skills necessary for life.

In God's providential love in creation and redemption, God's desire is for human beings to grow to mature personhood as embodied, historical and interdependent beings, according to the pattern given in Christ. Thus, a healthy intimacy in families allows individuals to come to understand, appreciate and use their own bodies in ways which are fundamental to growth in personal maturity and to a sane and happy life. Maturity also comes from the discovery that 'I' have a story and am part of an ongoing story, that I alone do not constitute myself but am also constituted by others. In particular, there is a givenness to my existence which I come to acknowledge in the form of forebears, parents, siblings, kinsfolk and also neighbours, church and a wider community.

So we can say confidently that family life is a God-given context for nurturing human beings to full personal maturity. At its best, it provides protection and sustenance, a sense of belonging, the safety of intimacy, examples to imitate, training in virtue and the skills of life, friendships to enjoy, rituals to help with times of change, and an openness to the divine.

Marriage

A central place in the Christian understanding of the family has to be given also to the institution of marriage. It is seen as a relationship undertaken in a context of wider communal support and obligation. It is based on the mutual promise of the partners to lifelong fidelity to each other, expressing itself in a love which is unconditional: in sickness and in health, for better or for worse. It is a relationship which involves, not just a sharing of interests but a sharing of selves, body and soul, as part of the common life of a community.

Christians have come to understand this relationship as covenantal because it is seen as an expression of the more fundamental love relationship into which God calls all people. This implies a very exalted view of marriage. It is based on the belief that the nature of God is a clue to the 'mystery' of marital love and, conversely, that marriage reveals something of the nature of God. In a nutshell, when Christians try to express something of the depth and long-suffering nature of the love of God for humanity they find marriage to be a powerful analogy; and when they try to articulate what is involved in marriage they say 'Love your partner as God loves you!'

Children

Also central to the Christian understanding of the family is the place of children. From a Christian perspective children are a gift and blessing from God. But in our increasingly individualist and materialist society, a number of factors and forces have led to the idea that children are a 'problem'. They are sometimes talked about as if they are a drain on personal and economic resources, limit the freedom of adults to pursue their careers or personal interests, make it more difficult to find a new sexual partner, add to the social security burden of the state in times of high unemployment, and so on.

What needs to be recovered is a more profound understanding of the nature of love. The love that a man and a woman express toward each other in sexual intercourse is not for each other alone, nor does it come from each other alone. Rather, since God is love, human love comes from God and is one of the ways in which humans worship God. Through sexual intercourse adult human beings are given the privilege of co-operating with God to make new life possible and thereby to help make the future possible. The family then becomes the intimate community where that new life which children embody is celebrated, nurtured and trained. On this view, children are not obstacles to happiness and fulfilment. Rather, they are one of the most important ways a couple can achieve happiness and fulfilment. Of course, this is not an easy option. It involves much sacrifice and sheer hard work. That is why having children is thought of in the Christian tradition as a special calling which people ought not to enter upon unadvisedly. It is also why families do best when they do not go it alone, but belong instead to a wider community where they can find extra resources and much needed support and guidance.

Diverse family forms

Christians celebrate the goodness and providence of God both in creation and in the process of history. One dimension of God's goodness is clearly to be seen in the rich diversity of creation and the variety of ways in which human beings live together in their different cultures and societies. This variety of patterns of human community exists likewise in those primary communities we call 'families'. The cross-cultural researches of anthropologists and sociologists and the findings of historians of the family help us to appreciate the diversity and to recognise that whatever we affirm as being good and true for family life has to take this seriously.

This has important implications. It suggests that no single form of the family is a kind of God-given ideal, in relation to which every other form has to be compared and evaluated. For this reason, Christian citizens of the modern western world need to acknowledge quite explicitly that Christianity is not just for those who belong to nuclear families and who believe that nuclear families are 'the ideal'. What needs to be affirmed and celebrated instead is that the new life that God has shown to us in Christ is universal. It is God's gift to all people to enable them to grow into the image of God both as individuals and in their life together.

Certainly, the Christian Gospel impels us to accept the transformation, not only of our inner life, but of the forms and patterns of our corporate life as well. However, this cannot be taken to imply that there is only one form of the family which is right for everyone. The diversity of God's creation and the wide range of human experience do not support such a view. It is very important that Christian truth about people-in-relationship is not made captive to 'tribal' interests of one kind or another. Instead,

87

what is necessary is to develop and practise ways of living together which seek to embody the wisdom which Christians believe comes from God and is revealed in Christ and the Christian way.

This wisdom is deep and wide. It draws on biology and what the natural sciences teach us about gender, sexuality, reproduction and human development. It draws also upon history and what the humanities and social sciences have to say about what people past and present have found to be good and life-giving ways to live together and raise children. It draws upon the witness of Scripture and tradition to Christ as the wisdom of God who gives life and light to the world. This wisdom is God's gift to humanity. It is for people in nuclear families and people in extended families. It is for people whose families are dispersed. It is for lone-parent families. It is for people in a cohabiting relationship. It is for people in a same-sex relationship. It is God's gift to all humanity in all its diversity.

This does not mean that 'anything goes' in forms of family life. But it is very important not to allow difficulties we may have in accepting differences between ourselves and others to lead to feelings of defensiveness and hostility, on the assumption that our own position is the last barrier against a tidal wave either of moral chaos or of moral oppression. What is called for instead is a genuine search in partnership for that true wisdom which Christians call 'the mind of Christ'. This is a special priority in an area of life like the family where vested interests of so many kinds make the task of wise and just discernment difficult, and where the resources of Scripture, tradition, reason and experience do not speak with one voice. Seen in this light, our vocation is not to shout at each other from entrenched positions, but to walk alongside each other so that we can share what wisdom we have about the family in a spirit of humility and love.

Church and family

The Christian Church is the company of people who are called to bear witness to the truth of the Gospel. That Gospel is the good news that human sinfulness and the corruption of relationships are not the end of the story. God in Jesus Christ has taken on human flesh and in his suffering, death and resurrection has brought reconciliation and new life. This new life is made possible by God's Spirit, given by God to all who turn to God through faith in Christ. It is open, not just to individuals on their own, but to people in all their relationships as well. Acceptance of the forgiveness offered by God becomes the basis for living in relationships of mutual forgiveness. Receiving the Holy Spirit makes possible the transformation of relationships blighted by sin. Becoming members of the Church gives access to God's grace through hearing God's Word and receiving the sacraments which unite believers with God and bind them to one another in love and mutual care and respect.

Theologically speaking, therefore, the community of the Church is even more fundamental than the community of the family. When we speak of 'the family of the Church', we are trying to express the intimacy of personal relationship with God our 'heavenly Father' and with our 'brothers' and 'sisters' in Christ which belonging to the Church makes possible. But in so doing, we are sometimes in danger of making the natural family the dominant model for church relationships. This idea can be reinforced liturgically if too much prominence is given to 'family services', where the impression can be given – however unintentionally – that the Church is there solely for the benefit of parents and children in nuclear families. It is also common for politicians and community leaders to call on the Church to teach people 'family values', as if the Church only exists to be a kind of voluntary association for the support of marriage and family life. While the Church has much to offer in this area – as this report seeks to show – the mission of the Church cannot be reduced to matters of family life, however important they are. Rather, it is as the Church continues to witness to the grace of God in Christ that it is able to contribute to the strengthening of marriage, to life in families, and to the common life of society as a whole.

Thus, it is by being the Church that Christians are able to gain the spiritual discipline, knowledge, skills and virtues which contribute to strong marriages and stable family life. It is by learning how to worship God that Christians are able to resist the idolatry of the family and the household consumerism so prevalent in secular society. It is by learning in Church the ethic and practice of neighbourly love that Christians are able to grow into strong communities, embracing people of all kinds, including those marginalised by age or race or class or sexual orientation. It is by learning about the liberating justice of God that Christians are able to resist the 'captivity of the family' and stand against patterns of marriage and family life which are unjust and in need of transformation.

One task of the Church is to be an example of the kind of community which families and households might also be. Another task is to support and (where necessary) help reform families and households to enable them to be places where justice and neighbourly love are fostered and where old and young, men, women and children can grow into the image of God. This should also include developing church life so that its liturgies, language and patterns of ministry better support healthy domestic patterns. Important at the level of theological reflection will be a rediscovery of relatively neglected areas of thought, such as the theology of friendship. For here are seeds for creative thought and practice able to move people towards patterns of nurture, co-operation and interdependence which are more life-enhancing and open to the Spirit.

But the process cannot only be one way, from Church to family or household group. For if the small-scale society of families is given by God in creation as a source of nurture, healing and grace, then it will necessarily be the case that household groups have a lot to offer to the Church about the nature of loving relationships and the practice of mutual acceptance, interdependence, and neighbourly love. If the Church is able to offer the sacraments of Baptism and Eucharist to members of families in whatever form, they in turn can offer to the Church gifts of hospitality, seasoned friendship and wisdom honed by the pain and joy of intimate relations. Without this the family loses its ties to the wider society and the transcendent dimension of our common life, and the Church loses its rootedness in small-scale human sociability and what could be called the sacraments of everyday life.

Sin

Like any community or social institution, the family can become perverted by sin. Sin is that basic alienation from God which blights all relationships. Where God offers life and is the source of life and love, sin brings only death. Its effect on marital and family ties is disastrous and all pervasive. Gender relations in family and society become distorted, sex and the human body become marketable commodities, and men and women become rivals or turn away from each other. Partners deceive one another through adultery, or other acts of unfaithfulness; they may become indifferent to each other or violent. Parents neglect their responsibilities to their children, or try to live through their children, or manipulate and abuse them. Children, when they grow up, neglect or abuse their ageing parents. Church and society start to idolise the family, and household consumerism becomes a way of life. Religion becomes a private, family affair, a matter of personal preference or family custom only, and God becomes reduced to the level of a household or ancestral deity.

Relevant here also is the way in which ideas and images from the Bible and Christian tradition become interpreted in ways whose effect on domestic relations is pernicious, even though they were not intended to be so. For example, the rhetoric of sacrifice and caring that sometimes envelops 'the family of the Church' may conceal a heavy moral idealism and emotional load which neither the Church nor families are able to carry. This is particularly true of the way women have often been expected to be first and foremost nurturing, serving, listening people, meeting the needs of others, to the detriment of their own health and well-being.

Sin is a word which often seems unhelpful today. We tend to see wrongdoing more as the result of particular circumstances than the result of wilful decision. But the strength of the word 'sin' is not only that it describes something real but also that it challenges us to face up to our own responsibility for the wrong we do, and stops us making endless and self-deceiving excuses. To remove from a person responsibility for their actions is to deprive them of their identity. There may well be mitigating circumstances, and there is certainly sinfulness within structures as well as individuals, but in the end our humanity also demands that we learn to take responsibility for what we do.

Theological reflection on the family will be deficient if it fails to tell the truth about the family. Part of that truth is unpalatable: for it is about human sin in the lives of individuals and institutions. More than ever before, we need the moral courage to see sin for what it is and for the effects it has on our families and households.

Salvation

Salvation is about freedom from sin in order to live for God. This freedom, won by Christ through his death for us, is open to all people in every part of their lives. In the teaching of Jesus, it is likened to the return of a prodigal son into the welcoming arms of his father. In the words of St Paul, its consequence is that 'nothing shall separate us from the love of God in Christ Jesus'. That love shown in Christ makes new life possible. It enables resurrection from the dead. Relationships that have died can come alive again. Families that have fallen apart can be renewed. Societies where relations between men and women are systematically distorted or where the concerns of families are neglected can be transformed. In the faith of Christians, this is God's work of judgement, redemption and reconciliation. It is a work in which Christians and all people of goodwill are called to participate.

How does the work of salvation express itself in relation to the family? It can be shown in various ways. It manifests itself when Church and society learn to see their ideals about the family in the light of what it means to be a disciple of Christ: 'Whoever loves father or mother more than me cannot be my disciple.' It happens when a husband and wife or a parent and child learn to forgive one another: 'Forgive us our sins, as we forgive those who sin against us.' It happens when barriers of hostility or indifference separating one generation from another or one family from another are broken down and people discover a unity in love: 'In Christ there is neither Jew nor Greek, slave nor free, male nor female, for you are all one in Christ Jesus.' It happens when family members learn to act for the good of their neighbour – whoever he or she may be – in a spirit of self-sacrifice: 'Love your neighbour as yourself.' It happens when rich households and societies share their wealth with households and societies that are poor: 'In as much as you did it to one of the least of these my brothers, you did it unto me.'

Salvation is not just about the eternal well-being of the individual soul. It is also about the well-being of the community. It is about being made whole as human beings created in the image of God to share in the life of God. This 'being made whole' is something which concerns relationships as well as individual selves. That is why, from the very beginning, the followers of Christ sought, in ways appropriate to their own time and place, to work out their salvation in the context of their life together in families and household groups. Our task today is to do the same in ways appropriate to our time and place.

Some practical implications

The preceding reflections have important practical implications, some of which may be briefly mentioned here.

Values and norms

It is a clear Christian duty to identify and uphold values and norms which help to define what is conducive to human nurture and fulfilment, both for the individual and for the public good. These values are Christian values in the sense that they take their shape and texture from the Christian story and find definitive expression in Christ. But they overlap with the values shared by all people of goodwill. Such values are: love, neighbourliness, friendship, faithfulness, forgiveness, acceptance, self-sacrifice, human dignity, reverence for life, social justice and care for the

92

poor. The Church should do all it can to teach these values as embodied in Scripture and tradition and to demonstrate and celebrate them in its liturgies and common life.

Authority and roles

Within this context, it is essential that Christians contribute to the exploration of appropriate patterns of authority in family life. This may mean listening with humility to the feminist critique of patriarchy, a critique which has strong roots in the Christian tradition. The Church in particular, and society in general, can no longer tolerate a sexual division of labour which marginalises women and disenfranchises them from the mainstream activities of public life. Nor, on the other hand, should the major contribution of parents and grandparents in the domestic sphere be minimised by the assumption that it is only what happens in the world of paid work which is important. The Church must also attend with great urgency to the needs of men, helping them to find new ways of expressing a masculinity that is strong without being domineering, tender without being weak, and open to the whole range of human emotions. Jesus himself provides the perfect pattern for such an expression of masculinity.

What is needed is a re-evaluation of the contributions of men and women to our common life, not on the basis of gender differences reinforced by assumptions about the separation of the public domain from the private, but on the basis of considerations of justice and the building of the common good. This process will mean addressing the changing roles involved in the shared task of parenting. It will also mean making the effort to discover better patterns of parenting, in which parents exercise the moral courage and responsibility required to induct their children into the traditions and values which they hold dear because of the contribution they make to true human growth.

Structures

Christians will also want to discern what forms and patterns of human relationship are most conducive to human flourishing. This will include how they take responsibility for people who are abused and marginalised as well as how they take responsibility for their children. It is as right and proper to be concerned about structures, institutions and traditions as it is to be concerned about values and norms, since values are meaningless without a concept of family and society. In this context, Christians have an important contribution to make in interpreting and upholding the ideal of marriage and in practising forms of family and household life which enable men and women to live whole and wholesome lives and which provide for the nurture of children and the care of elderly people.

Too often, in recent times, the family has been reduced to being primarily a unit of consumption in a social system whose values and interests are governed by the market forces of consumer capitalism. The Church can be one of the voices resisting this trend. It can do this by calling people to reorder their lives in families, communities and work-places along lines which are not competitive and exploitative but are instead directed towards all that makes for the common good. The bottom line in our common life must not be financial profit and material comfort. From a Christian standpoint, it must be concerned with welcoming the stranger in justice and fidelity – whether that stranger is our partner, our parents, our children, our neighbours and fellow citizens, or people in other countries to whom we are tied by bonds of common humanity and co-responsibility for the future in the care for creation.

Hospitality

Christians will want to develop practices of hospitality in their family life which build strong bridges between the private sphere of the home and the public sphere of the local community and the wider society. Understood in Christian terms, hospitality is a protest against the selfishness, individualism and sentimentalism of much contemporary family life. It is a basic means of following our Lord's command to love our neighbours as ourselves. It is a way of helping the poor, sheltering the homeless, harbouring the refugee and making the stranger welcome. In this context, the exploration of new forms of household living will be important. For some this may lead to experiments in communal living, for others it may mean moving to patterns of extended household, for the majority it may open up new ways of living as nuclear families, more open to the neigh-bourhood and to the needs of strangers. There is more reflection on this in Chapters 6 and 9.

Spheres public and private

We cannot afford to accept any longer the divorce between the private sphere of the home and the public sphere of work and politics. Nor should we accept the common view of the home as some kind of escape or haven of peace from the working world of amoral competition and consumption.

The effect of this is to trivialise household and family life as having no significant contribution to make to the good of society or to individual growth. In consequence, families do not learn the skills of hospitality and practical engagement which would enable them to function more effectively as agents of nurture, shelter, material care and political vision in the public realm.

Separating the public and the private in this way has to be recognised as a disenfranchisement of the family which greatly impoverishes people's personal and social lives. Its consequences for society are significant also. Life in society becomes fragmented and morals become fragmented too, between private virtue and public policy. In addition, the human resources of skill, wisdom and maturity embodied in many retired and elderly people are largely lost to the common good. Its effect is to diminish women, since it is they who, traditionally speaking, are left at home to 'hold the baby' or who are encouraged to run themselves into the ground by taking on what is effectively a second job outside the home. Its effect is also to dehumanise men who are largely excluded from the private domain through overwork in the public sphere, or through the stigma of unemployment, or through an inability to engage effectively with the world of feeling and emotion.

The Church has an important role to play here, although it too must resist the temptation to become a private grouping, cut off from wider society. Through its worship of the one, true God who is Creator of all, and through its proclamation of Christ as Lord of all, the Church bears witness to the immorality of a political and socio-economic order which separates the public domain as the realm of amoral facts from the private, domestic domain as the realm of values, subjectivity and personal religious commitment. For if God is Creator of all and Christ is Lord of all, then every aspect of life has a moral and spiritual dimension, and 'objectivity' is a matter of seeing reality clearly in the light of the presence and rule of God.

But the role of the Church goes further still. For the Church is itself a kind of society. As such, the Church is well placed to envision, develop and practise the kinds of common life which will enable private life in families and households and public working life to interconnect in ways that work for the betterment of both. The Church can also help civic society to recognise that it exists primarily for the benefit of its weakest members, not least for children, elderly people, the poor and the stranger.

Friendship

This may lead to a greater recognition of the profound importance of friendship as a social bond. Friendship matters because it links people together by trust instead of putting them in competition with each other. It also matters as a fundamental social relationship which does not depend on sexual attraction or blood ties. It has the potential as well for overcoming antagonism in human relationships, whether between people of the same sex or across the sexes. From a Christian point of view, friendship is a fundamental social form for expressing and receiving the gift of love which comes from God and is grounded in God.

Duty

Another word which has dropped out of common usage is 'duty'. The main reason for this is probably that a sense of duty has often been used to force people into action which is against their own best interest, or into unjust suffering. For instance, a daughter may be made to feel it is her duty to devote her life to looking after her mother. A wife may feel she should stay with a violent husband out of a sense of duty and obedience to her marriage vows. An employee may feel duty bound to work long hours at the cost of his or her own health and the health of the family.

Yet life often does require sacrifice and this then involves putting one's own desires and ambitions to one side. Sacrifice is central to the vision of love that Christ has given us. Laying down one's life for one's friends, selling all that one has and giving to the poor, being a Good Samaritan, honouring father and mother – in all these areas sacrifices may well be necessary. This is the way that Christ set before us, to find life itself, calling us to take up our cross daily and to lose our life in order to find it.

Living in families involves sacrifice. A sense of duty is inevitably involved in making families work. Parents have a duty to care for, to nourish and to provide security where possible for their children. This will often involve sacrifice and the setting aside of their own needs for a time. The harm that can be done by the misuse of the obligation of duty should not allow us to escape the necessity of duty's claims upon our lives.

Inclusiveness in Church and society

When a lawyer asked Jesus the question 'Who is my neighbour?', Jesus did not give a straight answer. Instead, he told a parable which has become famous, the parable of the Good Samaritan. The striking thing about the parable is that, instead of showing who my neighbour is, it reveals how to engage in the costly business of being a neighbour to others.

This is the practical challenge to all in Church and society today: how to be neighbourly in the increasingly complex world of contemporary family and houschold life, and how to be a sign of hope and community in a world of alienation and anonymity. It is this most practical issue which needs to be explored much further. In the past, the approach of Church as well as society to people who seemed not to 'fit' has too often been typified by denial, exclusion and scapegoating. But now Christian discernment points in a different direction, one which is more honest and inclusive. It points us towards a different starting place: identification with those whose experience of relationships and family life has left them looking for a better way.

Chapter 6

Where we are now: exploring the tensions

I long for a Church that is not frightened of diversity and which recognises many kinds of families.

(from a submission by a woman in Sheffield)

Our third term of reference asked us to offer a Christian contribution to the debate by 'reflecting critically and theologically on current developments' in families. In the previous chapter we looked at some of the central resources of the Christian tradition which bear on contemporary family issues. In this chapter we move on to look at the broad implications of our arguments for a number of aspects of family life today. We look particularly at being a parent, women as mothers, men as fathers, childless couples, being single, cohabitation, gay and lesbian partnerships, and households. We conclude with one person's reflection on his experience of being part of a 'broken' family.

Being a parent

Being a parent is one of the most important tasks anyone can take on. Parents generally try to do the best for their children and put time, energy and commitment into their upbringing. What is clear, however, is that there are great pressures on parents today and a need for much stronger networks of support. There is also a widespread sense of uncertainty about how to be a parent, how to create the framework of consistent love which children need and how to set appropriate boundaries for children's and adolescents' behaviour.

The arrival of children heralds a major change in the relationship between a couple. There is likely to be less of everything for the partners when children arrive: less sleep, less money, less sex, less time for each other and their own relationship. The fact that many marriages break down when children arrive reflects the conflicting interests of parents and partners, a situation which has been called 'the parent–partner trap'.

Studies show that many couples with children feel less satisfied with their marriages than they did before the children were born. One reason may be that the arrival of children tends to mean that men and women return to more traditional roles in the home.[1]

There are other reasons why this conflict may be experienced more sharply now. First, our culture is both preoccupied with and dismissive of the rights and needs of children. Though for a while children are intensely demanding, families are not all about children; they exist for the nurture, growth and care of all their members. When children are made the sole focus, to the detriment of the competing needs of adults, this can create envy and dissatisfaction in adults, and lead to scapegoating and abuse of the child. Learning how to balance the needs and rights of the different generations is a central task of parenting. Second, the nuclear family made up of partners and children may be too small to sustain the emotional demands made upon it. Unless the family is embedded in a wider network of relationships, the number of emotional and practical tasks to be accomplished when children arrive simply becomes too great. Third, the way in which children are targeted as consumers of the latest trainers, toys, football kits or video games – and their parents as the people who will earn the money to buy all these things – can lead to conflict between parents and children and between the roles of parent and partner.

There has been a growing awareness of the obvious truth that there is no such thing as a perfect parent:

> We all want children to have the best start in life, but is it possible for parents to match up to the high hopes that often surround parenthood? Surely it is not realistic to expect everyone to be the perfect parent any more than we would expect every child to be perfect. The key issue is how parents can feel that they are 'good enough' in helping their children develop appropriate skills, knowledge and qualities, in the light of the many constraints and influences within families. The most critical of these factors will be firstly the effect of the parent's own childhood experiences, and, secondly, the social, environmental and economic circumstances in which mothers and fathers are trying to raise their children. Parents need to be supported and valued by society, as well as feeling that looking after their children is a valuable and rewarding job in itself.[2]

As we have shown, there are many different family structures in Britain today, and in Chapter 4 we listed a series of questions which summarise what families need to provide for their members. Whatever the structure of the family, these emotional provisions need to be 'good enough' if both adults and children are to flourish. These fundamental characteristics of a good enough family have particular relevance to parenting responsibilities. One of our respondents emphasised this, from the standpoint of anthropology. She wrote:

> *Anthropology [has] found very sophisticated kinship patterns, some of which supported households which were only loosely based on biological parenthood. In any case biological parenthood could not be determined with the degree of accuracy which now obtains. What really mattered was that every child was born into a cradle of interwoven rights and responsibilities from supporting adults and that these did not depend on personal likes and dislikes. As the child grew, it inherited a reciprocal basket of rights and responsibilities towards these very adults.*
>
> *(from a submission by a woman in London)*

At the core of good enough parenting lies this essential 'basket' of rights and responsibilities, transmitted by the parent and inherited by the child out of his or her experience of the parental relationship. The child has been listened to and loved, given time and attention, boundaries and freedoms, discipline and care. He or she has been treated with honesty, openness and respect, and has learned something of justice and of being forgiven. The child has received an experience of these things within a consistent and committed relationship, sufficient for him or her to flourish and to feel an essential part of the continuity of family life with its rights and responsibilities towards both the future and the past.

It is much better understood nowadays that being a parent involves some skills which have to be learnt. Parents may for example need encouragement to discover the fun and enjoyment of playing with their young children and spending time with them when they are older. Churches and voluntary and statutory bodies are much involved in the development of parenting courses, and this is discussed further in Chapter 9.

Christian reflection on the faithfulness and the grace of God has much to say about the nature of being a parent. When children are born they come into the world both dependent and defenceless. In the formative years they depend on the faithful care of their parents. If that care is not given children may be so damaged that they do not learn to have confidence in themselves or the outside world. The scars can last a lifetime. They can be seen in children who have lost (or never developed) a moral sense, or who have become so alienated that they never trust anyone. They can be seen in young people who look at all relationships in a fearful or manipulative way.

The relationship between parents and children nearly always carries the highest of hopes. Yet it is a complex relationship and is often fraught with pain and difficulty. How should we bring up our children? How should we guide them without being too heavy-handed? How can we give them a proper sense of their value and worth without leading them to arrogance? How can we help them to cope with our own anger, failure, resentment, favouritism? All these questions come to parents who are

> *For a relationship to work well, families must talk to one another and keep talking when difficulties arise. Parents must listen and try to understand. Above all they must show that whatever the disagreement they still love the child. Our family has survived a 17-year-old son becoming a father by just going on loving and supporting.*
>
> *(from a submission by a woman in Derbyshire)*

trying to do their best. Yet grace – the active love of God in our lives through prayer and faith – can show where we are in the wrong, and can restore parent and child to forgiveness and love.

Women as mothers

Most women still become mothers at some point, and though fewer women feel that this is the only job of any worth they can do, most look forward to experiencing motherhood as a positive new dimension to their lives. They value the chance to care for a baby, born of their own flesh; to have another person dependent on them, and loving them in return. They see motherhood as a way of growing up or maturing, perhaps as a sign of commitment to their partner. Children are seen as a miracle, a gift, an achievement, even though the day-to-day demands of looking after them may erode that sense some of the time.

Although couples may enter relationships with the expectation that housework will be shared equally, in practice women still tend to spend longer on housework than do men, particularly once children arrive. The assumption is made that housework and child-raising go naturally together, yet one source of frustration for mothers is that household tasks become much more difficult to do if there are small children to be amused or cared for at the same time. Conflicts over the state of the house often cause problems when children are teenagers. Indeed, though attention tends to be focused on mothers with small children, the stresses of parenting adolescents can be intense.

The isolation of mothers who are at home with small children is still a real problem. Those without their own transport, and who live some distance from sources of support and friendship, can find it very difficult.

These situations may arise for all kinds of mothers, but are particularly acute for those on low incomes. Those who live in poor housing, in high-rise blocks, or in bed and breakfast hostels, have the additional problem that being at home is in itself unhealthy and restricting. We note later some of the schemes which are set up to support mothers in such situations.

Mothers today are more likely than in the past to be working outside the home. One of the major issues for mothers is how they can manage the tension between their different roles at home and in the workplace. Chapter 7 notes the problems over finding adequate child care, but there are also questions about how well mothers can function when they *are* with their children, if they have many domestic duties, and are tired out by their jobs. Women may have very little time for themselves, but without that chance to recharge their batteries, the stresses are likely to increase.

Nonetheless, many mothers are determined to try to balance the different areas of their lives. They want to find some way of continuing in employment which uses their talents, and of having enough time for their own development, as well as being responsible for their family life. In this respect, they are witnessing to a Christian truth, that wholeness is found in a proper balance between work, rest, human relationships, and relationships with God. As we noted, the commandment to keep the Sabbath day holy reflects this need for balance. But in order to achieve it, mothers need flexibility from employers, and commitment from other family members to do their share within the home.

Mothers who choose and are able to stay at home often say they feel undervalued. Such perceptions are difficult to address, yet we hope that the emphasis we place on the importance of parenting will contribute to a valuing of mothers. Clearly they have a vital role in their children's development, and anything which can be done to support mothers in doing this task well is important.

Christians have a part to play in affirming the importance of mothers. In the past, Christianity has upheld an ideal of motherhood as the supreme achievement of women, and has taught that good mothers are unendingly giving and gentle, never complaining or thinking of themselves. It is important to restate values of service and self-sacrifice in an age which focuses on individual rights and needs. Yet if families are to allow all their members to flourish, then mothers too must have their needs respected. Part of the devaluing of motherhood is shown in the reluctance of Christians to explore images of God as a nurturing mother.

Given that this is a strand in the tradition of writers like Clement of Alexandria, St Anselm and Julian of Norwich,[3] it is surprising that it is so strongly opposed by many Christians. Understanding that all that is good in human motherhood is a reflection of the love of God might help us to affirm the value of what mothers do.

Men as fathers

The 1980s and 1990s have seen a new interest in the father-child relationship and in the role of men. This has arisen partly because of the changing lives of women, partly from a concern over the increasing numbers of children being brought up without a father-figure, and partly from a growing awareness of the crucial role that both parents play in their children's development. Major areas of research have included the inter-relationship of fathers' involvement with their children, their role as marriage partners and earners, as well as the effects of increased paternal involvement on the behaviour and emotional well-being of children.

Fundamental to this issue is the question of how to be a man when there seems so little on offer as a model for men between the 'macho' and 'wimp' images of masculinity. How is a man supposed to relate to his children and to his partner in ways which are not dominating and controlling and yet are other than a feminised version of maleness?

Most modern fathers do not want to be peripheral in the lives of their children. However many men who are in work find that their employment

> *One of the most hopeful things about family life today is that some fathers are beginning to be more involved in looking after their children.*
>
> *(from a submission by a man in Lancashire)*

practices and the norms and culture of their place of work prevent them from spending enough time with their families for them all to flourish as children and parents, women and men. This dilemma needs addressing, and there is evidence that some men are beginning to give their family a higher priority than promotion prospects at work.[4]

Despite the move towards equality in the workplace, it appears that there has not been a parallel move towards equality in the home. One study found that on average, full-time working mothers spent 28 hours alone with their children each week, while their partners spent only 6 hours.[5] As one researcher concluded:

Clearly there is a need for much more awareness of the qualities that men and women bring together and separately to the upbringing of children, both in terms of research and providing practical support and services, and in developing policies that enable mothers and fathers to share parenting and work responsibilities.[6]

We also need to devote more attention to helping men develop their self-awareness and social roles in ways which will release the creative potential of masculinity. There has been a modest, though important, development of groups where men meet and reflect on issues of masculinity and gender identity, violence and creativity, sexuality and self-worth. These are slowly beginning to be established within the Church.[7] The Church has its own difficulties in the area of sexual politics but it may be that out of its struggle to understand the meaning of masculinity and femininity, new initiatives will emerge which will be helpful to men both as fathers and partners and in being themselves.

Childless couples

'Will you be starting a family soon?' is a question which is often addressed to childless people.

A sizeable minority of people do not have children. Sometimes this is because they have chosen other priorities or do not feel that the particular commitment of becoming a parent is right for them. Often however it is because one or both of the partners is infertile. It is estimated that one in six couples have problems conceiving. Many of these couples will eventually conceive, sometimes through medical assistance. However, despite great advances, the success rates for some types of treatments are low, and many couples still find themselves unable to become parents.

The strong link between sex and procreation in western and Christian traditions means that couples who choose not to have children are sometimes made to feel that their relationship is incomplete, that they are being selfish or avoiding responsibility. However, sometimes remaining childless is a self-sacrificial choice undertaken to allow the couple greater freedom to commit themselves to the needs of the Kingdom of God.

Detailed study has been made elsewhere of advances in human fertilisation and embryology and the ethical issues which these raise.[8] What we wish to do here is to suggest that infertile couples need to be helped to see what being a family means for them. How can they be creative, nurturing and in a sense parental, even if they cannot be biological parents?

The British Council of Churches prepared an excellent report on this subject entitled *Choices in Childlessness*.[9] It argued that although children are one of the 'goods' of marriage, they are not the only one. A number of church documents since have acknowledged the pain of couples who are not able to conceive. Nevertheless much still needs to be done to raise awareness. Many infertile couples have found that their experience is not acknowledged or taken seriously. Their sense of loss and incompleteness may remain a painful secret which is difficult to share in the politeness of church communities. On the contrary, they are likely to find themselves at the receiving end of well-meaning but profoundly discouraging comments like 'When are we going to hear the patter of tiny feet?' The emphasis on children, the images of the mother and the father, 'family services' and Mothering Sunday services can be acutely painful for people living with the rollercoaster of hope and despair which is for many the experience of infertility.[10]

The submissions we had from childless couples suggested that they found many ways of coping with infertility. Some of them deliberately sought out contact with children through their godchildren, friends' children, play-groups, crèches and babysitting schemes. Others felt that this merely heightened the pain of their childlessness and was a reminder of their grief, and in any case a pale reflection of the joys of parenthood. They were more likely to seek other ways of caring, perhaps through their work and through their relationships with friends.

Attitudes towards childlessness are important for the families directly affected but they also tell us about the basic assumptions of the wider culture. Contemporary western culture assumes that children belong only to their parents and are their responsibility. This contrasts sharply with some other cultures, where the community as a whole recognises its corporate responsibility for its children. Our individualistic views leave us with several problems:

- those who do not have 'their own' children feel marginalised and often make prolonged efforts to overcome their infertility;
- it is more difficult for the community to share in the wider responsibility of caring for, disciplining and challenging 'other people's' children when, for example, they are truanting from school;
- it undermines the willingness of childless people to provide for the welfare, housing and educational needs of children who appear not to be 'their own';

- perhaps most serious of all, it deprives families with children of the support of others which could be so helpful to them.

In contrast to these views, we wish to emphasise the interdependence of those who are parents and those who are not. We suggest another approach, of 'these' children being 'our' children, who deserve the protection and support of the whole community and who will hopefully offer back to it their love, respect and care of the older generation. It would be revitalising for society if those who are childless could join in feeling responsible for these children who belong to all of us because of our common inheritance of life. Such an approach goes against the grain of contemporary assumptions and would require a profound cultural shift. But it seems to us to spring from a Christian conviction of relationship and community.

Being single

Six million people in Britain now live alone – one in four households – and one in every three church members is single.[11] Singleness takes different forms. There is the period in the life cycle when many young people leave home, and by living alone or with peers, begin to establish themselves as individuals. Later on in life people may be single either by choice or because a relationship has ended through death or breakdown. There are also people who are celibate.

Many single people have a strong sense of their own wholeness, self-worth and well-being from which they can reach out to form relationships. Working from the premise that it is people's own understanding of the term family that is important, rather than a definition imposed from outside, enables those who are single to feel that they have a full part in the experience of being family. We do not therefore view 'singleness' and 'family' as mutually exclusive, nor do we see singleness as an incomplete state on its way to becoming something else.

We do however acknowledge that some single people, whether never married or partnered, widowed, separated or divorced, would like to change their status and find it difficult to be single. They may feel lonely much of the time; if they do not have children they may mourn their childlessness. It is often hard (but extremely important) for those who are married or in stable partnerships to recall the painful experience of feeling alone and excluded from the world of couples from which they themselves may gain great fulfilment. Other single people may define themselves as being 'a part of a family', with their family membership and sense of belonging intricately tied into their relationships with their brothers and sisters, their in-laws, nephews and nieces or with close friends and their families. Still others reject the term family altogether and choose single-ness as a means of distancing themselves from a social institution that does not seem to them to be life-enhancing.

Christians, we believe, need to encourage patterns of life that are conducive to human nurture and flourishing under God. This means affirming people who are single, not just those who are married and live in families or households. The overwhelming emphasis in our culture on 'coupledom' has to be resisted. One sure sign of an inadequate set of social and moral values is the tendency to see singleness as a problem, or a failure to reach the ideal of a sexual partnership or 'married bliss'. Conversely, a sure sign of social and moral maturity is the clear recogni-tion that the single life is as valid as the married life, and that single people are often in a position to make the kinds of contribution to our common life which are more difficult for people who are married and have children. But the freedom which single people appear to have should not be over-estimated. They themselves are members of families which may make demands on them, such as caring for elderly parents. They may have their own careers to develop. Certainly they are responsible for managing their own households and cannot share the load as married couples can.

The Christian tradition of singleness has rich resources of practical wisdom in this area which need to be rediscovered and creatively reaffirmed. Some Christians feel called by God to a single life, in order that they may devote themselves to the opportunities for giving and receiving love that are different from those afforded by the calling to be married and/or to be

> *There are different ways of belonging . . . But we all share the same human need to love and be loved.*
>
> *(from a submission by a Mothers' Union group)*

a parent. For many, celibacy forms the creative core of their vocation and life-style. It is a state of life freely and deliberately chosen in order to be devoted completely to God's concerns. Celibacy gives meaning to their commitment, and, through the grace lavished by God upon all who make an offering of themselves to him, it provides the means by which they become spiritually fruitful. The dedicated single celibate person is often seen surrounded by others – children, women and men. Such people are much in demand because of their generous and easy involvement in the lives of others and their obvious fulfilment.

The submissions we received on the subject of sexuality and the single life reminded us how much attitudes have changed in the last 20 years. Young people are becoming sexually active earlier than in previous generations and are delaying marriage until, on average, 26. A recent survey of 19,000 people ranging in age from 16 to 59 indicated that a sizable minority of young people are now sexually active before 16. Of young women aged 16 to 19, nearly one fifth said they had experienced sexual intercourse before the age of 16. For young men the proportion was even higher – at over a quarter.[12] In many ways sexual freedom is much greater. But the spread of HIV has brought new threats, and the physical and emotional dangers of early sexual activity are becoming all too obvious.

A number of churches have prepared work on sexuality in recent years. *Issues in Human Sexuality,* the Church of England House of Bishops' report, was offered to the Church in 1991 as part of an educational process and invitation for continuing discussion.[13] It has become known for its reflections on homosexuality, but there is much thoughtful material also on singleness, sexuality, marriage and celibacy. We refer the reader in particular to the section entitled 'The Christian Vision for Human Sexuality'. This makes the point that an important principle in Christian thinking about sexual relations is that the greater the degree of personal intimacy, the greater should be the depth of personal commitment. In the Christian tradition this has been codified in the principle that full sexual intercourse requires total commitment, that is, in the words of the marriage service, 'faithful' and 'forsaking all others', 'to have and to hold, for better, for worse, for richer, for poorer, in sickness and in health, to love and to cherish, till death do us part'.

The report recognises that society today has largely abandoned this Christian definition of the link between intimacy and commitment and asks for more reflection. As a response to that request we make the following comments:

- First, the gap between the traditional teaching of the Church and the practice of the majority seems to us unlikely to lessen. It is likely to remain an area of great pastoral tension.

- Second, we are aware of the intense peer-group and media pressure on young people to begin sexual activity at an early age. We deeply regret the fact that sexual activity now begins so young and wish to support all those efforts made by parents, schools, churches and other bodies to help young people towards a mature understanding of sexuality and personal relationships.

- Third, we are aware of the many mature single people in contemporary society who do not feel called to be celibate and yet seek to live creatively and ethically in right relationships with others, with themselves and with God. We believe that one of the tasks facing the Church in the years ahead will be to develop a sexual ethic which embraces a dynamic view of sexual development, which acknowledges the profound cultural changes of the last decades and supports people in their search for commitment, faithfulness and constancy.

Cohabitation

I've just been going through the bookings for weddings in my church for next year. I guess that every couple is already living together – many of them for several years. It's no good pretending otherwise. It has made me decide that the kind of marriage preparation I used to give won't do any longer. I need to find a way of honouring their experience of each other, helping them affirm the strengths that their relationship already has and bring all of these into their new commitment.

(from a submission by a clergyman in Lancashire)

As Chapter 2 noted, while marriage is still very popular, cohabitation is becoming common both before marriage and between marriages. It is estimated that by the year 2000, four out of five couples will cohabit before they marry. The increase in cohabitation has been of concern to the Church of England, and the Working Party was particularly asked to reflect on what the response of the Church might be. We therefore discuss this issue at some length, drawing on the following:

- the General Synod debate on cohabitation in July 1992;
- the views of people who are themselves living in cohabiting relationships or who have children or other close relatives who are cohabiting;
- recent research conducted by the Family Policy Studies Centre, the Policy Studies Institute and the Joseph Rowntree Foundation;
- theological studies which examine cohabitation in the light of Scripture and the tradition of the Church;

- studies which suggest ways in which unmarried families may best be supported.

Three points are important to make at the outset. First, we are not discussing something that belongs out there to 'them'. Rather, it is something which affects 'us' personally as Christians in large numbers in terms of our own experiences and choices and those of our adult children. Several members of the General Synod in the 1992 debate acknowledged their experience of cohabitation, as lived out by their children. Their honesty gave the debate a remarkable quality of openness. Thoughtful reflection about cohabitation must acknowledge that all of us are part of the exploration into this form of family life. We must bring our theological and pastoral sensitivity to bear upon it from this insider perspective, so that each of us may discover more of what the Holy Spirit is wanting to reveal within the whole spectrum of our intimate relationships.

Second, there is a clear generation gap in many discussions about family life:

> When the attitudes of the older generations are compared with those of their children it is clear that older men and women hold more traditional views about marriage and family life than do their grown-up sons and daughters. The vital registration statistics – numbers of marriages, births etc – largely reflect family behaviour of the young, for it is they who are in the process of forming and building families.[14]

When older people talk about 'young people' *en masse* there is always the risk of falling into a disapproval which is too sweeping and simple (in this case not least because cohabitation is by no means only confined to the young or to this generation).

Third, as the statistical material in Chapter 2 made clear, there are several types of cohabiting relationships. The three types identified by the researchers are the young never-married couple without children, the post-marriage couple, and the never-married couple with children.[15] The motivation, characteristics and needs of these three groups are different and there are many further subgroupings within these broad divisions.

Why is cohabitation becoming more common?

A historical perspective shows that cohabitation has always existed. There have always been couples who have lived together without having been formally married in a civil or religious service. Indeed marriage 'without benefit of clergy' was the reality for the majority in Britain for centuries until the Hardwicke Marriage Act of 1753. In some minority ethnic communities cohabitation has continued to be a common family form; in parts of the African-Caribbean community, for example, living-together relationships have always been very common. Historically, Judaism made no distinction between cohabitation and marriage:

> *There is no formal marriage ceremony in the Pentateuch. The act of marriage in Biblical times was called 'taking', which was synonymous with sexual intercourse. Put bluntly sex meant marriage. To be precise, this is in the sense of a couple living together in a stable relationship (as in the modern sense of cohabitation) rather than having a one-night fling. Jewish law subsequently added two extra dimensions – the purchase/bride price and a written contract. However these are both later additions. Technically, Jewish law regards cohabitation as a legitimate form of marriage, although it would today prefer a formal marriage ceremony in a synagogue.*
>
> *(from a letter from Rabbi Dr Jonathan Romain, Maidenhead Synagogue)*

Some commentators have suggested that cohabitation today is a reaction to the clear failure of traditional patterns of partner selection, courting, marriage and setting up home. Many young people of marriageable age have seen and experienced the failures of their parents' marriages or those of their friends' parents, and are resolved to live with a partner in a different way. They have immensely high hopes for their own relationships and regard the prospect of a long-term commitment with real seriousness. The British Social Attitudes Survey found that 40 per cent of the British public as a whole would encourage young people to live together before marriage, and this figure rises to two-thirds among the under 45s.[16] It is thus possible that premarital cohabitation is becoming accepted as an institutionalised part of the mating process in the same way as the period of engagement used to be. It has been called 'a new stage in the life cycle'.

Contraception has reduced the fear of young people entering into sexual relationships before marriage. Young people who do not feel ready to marry (indeed they may have been advised by their parents not to marry young) but who do not wish to pursue sexual abstinence are faced with a choice – promiscuity with all its risks or a stable sexual relationship with one partner.

Another explanation for avoiding marriage is that couples do not want legal consequences to flow from their relationship. Although they are frequently ill-informed about the legal position, they want the freedom to determine by themselves their own obligations to each other and their children, to avoid the vows, declarations and rites of passage involved in civil or religious marriage – or at least until a time of their own choosing. Many want to be able to extricate themselves if things come to an end

> *After a first unhappy marriage I was for some years reluctant to marry again, although I loved the man I was cohabiting with. I had felt so trapped in my first marriage I did not want to run the risk of repeating the experience.*
>
> *(from a submission by a woman in Edinburgh)*

without the involvement of the law, in the hope that they may be spared the pain, expense and broken networks involved in a divorce. A study of cohabiting mothers found that fear of divorce was given as a reason for cohabiting by 30 per cent of the women interviewed.[17]

Some cohabit because they cannot face the effort or afford the cost of a wedding – 26 per cent in the study quoted. Others because they believe that cohabitation offers them the freedom of singleness with the pleasures of companionship. Women may cohabit because they believe that marriage makes them subservient to men with a loss of dignity and status. In the study quoted 21 per cent of women interviewed were hostile or apathetic to the institution of marriage and all its obligations.

Another explanation sometimes put forward is that behaviour is structured by tax, benefit and housing policies. It is however difficult to identify policies that are likely to be having a strong influence in favour either of marriage or cohabitation. Indeed civil policy appears to have become more or less neutral in respect of family form. For example, the Child Support Act places the same responsibilities for child maintenance on cohabiting and married parents. The tax system which did formerly offer some advantages to those who cohabited now no longer does so. In legal matters the position of a cohabitee is far less protected if the relationship breaks down. If the relationship is ended by death and there is no valid will, an unmarried partner does not have the same automatic entitlement to a share in the estate that a married partner has.

Legal discrimination against children born outside marriage has largely been removed, but such children may be disadvantaged because they can take their nationality only from their mother, and not from both parents as the child of married parents can. Married parents always have parental responsibility but fathers who cohabit must acquire parental responsibility by a formal agreement with the child's mother or by court order.

What are the concerns about cohabitation?

Concerns about cohabitation usually focus on two aspects, theological and social.

One area of concern has to do with the nature of love and the place of sex. The traditional Christian understanding situates sexual intercourse firmly within the context of the bond of marriage and therefore means that any non-married relationship involving sexual intercourse is wrong. Many Christians feel that the goodness of sexual intercourse is safeguarded by being kept within the special commitment of married love, and that it is put at risk once sexual intercourse outside the marriage relationship is considered permissible. For those who believe that all sexual intercourse outside marriage is wrong, all cohabiting relationships – whatever their qualities of love, commitment and tenderness – are flawed. The rise of cohabitation is seen as a sign of lack of discipline, a giving in to the spirit of the age. Other Christians take a different position and are ready to see what is good in a relationship, regardless of its marital status. They point out that the fruits of love, joy, peace, patience, gentleness and self-control can be harvested within cohabiting relationships as they can be in marriage. Marriage is no guarantee of their presence, nor cohabitation of their absence.

Another set of concerns focuses on the function of marriage within society as a whole. Some of the submissions we received argued that cohabitation poses a threat to the institution of marriage and the family as Christians understand them. Christian marriage is a community event. It is a solemn covenant made before God between a man and a woman in church, in the presence of witnesses and an ordained minister. In the service, the couple promise to love and care for each other 'for better or worse, in sickness and in health, till death us do part'. Cohabitation, on the other hand, tends to be an informal arrangement of a more private kind, involving consent but lacking the unlimited commitment of the vows of marriage. Instead of constituting a formal passage into a new social and legal status publicly acknowledged and confirmed, cohabitation is usually a relatively private expression of personal choice, an agreement between the man and the woman alone. As such, cohabitation can be seen as a step in the search for a fulfilling relationship. This may be good as far as it goes, but it does not go far enough if it fails to recognise God's desire for 'fulfilling relationship' to extend into the family, the Church and the wider society.

A third area of concern is that cohabiting relationships appear to create less stable relationships when converted into marriage. Those couples marrying in the 1980s having first cohabited were 50 per cent more likely to have divorced within five years of marrying than those who did not previously cohabit.[18] Children born to parents who marry after cohabiting may therefore be more at risk of going through family breakdown. However, the research in this area is difficult to interpret, as the evidence does not necessarily mean that cohabitation before marriage *causes* breakdown. It may reveal that those who cohabit and then marry are likely to have a rather different commitment to marriage from those who do not. It also seems that some cohabiting couples who are having relationship difficulties go on to marry because they think that this may ease their problems. For all these reasons, those who enter cohabitation with a commitment to marriage, in order to test out the partnership and their compatibility before marriage, may be deluding themselves.

It is also the case that some cohabiting relationships are fleeting and exploitative. Many cohabitations do not have the commitment to lifelong partnership that marriage does. Some cohabitations are not freely and equally entered into by both partners. In some cases they may be the best that one partner can achieve in the context of the other's unwillingness to marry. These factors mean that cohabitation risks being a more insecure relationship than marriage.

One child in six is born to a cohabiting couple and about half of all births outside marriage are to cohabiting parents. The never-married cohabitees who have children are more likely to have lower incomes, to be dependent on Income Support or Housing Benefit and unemployed, than is the case with married couples. It also appears that an increasing proportion of single, never-married, lone-parent families are separated after a cohabitation.[19] Indeed, most of the increase in the proportion of lone parents who are single is accounted for by cohabitation breakdown.

Finally, while cohabitation has become more socially acceptable, we have yet to establish a language and mode of behaviour with respect to the new form. Thus the couples themselves may find it difficult to present their relationship to the outside world. The lack of clarity in the status of the relationship can present problems for families and particularly for parents of the couple. How do they decide when a cohabitation becomes a marriage-like relationship? When should they acknowledge a cohabitation as equivalent to a marriage, by behaving as though they were parents-in-law and incorporating their child's partner into their wider family network? When a child arrives in a cohabiting relationship, grandparents, uncles, aunts and so on may feel confused about their status and they may feel deprived of straightforward contact. As the practice of cohabitation spreads these issues may become less difficult to negotiate, but there is still likely to be confusion for some time to come.

Steps along the way

The pattern for a Christian way forward was given by Jesus. It comes in the parable of the Prodigal Son, the story of the father welcoming back the son who rejected him. Jesus shows here that no one has grounds for boasting or self-righteousness in the way they live out their personal relationships. All relationships are marred by selfishness, greed and personal inadequacy. Life-giving relations begin and develop only as people 'come to themselves' in sorrow and repentance for the poverty and sinfulness of their lives, and discover in God the understanding, acceptance and guidance which make them new.

It is only in this spirit of humility, of acceptance and being accepted, that we can begin to consider properly the issue of cohabitation. Too often the Church has been censorious and judgemental in matters of personal ethics. On the other hand, the Church has often been met by a cynicism which blinds those concerned to the issues of moral and spiritual truth they need to face. The beginning of a meeting of minds and hearts is only likely to occur if the Church is honest about its failure to embody the love of God in its teaching and practice of marriage and family life, and if people in search of loving relationships admit that if they wish to find true fulfilment they cannot go it alone.

The wisest and most practical way forward therefore may be for Christians both to hold fast to the centrality of marriage and at the same time to accept that cohabitation is, for many people, a step along the way towards that fuller and more complete commitment. Such an approach has much to be said in its favour. First, it is a way of responding sympathetically and realistically to the increasing number of people who are seeking a different form of partnership from that traditionally accepted. As we have suggested, many people today want to avoid the long-term, legal commitment of marriage because they do not want to fall into the same 'trap' their parents fell into. The risk is regarded as too great. The divorce rate is very high. The awareness of domestic violence and sexual abuse in marriage is greater than ever before. Many women, in particular, want to avoid marriage because they believe that being married will leave them marginalised in a male-dominated society. Fears like this need to be respected, for they are grounded in sober, harsh reality. In such a context, cohabitation can be seen either as a way of 'testing the waters' before anything of a more long-term nature could ever be contemplated or as a clear alternative to an institution that, for many, has failed.

Second, taking a 'both-and' approach is a way of recognising that some forms of cohabitation are marriages already in all but name. Theologically and morally, what makes a marriage is the freely given consent and commitment in public of both partners to live together for life. A wedding ceremony serves to solemnise and bless the commitment that the couple make to each other. The rite of marriage is a grace which each partner bestows upon the other. It is not something bestowed by an ordained minister or the Church. This being so, it is important to acknowledge that, in terms of the theology of marriage, cohabitation which involves a mutual, life-long, exclusive commitment may be a legitimate form of marriage, what might be called 'pre-ceremonial' or 'without ceremonial' marriage. The wedding ceremony may loom so large in people's concept of marriage that they fail to see what marriage really is and that it is quite possible to be married without an elaborate ceremony. Indeed, some cohabitees give as their reason for not 'getting married' (in the sense of having a wedding ceremony) their moral objection to the high cost and conspicuous consumption which wedding ceremonies often involve.

Another reason for regarding cohabitation sympathetically has to do with changes and developments in modern life.

- Issues relating to the quality of life, including the quality of people's intimate relations and sexual experiences, are taken more seriously.

- The advent of contraception makes optional the link between intercourse and procreation.

- The shift in gender-role stereotypes, due in part to the mass entry of women into the workforce in the post-Second World War period, has led to a tendency for men and women to marry later.

- The women's movement has gained momentum over recent decades.

Such changes are significant and positive. Indeed, Christians have often played leading roles in bringing them about. While none of these changes is hostile to marriage, they have gone hand in hand with a marked rise in the popularity of cohabitation, with marriage – whether for the first or second time – viewed as a still more serious commitment to be postponed until later and involving the raising of children.

The first step the Church should take is to abandon the phrase 'living in sin'. This is a most unhelpful way of characterising the lives of cohabitees. It has the effect of reducing cohabitation in all its complexity of intentions and variety of forms to a single, sensationalist category. Theologically and ethically it represents a serious failure to treat people as unique human beings. It perpetuates the widespread misconception that sex is sinful and that sin is only about sex. It can also lead to a denial of ministry. Some clergy for example, continue to refuse to baptise the children of parents who are unmarried.

A more positive approach, involving a genuine recognition that some people choose cohabitation as a way of expressing their deepest commitments, could transform the current awkward embarrassment. What little research there has been into the experience of cohabiting couples within the Church, makes depressing reading. Le Tissier conducted a survey of cohabitees – Christians and non-Christians – about their perceptions and experiences of their contact with the Church. From her 111 responses, she found that almost all felt the Church's attitude towards them was negative. The group fell into two categories: those who had had no contact with the Church and consciously avoided doing so because they assumed that that contact would be negative; and those who had had actual negative experiences from going to church and had felt actively rejected. Le Tissier comments:

> It is evident from statistics that a large proportion of those the Church is going to try and evangelise in the 1990s will be cohabitees. It is equally evident from the survey of cohabitees presented here that many of them do not attend Church because they either fear being rejected or they have been rejected because they are cohabiting. If, then, the Church envisages a future where the general population are open to evangelism it will need to change its approach toward this large (and increasing) sector of society, since the present approach is clearly failing.[20]

The attitude which Le Tissier summarises as 'accept them when they come to Church but tell them they are wrong and make them get married' is unlikely to encourage people to feel that the Church can be a source of strength to them.

In conclusion

The Christian practice of lifelong, monogamous marriage lies at the heart of the Church's understanding of how the love of God is made manifest in the sexual companionship of a man and a woman. The increasing popularity of cohabitation, among Christians and non-Christians, is no reason to modify this belief. On the contrary, it is an opportunity and a challenge to the Church to articulate its doctrine of marriage in ways so compelling, and to engage in a practice of marriage so life-enhancing, that the institution of marriage regains its centrality.

At the same time, the widespread practice of cohabitation needs to be attended to with sympathy and discernment, especially in the light of the enormous changes in western society that have taken place recently and the effect these have had on the understanding and practice of personal relationships. Anxiety among churchgoers about cohabitation is best allayed, not by judgemental attitudes about 'fornication' and 'living in sin', but by the confident celebration of marriage and the affirmation and support of what in cohabiting relationships corresponds most with the Christian ideal. Being disapproving and hostile towards people who cohabit only leads to alienation and a breakdown in communication. Instead, congregations should welcome cohabitees, listen to them, learn from them and co-operate with them so that all may discover God's presence in their lives and in our own, at the same time as bearing witness to that sharing in God's love which is also available within marriage.

Lesbian and gay partnerships

Gay men and lesbian women form a small minority variously estimated at 1 per cent, 2 per cent, 4 per cent, 6 per cent and 10 per cent of the general population. The way in which gay and lesbian people view the concept of family is complex and involves political as well as social and personal dimensions. The way in which Christians view those who are gay or lesbian is also complex. As with other kinds of families, we have been greatly helped in our reflections by submissions received both from agencies and organisations, and from lesbian and gay people themselves.

Gay and lesbian partnerships face the difficulty of being a minority group and of often experiencing sharp prejudice. Homophobia is a pervasive evil in society, lurking near the surface both within the Church and in the community at large. It forms part of the context of life for all gay and lesbian people and can undermine their well-being and erode their confidence. In *Issues in Human Sexuality,* the Bishops called for urgent steps to be taken to overcome homophobia.[21] Gay and lesbian individuals and families often suffer from the rejection or incomprehension of their church community, in much the same way as cohabitees. The following submission graphically illustrates this point:

> *I believe strongly in committed monogamous relationships, whether they are gay or straight. In that setting relationships can grow. I think the quality of a relationship matters far more than who it is between, and the Church could do with putting more energy into encouraging people to seek quality relationships, in which they are able to be whole, healthy individuals, than pointing out precisely who is allowed to do what with whom. I don't think anyone is set free by such prescriptiveness.*
>
> *I'm aware of feeling angry at the Church for the way it heaps guilt and a sense of failure onto people who hurt enough already, and makes it so hard for those who are seen as 'different' to celebrate their everyday lives. It is no wonder people leave or are not there in the first place. The Church needs to address the fact that it is capable of alienating many through the way it puts across its views on an issue such as the family.*
>
> *(from a submission by a woman in Birmingham)*

Gay and lesbian couples may be ambivalent as to whether or not they wish to be regarded as a 'couple' or a 'family'. They hold a spectrum of views, ranging from those who consider their relationship as being a marriage, to those whose choice of a same-sex partner is in part a statement made against the institution of marriage.

The subject of gay and lesbian partnerships arouses very strong feelings, both inside and outside the Church. It seems likely that churches will continue to hold ambivalent views about homosexuality for some time to come. It is not our place to look in detail at the theological approaches to gay and lesbian people, and once again we refer the reader to recent material. Rather, we reflect on what can be said about gay and lesbian people as members of families, as people who create their own households, and who need the kind of support of the wider community that has been described elsewhere in these pages.

We make three comments. First, we believe that it is important not to generalise about gay and lesbian relationships as though they were either all equally conducive or detrimental to human flourishing. As with heterosexual relationships, we do not believe that casual, promiscuous, adulterous or exploitative sexual relationships have any place in promoting human well-being and they cannot therefore be acceptable for gay and lesbian Christians either.

Many gay and lesbian partnerships and family groups are however built on the desire for commitment and interdependence. Many are able to create relationships of high quality, capable of expressing love, joy, peace, faithfulness, endurance, self-sacrifice and service to the outside world beyond their relationship. These families, we believe, should be given encouragement and support in the living out of their commitments to each other and to their children.

Second, we believe that gay and lesbian families ought to find a ready welcome within the whole family of God and not merely within those churches where there are already a number of gay and lesbian families who create an accepting and hospitable milieu for others, important though this is. As one of our submissions said:

> There are men and women in our churches who are homosexual both in orientation and practice who regularly attend church and who see their Christian belief as an important part of their life. It is sad that for a large section of them their sexuality has to be a matter of secrecy, falsehood, repression and conflict. Expectations of healing and/or deliverance, requirements of sexual abstinence, pressure into inappropriate relationships and the lack of any positive acceptance of the contribution of gay men and lesbians within the congregation – all these can lead to the church becoming a place where love is proclaimed but not experienced and where acceptance is based on clear expectations and adherence to rules.
>
> *(from a submission by a man in the East Midlands)*

We are also aware of the gifts which lesbian and gay families have to offer to the Church and to the wider community and of the particular perspectives lesbian and gay people may have on human relationships.

Third, for the Church to be able to understand gay and lesbian relationships, it must work hard to undermine the many myths and prejudices that still abound. Gay men in particular are still often regarded as being synonymous with child abusers. Lesbian or gay parents are viewed by some as incapable of providing a suitable environment for bringing up children. There is a need for continuing research, but some limited studies of the effects of gay and lesbian parenting on children demonstrate that neither in terms of sexual identity, sexual role, nor sexual orientation are children confused or disabled, nor do they do less well academically or relationally than their peers in heterosexual families.[22]

We therefore support the House of Bishops' hope that there will be a continuing growth in understanding and support of gay and lesbian people and a fuller integration of all that they may be able to teach and give through their own particular perspective.

Households

In its submission to the Working Party, the Jubilee Policy Group, made the following comment on family values:

> *Family values are usually used to sum up all that is good, commendable and traditional about human relationships between people within the same family. However, a more helpful and more inclusive term would be 'relational' values because family values are essentially healthy relationship values, such as trust, fidelity, honesty, truthfulness, commitment, continuity, compassion, self-sacrifice, forbearance, kindness, generosity, sharing respect, understanding, loyalty, co-operation, solidarity. These contrast with values associated with independence and individualism such as freedom, choice, fairness, privacy; 'citizenship' values such as equality of opportunity, access to resources or abiding by the law; or materialist values such as financial success, celebrity and convenience.*

The relational values listed in this statement do indeed, we believe, lie at the heart of family values and closely resemble the 'fruit of the Spirit' described by St Paul. They often also form the basis of the committed living arrangements described by many of our respondents:

> *Sitting in the audience at a school concert the other night I struck up conversation with the person next to me. 'Do you have a child at school?' she enquired. I was about to say 'No', then stopped, thought, and said, 'Yes, I am the guardian for two young people'. On Mothering Sunday the two young people informed me that there was something in my room for me. On my desk there was a pink carnation in a vase, with a note giving me their love. When I thanked them they said that they wanted to let me know that they recognised that the day was special and that I had a part in it.*
>
> *A year later on Mothering Sunday I received a bunch of flowers. It made me think. Two anecdotes but making the point that family is about more than flesh and blood, and it comprises more than just a man and a woman who may or may not have gone through a legal ceremony that declares them to be husband and wife. I live as part of a group of four people, of varying ages who at this moment in time, perhaps for the rest of our lives, have made a commitment to each other.*
>
> (from a submission by a woman in Liverpool)

121

We were struck by the number of people who wrote to us about their positive experiences of living in what they called 'households'. Young people may share households with other young people for a time, or live with other families. Other people may live in households where a commitment to others has been formalised. One respondent wrote:

I share a house with Penny and her two children. Her husband died a few years ago and two years after I became a member of the household. I have taken on much of the responsibility for the children. I collect them from school, take my turn in the shopping and the cooking. When Penny goes away for work duties I am what might be called 'the parent' and operate in what would be regarded as a parental role.

This arrangement has brought me great riches. Some people might say that it is not a family in a strict sense – we are not bound by blood or marriage. But it is a family in the sense that we offer long-term commitment to each other. Penny and I expect to remain in partnership for the rest of our lives, and all of us care for each other and feel a responsibility for each other. I have been able to explore a role that would otherwise not have come my way – the gift of loving and being loved by children. And Penny has received the gift of knowing that she is not alone in the joys and responsibilities of bringing up her children. A gift she readily acknowledges and has termed 'domestic partnership'.

I never expected to be 'in loco parentis'. It has not always been easy but it has been something of a discovery. Parts of me have come to the surface that had not had the opportunity to before. Lest I sink into sentimentality some of the parts have not been too laudable. Attending to and taking one's place in the queue with the needs and demands of others is not easy. It is easier to live alone. Whether that way of living gives the best chance to discover potential is another matter; I am of course not saying that household living is the only way to realise talents. It is a way, and perhaps more inclusive than family living.

(from a submission by a woman in Southampton)

It will probably always be a minority who choose the commitment of living in this kind of household. At their best they are places of care, commitment and responsibility and can have great qualities and strengths. Households often expand the boundaries of the family beyond the relationships of blood and marriage. They can allow members to have the occasional break from their main roles with the knowledge that the other members of the house are ready to share the task with them.

The 'birth parent' in the household we heard about is able to meet professional commitments, sometimes involving being away from home for a few days, because of the secure knowledge that there is another adult member of the household able to care for the younger members of it.

Households can challenge many of the assumptions behind the nuclear family and can be a model for extending the intensely private kinds of families which are now so common. Many people wrote to us of the impossible burden they felt they carried as parents, and of the loneliness of the task. Others lamented the loss of the extended family and the committed care it offered and were eager to encourage the building of community in as many ways as possible.

The concept of friendship is important in relation both to families and to households. It may not be necessary to live under the same roof all the time to be regarded and to regard oneself as a member of a household. One respondent wrote:

> *I was a member of a household for several years, an extended one. We did not all live together (three members did, three did not); we had a commitment and care for each other. We have now dispersed geographically, but the commitment and affection remains, for some members in the tangible role of executors of each other's wills! We do not expect to remain a household for the rest of our lives, the bond being that of friendship.*

He continued:

> *At their best, households are about love, commitment, trust, care and community – all Christian concepts. Love does not presuppose a sexual relationship but does run very deep and is at the heart of the friendship relationship between household members. Friendship is often the bond that binds marital partners together also, especially in the longer term and latter years of a relationship that can often last half a century. Perhaps the first household – a flexible and mobile one – was Christ and the disciples, those named and those un-named.*
>
> *Households are not necessarily an alternative to the family and for many the family is the main place where people give and receive care. But they show that families do not have to be built on blood or marriage. I think that society has already found that units such as households are an increasingly viable and enriching way of living, that meet the needs of their members and provide children and older people within the unit with love and security. We have been given friends and family, blood relationships and non-blood relationships to cherish and challenge us. Such gifts must not be wasted.*
>
> *(from a submission by a man in Northumberland)*

The boundary around who belongs and who does not may be more fluid than in other kinds of family and may make it easier for outsiders to join for as long as they need to belong. The likeness between households and communities may be strong, and Christians have traditionally been at the forefront of experimenting with ways of creating community that answer both the need to create family and the need to reach out from family to the outside world. We see these experiments as being very valuable in enshrining and demonstrating relational values within society and in challenging all families with their importance. These we believe are being worked out in many small-scale and unassuming ways by Christians and others who are living out their commitment to others in households and communities. We note too the more formal examples of community life, including that practised by religious orders. From their many new developments in community life much can be shared and learned. We commend the continuing outworking and dialogue between these different forms of living.

One man's story

We conclude this section by quoting in full a submission that we received from a clergyman in Bedfordshire:

> *Christians have a proper concern for the stability of families, and we are right to see family breakdown as a symptom of human sinfulness. However, it is a fundamental insight of the Christian doctrine of redemption that God is able to bring good out of evil, and to use the experience of brokenness as a source of insight and vocation. All of us share in the sinfulness of the human condition in one way or another, and it is wrong to single out family breakdown as a particularly unacceptable form of human sin, or as a unique handicap in the formation of personality. I would like to suggest that there are some insights into the relationship with God and the world which perhaps come more easily to those whose experience is of a broken family than to those who have only known harmony in the home.*
>
> *My own father was a prisoner of the Japanese, and I did not see him until I was four years old. At that stage, the formation of a satisfactory relationship with him was inevitably difficult. Tensions developed between my parents which led to the breakdown of the marriage when I was 11 years old, followed by divorce a few years later. My brother and I were brought up by our mother; our father subsequently remarried, and I saw very little of him until a few years before his death when we got to know each other better, and some measure of healing and reconciliation was achieved.*

These experiences inevitably left their mark upon my own develop-ment, and also on the way in which my faith developed. To some extent it may be true that God served as a projection of my absent father. But then I began to notice how frequently the theme of family breakdown occurs in the Bible. The people of the Bible lived in insecure times, and their history was characterised by slavery, war and exile. Stories of marital infidelity abound, and in the case of David and Bathsheba, although adultery is regarded as a grave sin, particularly as it led to the murder of her husband, it is not regarded as disqualifying David from his calling to be the leader of Israel. Other forms of family breakdown, particularly the separation between parent and child, assume the role of major biblical themes.

The story of Joseph has always affected me very deeply. Family breakdown follows from the jealousy of the brothers, and the selling of Joseph into slavery in Egypt. But within the context of the providence of God, the breakdown is necessary in order to put Joseph in the position where he can become the instrument of salvation at the time of the famine. Family reconciliation is indeed part of the redemptive purpose of God in this story; but it is significant that it cannot occur until the providential purpose of Joseph's separation from the family has been achieved. When Joseph does eventually meet his brothers again, he tells them not to blame themselves for what they did, since it was God who sent him to Egypt to save lives. The family breakdown thus served God's purpose of bringing healing and hope to a much wider community than that of the family itself.

The Joseph story is very little used in the New Testament, which is surprising in view of the fact that Joseph seems almost like a Messianic figure – a representative Hebrew through whom new life is brought to the Gentiles. However the story does seem to underlie the parable of the Prodigal Son. Here again, we have the theme of family separation. This time the younger son separates himself from the family through his own greed and impatience, and he experiences the alienation of the far country – a mirror of Joseph's experience in Egypt. When the son returns, his father's comments, 'This my son was dead and has come back to life; he was lost and is found,' recall the joy and unbelief of Jacob in discovering that Joseph was still alive, 'It is enough; Joseph my son is still alive; I will go and see him before I die.'

Both these stories are major parables of the relationship between God and the world. That relationship, though described in the vocabulary of the family as being like the relationship between a father and his children, is essentially a broken one. Whether we interpret this in terms of a 'fall' at the beginning of human history, or of an evolutionary process involving pain and suffering, in which love has to arise out of and overcome brokenness, it is important to note the significance of using family failure (rather than family success) as an image of our relationship with God. The consequence of this is that the experience of family breakdown in our own lives does not necessarily distort our experience of God; on the contrary it can lead to a more accurate and realistic understanding of the relationship between God and the world – one which is aware of the dimensions of tragedy and alienation which characterise the universe, and to which those who have grown up in secure homes can sometimes be insensitive.

None of this undermines in any way the imperative which is laid upon us all to build strong marriages and loving, committed families. But it does mean that, where breakdown has occurred, insights can be gained into the grace of God which may not be otherwise available. Looking back on my own experience, I would want to express profound gratitude for it, and not see it in negative terms. In its pastoral work with broken families, especially with the children of broken families, it is important for the Church to be aware of the theological advantages which such people may have over their more secure counterparts, and not to see them simply as victims of deprivation.

PART THREE

Helping families

Chapter 7

Families and social policy

The central goal for family policy and for other areas of public policy affecting the family should be the facilitating of committed and stable relationships including parenting.

(from a submission by the Jubilee Centre)

We have argued throughout this report that families are embedded in neighbourhoods and communities and wider society. None of the families described in our street in Chapter 1 is an isolated unit; each of them makes a contribution to the neighbourhood and beyond. All of them have needs which they cannot meet alone. Their well-being depends to a considerable extent on the society around them. At the same time the well-being of society depends on the healthy functioning of families.

We have also argued that the Christian tradition has always had a concern for these connections between families and society. As Chapter 5 showed, Christians are called to be as passionately interested in how societies organise themselves and the justice of those arrangements, as we are in personal ethics or in the quality of relationships within families. Christians are called to have a particular involvement with the poor and with people who may find it difficult to make their voice heard.

Our fourth term of reference asked us to look at these crucial links and 'to make recommendations for action in public policy and the Church'. This chapter considers some of the key issues in social provision. It is clearly impossible in a report of this kind to discuss the full range of policies as they affect families. So we consider briefly some basic principles and areas of provision and go on to highlight a number of concerns. Chapters 8 and 9 address the role of the Church and the local community in helping families.

What do families need?

What do families need in social and economic terms to survive, to thrive and to be able to fulfil their caring roles?

Perhaps the first requirement is an ordered society which determines, in the public interest and with due recognition of the rights of all, what is and is not lawful behaviour. Society needs a framework of laws which regulate citizenship and/or the right of abode; record births, marriages, divorces and deaths; and provide for the ownership of property. Other responsibilities include taking steps when families are falling short in ensuring the well-being of their members. The most obvious example of this is the duty of local authorities to investigate where children are believed to be at risk of significant harm. Families need a safe environment, so provisions for dealing with crime, including racial attacks, must be in place and enforced.

The second requirement relates to the essential material needs of families. Families need:

- a sufficient and reliable income either from employment or from social security or from private means, in order to keep themselves fed, clothed and warm, and to meet other household expenses;
- secure housing;
- access to schools for their children, day care when they need it and help and support when looking after the children is difficult;
- access to preventive health services and to health care in times of illness;
- special help when it is required, for example after the birth of a baby, or when someone is chronically ill, disabled or mentally ill;
- support during times of family tension and difficulty and, when necessary, access to arrangements for dealing with separation, divorce and responsibility for the children, including child maintenance;
- a secure environment in which spiritual, mental and imaginative growth can take place and relationships be fostered through sport and through play.

While the private market has a part to play in providing for these needs, many of them have to be met through collective arrangements, organised and administered by national or local government on behalf of society. In turn, families help to finance these provisions through taxes, national insurance contributions and other charges. How these needs are to be met is the subject of vigorous debate in an open society. But if they are not adequately addressed, then families will suffer and so will society. If the resulting strains on the family are too great, relationships within the family may be badly affected, sometimes to the point of a break-up of the family unit.

A sufficient and reliable income

Employment

For most people of working age, the most satisfactory way of acquiring a sufficient and reliable income is through secure employment with adequate payment.

Until the late 1970s and early 1980s most men thought in terms of finding a steady full-time job, often expecting to spend their whole working lives with a single employer. This has changed. There has been an escalating trend towards planned redundancies, lay-offs, short-term contracts and part-time jobs. Employees have to be much more flexible, to reckon to change their employment, and even their occupations, much more frequently, and to work irregular hours. There has been an erosion of job security across the social spectrum, though its impact has been felt in different ways.

The number of manual jobs, particularly in traditionally labour-intensive heavy industries, has diminished. Many high-wage jobs for manual workers such as miners have gone, often to be replaced, if at all, by low-wage employment. Many unskilled workers now have to live with the anxiety that they may never find work again. Many young people who leave school without qualifications or skills have to face the real probability that they may never find secure employment at all. This changes the way the traditional male role of family breadwinner is perceived. It also alters the balance within many families since much of the growth in employment has been in employment for women. Moreover, great stress can be experienced by husbands and wives who have different patterns of shiftwork and cannot spend much time together.

Amongst skilled and professional workers, the reduction in job security has often been accompanied by an increase in working hours. Employers often want their employees to work very long hours, and this has created a new work ethic which can conflict with family life. Time spent travelling to work also means less time for the family. Employers may require workers to move often, which can cause strains in families, particularly where there is a conflict between the careers of husbands and wives. Constant moving can disrupt children's education and makes it more difficult for families to make friends and put down roots in their local communities.

The increasing number of mothers in the labour market in part reflects the changing role of women in society, but the primary motivation has been the need to bring more income into the family. Over the last decade there has been a dramatic increase in the number of women who are combining motherhood and employment.

- By 1992, 63 per cent of married mothers were in paid work, 21 per cent full time and 41 per cent part time.
- Some 42 per cent of lone mothers were employed in 1992, 17 per cent full time and 24 per cent part time.
- Among married mothers with a child under five years, the proportion in employment has increased from 27 per cent in 1977 to 47 per cent in 1992, 14 per cent full time, 33 per cent part time.
- Three-quarters of all married mothers with a child over five years are in paid work, 27 per cent full time, 47 per cent part time.[1]

Part-time employment has many advantages for women with children because it allows them more scope to combine paid work and family responsibilities. But it also has disadvantages. Low pay is particularly common among part-time women workers. This is because many of the jobs are in the service industries where wages are typically low and because the hourly rates of pay for part-time workers are often set at a lower level than those of full-time workers in equivalent jobs. Promotion opportunities are more limited and the extent to which part-time workers receive employment protection through the labour laws is restricted by rules related to hours of work and years of service.[2]

Official policies in this country see the changed and more flexible labour market as highly desirable because it will create more jobs. But the other side of the coin is more insecurity for many of those in work who are trying to earn their living and support their families. The majority of European Union countries have decided that the pursuit of greater flexibility must be qualified by measures to protect the wages and working conditions of those in employment – hence the Social Chapter adopted by the other 11 EU members and in all probability in the future by the new EU member states. The UK has opted out of the Social Chapter, has abolished most of the Wages Councils which set minimum wages for some of the lowest paid occupations, has reduced employment protection rights, and has experienced – and indeed encouraged – an increase in low-wage employment.[3]

There has been some recognition among major employers of the need to develop more 'family-friendly' policies in the workplace, in particular policies which allow more time for the demands of parenthood, for both fathers and mothers.[4] We would wish to encourage this trend and see it extended to a wider range of workplaces.

Unemployment

The persistence of high unemployment from the late 1970s through to the present day must be a cause of major concern. While the rate has fluctuated in recent years, it has never been lower than 1.6 million (in 1990)

> *I recently lost my job, and I know that my family paid the price.*
>
> *(from a submission by a man in Newcastle)*

and in some years has been as high as three million.[5] Unemployment is acknowledged to be a major cause of poverty. It can have devastating effects both on individuals and families, not only in income terms, but because of its impact on self esteem and the stresses within the family which unemployment creates.

A number of features of present-day unemployment cause us particular concern.

- While some people are able to move back into work fairly quickly, one million unemployed people have been out of work for more than 12 months. In January 1993, over half of long-term unemployed men were aged 25 to 49 years – the years in which people are generally raising families.[6]

- Figures for 1993 showed as many as 100,000 16 and 17-year-olds who were neither in work or training. These were calculated by the (independent) Unemployment Unit. Government figures for those receiving benefit were only 17,400.[7]

- Among both minority ethnic groups, and people with disabilities, unemployment is significantly higher than the average.[8]

- While unemployment is falling at present, recent studies have pointed to a new and worrying development: the widening gulf between the growing numbers of families with two incomes from work and an increasing number of households where no one has a job.[9]

- The economic recovery will probably do little to close the gap between these 'work-rich' and 'work-poor' households – since new jobs will tend to go to homes where one partner is already working. In a study of couples, 60 per cent of women with employed husbands were in paid employment, in contrast to 33 per cent of women with unemployed husbands.[10]

- An undesirably large proportion of those who do find work find it is temporary or insecure employment and many return to unemployment within a matter of months.[11]

The number of people wanting employment but unable to obtain it represents a major challenge to building a society where families can thrive and creative instincts flourish. We recognise that social and economic policies offer no easy solutions to the problem of unemployment and how it can be achieved together with other objectives such as low inflation and a competitive economy. However, society does sometimes have to make choices between economic objectives and these must depend on social priorities. We believe that a high priority of economic policy must be to bring down unemployment and in particular to reduce long-term unemployment and unemployment amongst young people.

Social security

All families experience variations both in their income and in their expenditure. In our view it is right that the state should intervene to sustain family incomes by providing Family Credit for low-paid families, Unemployment Benefit for people who are temporarily unemployed, Income Support for those who are unable to work, Child Benefit for dependent children, disability benefits for people whose prospects of work are inhibited by disability, and pensions for elderly people.

In recent years there have been a number of changes to the social security system that have affected families. These have often been small changes designed to save public expenditure but in their cumulative effect quite important for families. Perhaps the most important of these was the decision taken in 1980 to break the link between benefits and earnings. Since 1980 most benefits have been uprated by inflation only. Thus as earnings have moved ahead of prices, the living standards of those who must rely on benefits have declined relative to the living standards of those who work. In our view this drift in the comparative value of social security benefits cannot be allowed to continue without isolating those on benefit from the rest of society and destabilising the inter-generational contract implied in a 'pay as you go' scheme. The social security system reinforces social cohesion and helps to protect the vulnerable. If it is allowed to diminish in relative value it will undermine social solidarity in this country – a point emphasised by the report of the Joseph Rowntree Foundation *Inquiry into Income and Wealth*.[12]

Another change has been the drift from reliance on contributory benefits to selective and income-related benefits. The latter benefits are not claimed by all those entitled to them and create poverty traps in combination with the tax system when they are withdrawn as earnings rise. The increase in real housing costs in recent years has tended to work against the Government's attempts to reduce the impact of the poverty and unemployment trap.

There have been constant incremental changes for unemployed people, among which have been the abolition of earnings-related Unemployment Benefit, the abolition of child additions to Unemployment Benefit, culminating now in the proposal to replace Unemployment Benefit by a Job Seekers Allowance. There has been a massive increase in the numbers of people, including unemployed people, dependent on Income Support. The majority of lone parents were certainly worse off as a result of the introduction of Income Support,[13] but other claimant groups also suffered from the replacement of additions for special needs by the cash-limited and mainly loan-based Social Fund and by the fact that they had to pay water charges and, now, 8.5 per cent VAT on fuel for the first time.

One of the most dramatic changes in the Income Support scheme was the ending of entitlement for most 16 to 18-year-olds. The idea was that young people of this age should be supported and subsidised by their parents. They should either stay on at school or enter the Youth Training Scheme (YTS) where there was an intention that places should be guaranteed for the whole age-group who needed them. However, there is evidence that YTS has not succeeded in delivering either the quality or the quantity of training that is required and young people have had to fall back on the resources of their parents. Young people who have been in care, or are unable to live with their families, perhaps because they have been thrown out, seem to be falling through the net. Although a severe hardship scheme was eventually established, it has proved cumbersome and far less effective than a straightforward right to Income Support, even with work-related safeguards. One result has been a large increase in youth homelessness in the last decade or so.[14]

It is possible to see social security benefits as a drain on public resources, but we prefer to see them as an expression of a commitment by society to stand by people in times of need. We recognise the need for efficiency and fairness in the distribution of benefits, and we recognise the risk of benefits in certain circumstances acting as a deterrent against proper self-reliance. We are nevertheless concerned by a number of aspects of recent Government policy. For example:

- Although the level of Child Benefit is now linked to prices, we regret the fact that for a time during the 1980s its level was frozen. The overall level of financial support for families with children has diminished over time. We see Child Benefit as a recognition of the importance of parenting and of the expenditure it involves, even in the case of families which are comparatively well off.[15]

- We are deeply concerned about current legislation in relation to the entitlement to benefits of most young people aged between 16 and 18. This is a difficult time for many young people and for their parents, and the current regulations can distort family relationships and cause much real hardship.

- We are concerned about the Government's proposals to tighten the criteria for entitlement to Unemployment Benefit. This may increase the hardship faced by those who genuinely cannot find work and will increase the insecurity felt by all those who know that their jobs are at risk.

Housing

Having a good place to live is one of the most important bases for family life. Housing provides security and stability, and a familiar environment that is particularly important for young children.

At the beginning of the First World War, nine-tenths of all accommodation was privately rented; now the proportion is only 8 per cent. Between the two dates, slum clearance, the sale of better standard properties into owner-occupation, and the lack of incentives to develop new privately rented homes all contributed to this steep decline. Efforts by successive governments since the 1970s to reverse this trend have had only limited effects.

Although all local authorities were able to build houses for rent from 1900, the biggest expansion in this sector came after the Second World War. Council housing represented over one-quarter of the housing stock in 1961. By 1990, this had declined to one-fifth. An alternative provision of low-rent housing by housing associations was stimulated in 1974 by legislation which enabled the associations to receive up to 90 per cent of the costs of developing accommodation.

Changes in legislation have reduced subsidies for building low-rent accommodation both in the local authority and housing association sectors. Measures have also been taken which have allowed rents to approach 'market' levels in both the public and private sector. The Government decided that these increased rent levels would be met

> *To have a home of one's own is a basic necessity . . . Homelessness is the most acute form of marginalisation in society, and few relationships thrive in these circumstances.*
>
> *(from a submission by Shelter)*

through Housing Benefit for people on low incomes. The 'burden' of housing costs was transferred from the Department of the Environment to the Department of Social Security. The Department of Social Security has plans however to cap its Housing Benefit bill, which has escalated in recent years.

It is very difficult for young people starting work for the first time to find rented accommodation at a price which they can afford, particularly in rural areas.[16] This often forces them to continue living in their parents' home at a time when they might do better learning to fend for themselves. These difficulties are compounded when two young people are ready to start life on their own, because learning to be a couple in the inhibiting atmosphere of a parental home can be stressful.

The major form of housing tenure has become owner-occupation, which stands at just under 70 per cent. Traditionally owner-occupation has offered security of tenure and freedom from harassment. There has been a degree of choice about location and style of accommodation. In addition, there have also been considerable financial benefits through tax relief on mortgage interest payments and the acquisition of a capital asset. Owner-occupation was given a further boost by the Right-to-Buy policy in 1980 for people in local authority accommodation. Great difficulty has however been experienced by many families in maintaining mortgage repayments during times of unemployment. A stagnant housing market has made it difficult for people to move to take up work, and for others the capital value of their property is less than the outstanding mortgage loan. Many families cannot meet their mortgage obligations from a single salary and this has put pressure on families for both partners to find work.

Further pressures will arise if proposed new measures to restrict severely the payment of mortgage interest for those on Income Support are implemented.

The chances of families having accommodation which is secure have decreased markedly in recent years. The ultimate manifestation of such insecurity is homelessness. Between 1981 and 1991 the number of households accepted by the local authorities as homeless and in priority need doubled. Some 78 per cent of these were families with dependent children or households including a pregnant woman.[17] It was estimated that in 1990 alone a quarter of a million children were among those accepted as homeless.[18] Local authorities have statutory duties towards homeless people. Families accepted as unintentionally homeless by the local authorities have a right to permanent accommodation, probably after a period in temporary accommodation. In 1993, of over 58,000 households in temporary accomodation, 41,000 were in short-life housing, 12,000 in hostels and 5,500 in bed and breakfast hotels.[19]

The Churches' National Housing Coalition – along with many other organisations in the field of housing and homelessness – believe that the relative neglect of affordable rented housing must be reversed. All available resources should be used – council housing, housing associations and private landlords, and through new home building for rent and by bringing empty property back into use. Given that families need stability in order to flourish, we recommend that the Government reviews its housing policies in order to achieve a clearer and fairer strategy.

Families with children

Children under five

The parents of children under the age of five who have chosen or need to work outside the home must find child care which fits the demands made on them by their employment. Children under the age of five need care which is appropriate to their educational, social and developmental needs. The debate about child care must address these sets of needs simultaneously.

Many families need two incomes to meet household costs; for them, and for many lone parents, going out to work is not an optional extra but a financial necessity. This makes the availability of child care a crucial consideration; indeed a recent magazine survey of 14,000 parents revealed that their major source of anxiety was how to combine parenthood and work.[20]

138

The majority of working parents rely on an informal network of friends and family to provide child care. One parent may look after the children while the other works. Sometimes grandparents are willing to care for the child if they are living nearby and are not working themselves. In 1990, relatives, friends or neighbours provided child care for almost two-thirds (65 per cent) of employed mothers with a youngest child under five. It was estimated that in 1990 less than 10 per cent of children under 4 had places in any form of non-family child care. An increasing proportion of under 5-year-olds now attend state nursery or state primary school on a full or part-time basis, (in 1992 just over half of all under-5s). Many others use playgroups or private nurseries instead or in addition. Even so parents often find this provision difficult to reconcile with the working day.[21]

The Government's policy is that it is the responsibility of parents to arrange and pay for the child care they need to enable them to go out to work. Public support for child-care services for children under five is confined to local authority day nursery and nursery school provision, grants to certain playgroups, and support for registered child-minders. This policy has led to an *ad hoc* pattern of provision with little assurance of high quality. Good quality child care is expensive, and only parents earning well above the national average can afford to pay market costs. The Government has started to address this by announcing a disregard which takes into account some of the costs for child care for some parents on Family Credit and this is a welcome step.

Some working parents are helped by their employers, but in 1991 only one per cent of working women with a child under 5 years worked for an employer who provided child-care facilities. A further one per cent of working mothers received some sort of financial contribution or subsidy from their employer for child care.[22] Some employers have developed imaginative new ways of helping parents. All this is useful but any child-care system which places too much responsibility on employers could be expected to reduce their profitability and encourage employment policies which discriminate against the parents of young children, for example the hiring of temporary staff on a casual basis.

Studies have concluded that high quality pre-school education can lead to lasting cognitive and social benefits, especially for children from disadvantaged backgrounds. It is likely that the investment in such education will 'pay off' in terms of later economic savings to society.[23]

There is also a growing consensus amongst early-childhood specialists as to how the needs of pre-school children can best be met. It shows that a curriculum should be developed within which children are able to be active learners, learning through first-hand experience with plenty of opportunities for play and talk. The involvement of parents as equal and respected partners, the training and retraining of staff because the children's needs are complex, and integration with other services for parents and children are also important. A common set of minimum standards needs to be developed in accordance with these principles, for implementation throughout the spectrum of provision, in nursery schools and classes, day nurseries, playgroups, and workplace crèches. Pre-school experiences need to be seen as important in their own right, and not merely in terms of preparing children for primary school.

The development of a social policy which properly addresses the needs of families will require radical changes in provision for children under five. At present, provision in Britain lags behind every other European Union country. One study comments:

> It seems shameful that at the end of the twentieth century, after countless reports from researchers and national committees, we are still having to make the case that a child's early years are of crucial importance. It is now well established that a high percentage of children's learning takes place in the first five years of life, and that this is the time when attitudes are formed, when relationships are made, when concepts are developed, and the foundation for all skills and later learning are laid.[24]

Child-care problems do not cease when children start at infant school. The duration both of the school day and of the school year is too short to allow parents to work full-time without anxiety. About 20 per cent of all 5 to 10-year-olds, some 800,000 children, are left alone after school or during holidays while their parents work.[25]

Any new system will need to take full account of working parents' need for child care. This will mean the provision of care for many more children under the age of three, an expansion of nursery education or playgroups to provide places for all the children aged three and four whose parents wish it, and the provision of care to supplement the school day and the school year for both nursery school and primary schoolchildren, preferably on the same site. We welcome government pledges to extend nursery education to 4-year-olds and the assistance Government has given to promote out-of-school programmes. Action will also be needed to improve standards in playgroup and child-minding provision. Implementation will be expensive; the Government will need to recognise the value of investing in families both in the present and for the future.

Schools

Schools share with families the responsibilities of bringing up children of compulsory school age. Section 17 of the Education Act 1988 states:

> The curriculum should reflect the culturally diverse society to which pupils belong and of which they will become adult members. It should benefit them as they grow in maturity and help to prepare them for adult life and experience – home life and parenthood; responsibilities as a citizen towards the community and society nationally and internationally.

The formality of these words is brought to life by concerns expressed about schools by Scottish parents in a recent survey.[26] These parents want schools:

- to provide for the well-being of their children to enable them to be happy, safe and successful;
- to give them the fullest opportunity to learn;
- to help them get on well with other pupils within a framework of acceptable behaviour;
- to ensure they are treated fairly;
- to give guidance and help in making choices.

Schools are children's own communities. They give opportunities for learning independence and socialisation skills alongside formal education. Parents need to be involved in their children's schooling, both because they must have confidence in what goes on in these communities, and also because they need to relate to their children throughout their schooling years. Parents need to acknowledge that difficulties at home can sometimes lead to children being physically or verbally abusive to teachers. For schools to become really caring communities, there must be good home-school liaison and communication and a willingness to work through problems.

Concerns that have been expressed about deteriorating standards of behaviour and rising crime among young people must be set alongside the many positive achievements of the young. More young people are gaining qualifications, and at higher levels, than ever before, and many show a high degree of maturity. Credit must be given to the commitment of schools in developing a caring and moral ethos, for example in promoting anti-bullying policies, tackling racism, and encouraging children to have a share of responsibility in how the school is run. Many schools actively encourage engagement with the local community involving pupils of all ages, their families and teachers in community service, such as working with disadvantaged people, or in projects to improve the local environment. In many areas of social deprivation, schools have a dual role, both to encourage pupils to achieve in an environment where good exam results and records of achievement do not bring their reward in terms of employment opportunities, and to create and maintain a school ethos which reflects values that may be difficult to find outside the school gates.

There have been many recent changes in the way education is delivered, such as the introduction – through funding arrangements and the publication of exam league tables – of competition between schools. Where local resourcing is insufficient, these may disadvantage the most vulnerable schools. However there is also an increasing awareness that it is not just high academic achievement that makes a 'good school'. Parents and carers want children to succeed within a caring environment. It is in the area of assessing quality in schools that the greatest strides are now being made; the concept of 'value-added' has become widely acceptable. The introduction of the testing of the academic achievement of children from the age of seven is well known; alongside this must be placed the emphasis on schools fulfilling the requirements of the Education Act 1988 quoted above, which forms part of the guidance to the new teams of inspectors of the Office for Standards in Education.

> The overall judgement about a school should be based on evaluation of the quality of education provided, the standards of work, the efficiency of management and the effectiveness of the school community in providing for the spiritual, moral, social and cultural development of pupils.

There are also many changes in further and higher education, especially to do with funding (including the problems arising for many students from the introduction of student loans and the fact that student grants have fallen in real terms). One recent positive element has been a willingness on the part of institutions to develop open learning, encouraging people from all backgrounds, and those without formal qualifications, to get involved in further study. This has been particularly useful for women who have been given the opportunity to return to learning after having children. In spite of tumultuous change, problems of resourcing, low teacher morale and other factors, these are good days for families and education. Never before has there been such broad access to lifelong learning.

Support for families with children

The relationship between the responsibilities of families for the care of their children and the responsibilities of the state are comprehensively defined in the Children Act 1989. The Act enshrines a number of guiding principles which include the following points.

- The welfare of the child is the paramount consideration.
- Wherever possible children should be brought up and cared for within their own families.
- Parents with children in need should be helped to bring up their children themselves.
- This help should be provided as a service to the child and his or her family and should:
  - be provided in partnership with the parents;
  - meet each child's identified needs;
  - be appropriate to the child's race, culture, religion and language;
  - be open to effective independent representations and complaints procedures;
  - draw upon effective partnership between the local authority and other agencies including voluntary agencies.[27]

We strongly support the principles enshrined in the Children Act, but would welcome greater resources being made available to families with children. In particular we would like to see more preventative services and more support both for parents who are separating or divorcing and for those whose children are in trouble with the law. Local authorities, in particular social services departments, generally do impressive work with families. But they often do not have the resources to intervene to help children who are in need, and this actively discourages them from defining those children as being in need. Despite these reservations, the Children Act does represent a most valuable step forward in balancing the needs of children and the responsibilities of families, and we welcome its enactment. In Chapters 8 and 9 we look in greater detail at support for families.

Crime and the family

The relationship between crime and the family is complex. Members of families may be either the victims or the perpetrators of criminal acts; and criminal acts may take place within the family itself.

Families may experience crime through its direct impact on the family as a whole (for example a burglary) or through its impact on a family member (for example personal assault). Age, gender and life-style are important factors in determining whether a person becomes a victim of personal crime. Where a family lives is a factor in determining the risk from household crime.

Young men are the most likely victims of violence and robbery; women are more likely to be the victims of theft from the person, sexual assault and domestic violence. The risk of violent assault is least likely for women and men over 60. Families living in inner-city areas are at the greatest risk from household crime. Members of minority ethnic families are more

---

As well as the difficulties experienced by their white counterparts, black families are subjected to the added dimension of racial discrimination and harassment.

(from a submission by the General Synod's Race and Community Relations Committee)

---

likely to be victims of both household and personal crime than white people, and are particularly vulnerable to racially motivated attacks.

For some families, including those from ethnic minorities, the experience of crime will be repeated. Research in recent years points to the increased likelihood of those who have been victims on one occasion becoming victims again soon after.[28] Repeat-victimisation is highest in areas which suffer the most, and the most serious, crime.

Fear of crime is a significant factor in many people's lives. Many women and elderly people feel that it is unsafe to be on the streets after dark; and children's freedom to play and explore is restricted by parents anxious about their safety. Home Office research suggests that more people are affected by the fear of crime than by crime itself.[29] Measures need to be taken therefore to reduce unfounded anxiety about crime, as well as to reduce both opportunities for offending and risks of victimisation.

The recent emphasis being given by central and local government to community safety is to be welcomed. Initiatives to enhance the safety of communities must include attempts to address and redress the social factors that contribute to offending behaviour.

Perceived increases in crime, and offending young people in particular, have fuelled the debate about family values, with the family being seen as the key influence on whether children become offenders. However care needs to be taken. The true extent of crime in our society is not known; therefore we do not know for certain the total number of offenders and its distribution by age and gender. The evidence available from the annual Criminal Statistics indicates that the vast majority of offenders are under 25 and male; that the peak age for known offending is 18 for males and 15 for females; and the vast majority of offences committed by young people are offences against property, mainly theft or handling stolen goods. The available evidence also suggests that there has been a fall in the number of juveniles (aged 10 to 16) known to be committing offences in England and Wales over the past ten years; this fall can only be partly accounted for by the fall in the number of juveniles in the population.[30]

There is no single answer to why young people offend, nor simple solutions to the problems raised by their offending. Poor parenting, school failure and economic deprivation have all been identified as important predictors of offending behaviour.[31] These need to be addressed within social crime prevention strategies. As the report *Crime and the Family* makes clear, the quality of care and supervision children receive in their home is crucial.[32]

Difficulties, stress or dysfunction within families may also lead to criminal acts within the family group, ranging from minor thefts and criminal damage to the most serious offences of violence against the person. Acts of minor theft (for example pilfering from mum's purse) occur in many families as children grow and test boundaries, and most often can be dealt with by parents. In some families, however, thefts or other criminal acts become persistent and are a symptom of a deeper problem requiring help from skilled professionals.

The most serious acts of violence against the person (rape and murder) occur more within families than elsewhere. Around 60 per cent of female homicide victims and around 20 per cent of male homicide victims are killed by partners or other members of their families (mainly parents).[33] There is now growing awareness of the extent and effects of domestic violence, and of parental abuse of children, both of which are addressed elsewhere in this report.

Delinquency and the levels of crime in a society are by no means simply due to a new breakdown in morality or widespread failure in the family. Nonetheless, policies which help families to function well could make a worthwhile contribution to the reduction of crime, whilst measures for crime prevention would be of substantial assistance to families.

Health care

Overall, the health of the nation has significantly improved during the twentieth century. People live longer, fewer children die in infancy, and many of the serious illnesses of childhood are no longer a threat. Women are much less likely to die in childbirth, and reliable contraception has made a tremendous difference to their lives, freeing them from continual child-bearing. Many formerly fatal diseases are now treatable. Advances in medical technology have saved many lives, and made it possible for life to be created in new ways through different kinds of assisted conception. Expectations are high that there is, or should be, a cure for everything, and the growing cost of health care leads to difficult decisions about priorities and rationing.

Despite the positive nature of the overall picture, there remain some matters of concern. The large increase in cases of childhood asthma is a particularly worrying trend for families. There are wide differences in the health of the poorer and the more affluent sections of the population as shown in the reports *Inequalities in Health*[34] and *The Health Divide*.[35] Families of semi-skilled and manual workers experience the greatest health disadvantages. Differences exist before birth. Babies born to parents in Social Class V are likely to have lower birth weights than babies born to parents in Social Class I and, as a result, are almost twice as likely to die in the first year of life. The incidence of illness for children in low-income families is higher than average. Research indicates that children from manual-class backgrounds are more likely to have had pneumonia by the age of five, and at the age of ten, they are likely to have had chronic coughs, higher rates of absence from school, or behavioural problems. It is clear from a recent report that these problems persist and may even have worsened.[36]

The existence of a totally free and comprehensive health service would in itself do little to prevent people becoming ill. Poor housing, unemployment, lack of an adequate and varied diet, pollution, the use of alcohol and tobacco, all have a deleterious effect on health.

In 1992, the Government published a White Paper, *The Health of the Nation*,[37] which set national targets for improvement in health. These included reducing the numbers of teenage conceptions, smoking among

11 to 15-year-olds, and the incidence of obesity among children and adults. Success in achieving the targets relies on the development of healthier life-styles. This is not straightforward for many people. For example, research has shown how difficult it is for families on low incomes to afford an adequate diet.[38] Parents often go without food to give their children better nourishment. The ease with which children can become more physically active depends on the safety of their external environment and the availability of affordable recreation. Children of low-income families are debarred from many leisure facilities by the prices charged.

It is clear that good health does not simply depend on individual behaviour. Concerted Government action will continue to be needed through a range of social policies if these concerns about health are to be properly addressed.

Special help for families

Maternity and paternity entitlements

The birth of a baby is one of the most important events in family life, and it is essential that provision be made for it. Financially-supported maternity leave is 18 weeks in the UK, which compares favourably with France, Luxembourg and the Netherlands (16 weeks), Belgium, Germany and Greece (15 weeks) and Ireland (14 weeks). However, in other respects, provision in the UK compares poorly. In Germany, Austria and the Netherlands, for example, women are entitled to 100 per cent of their normal earnings for the total period of statutory leave. While there have been recent improvements (October 1994) in the UK provisions, as a result of the European Union Pregnant Workers Directive, it remains the case that in this country only a proportion of women receive earnings-related pay (at 90 per cent of earnings) and only for 6 of the 18 weeks maternity absence. The remaining 12 weeks, and the whole 18 weeks for other women are paid at a lower – if for some an improved – rate.[39]

When we consider the poor level of maternity provision for employed women in the UK alongside the paucity of child-care provision, it is clear that the needs of the family are not receiving sufficient attention. Where there is poor maternity provision, women need to return to the labour market in order to maintain the household's income. As we noted earlier, however, this is difficult given the lack of child care which fits the needs of employed mothers. Many women face hard choices, and would prefer to have a longer break before returning to work, or would like to go back to work part time. The situation for working mothers is made more difficult by the absence of statutory family leave provisions in the UK. Five countries of the European Union provide a child-rearing allowance to enable either the mother or the father to be at home to care for the new baby for varying periods, some as long as two years. The UK Government, on the other hand, has for some time resisted the introduction of an EU Directive on parental leave on the grounds that the cost to employers would be too high, and that this is a private concern which is to be negotiated between employers and their employees.

It is true that there is some evidence that contractual arrangements for paternity leave are becoming slightly more widespread, but the period of leave tends to be short, two or three days. Leave for family reasons, where it is available, is often discretionary, and pay during parental leave is rare. We encourage employers to develop both parental leave and leave for family reasons more fully. We would like to see a more thoroughgoing government review of the needs of families at the time of childbirth and early child-rearing, and more attention to the need to enhance the role of fathers at this crucial stage in family life.[40]

Help with caring

One of the primary functions of families is to care for their members. But there are bound to be occasions when the degree of care that is needed by a particular member is so great that the family finds it very hard to respond, or can do so only by making inordinate sacrifices.[41]

In recent years, new responsibilities have fallen on families, particularly on women, who may be caring for more severely disabled or mentally ill people, and for longer periods than before. The principle of moving people out from institutions into the community has largely been welcomed, and carers often value the chance to care for their relatives in their own homes. But the support services they need have not always been readily available, and this can cause severe stress to families, as well as to the wider community.[42]

A particular burden falls on children and young people in this country who are themselves carers. It is estimated that 10,000 children and young people under 16 years have responsibility for the physical care of one of their parents.[43] But whether the carers are young or old, all families which include someone with a disability need economic security and extra support.

The National Health Service and Community Care Act 1990 is concerned with meeting the needs of groups such as elderly people who are frail or confused, people who are physically or mentally handicapped or mentally ill, and people who misuse alcohol or drugs. Under the Act, local authorities are required to undertake an assessment of the social care needs of their populations (for home helps, meals on wheels, bathing, visits from the district nurse, day centres, respite care etc.) and to ensure that services are available for meeting them. Local authorities are then required to undertake individual assessments of people who need care, and to draw up individual care plans, in consultation with the individuals concerned and their carers. Local authorities then purchase care, as appropriate, from providers in either the statutory or independent sector. Some of the help is offered free of charge and some on payment.

As a framework, community care has been generally welcomed. However, concern is now being expressed about the adequacy of the care that is available. To some extent this is a consequence of the confusion which inevitably accompanies any large structural change, but the main constraint is the level of financial provision made by national Government. Local authorities argue that they do not receive sufficient funding from Government, and the Government maintains that it is the responsibility of local authorities to manage community care within the resources that they have available. In any event, it is our view that increased resources are needed if families are to be properly supported in their performance of this important task. A crucial test of any society is how it cares for its vulnerable members.

Support for families experiencing difficulty

Procedures for separation and divorce

While believing that marriage should be entered into as a lifelong commitment, the Church of England recognises that many marriages do break down and that the civil law must make provision for such breakdowns. In 1966, *Putting Asunder*[44] recommended the replacement of the matrimonial offence with the principle of breakdown as the ground for divorce. *Putting Asunder* was referred to the Law Commission which responded with *The Field of Choice*. In this Report the Commission considered that a good divorce law should have two objectives:

> To buttress, rather than to undermine, the stability of marriage; and when, regrettably, a marriage has irretrievably broken down, to enable the empty legal shell to be destroyed with the maximum fairness, and the minimum bitterness, distress and humiliation.[45]

149

More recently the need to discharge responsibilities towards children of the family and to minimise the harm suffered by them as a result of divorce have been recognised as additional aims.[46]

The current law, introduced by the Divorce Reform Act 1969, made irretrievable breakdown the sole ground for divorce. However, irretrievable breakdown has to be established by proof of one of five facts. Three of these facts involve fault, namely adultery with intolerability, intolerable behaviour and desertion; while the remaining two facts rely on periods of separation. Many couples, especially those with young children, are not in a position to undertake a formal separation, and many do not wish to wait. Being forced to blame each other for their marriage failing does not encourage a husband and wife to work out their differences and try to save their relationship. Moreover, the inability to respond effectively to charges of blameworthiness can create a real sense of injustice and grievance.

The present law also offers opportunities to one party to use a bargaining chip to gain an advantage over the other. For example, if a person is willing to consent to divorce the period of separation required is two years, but if consent is withheld the other party must wait for five years. The threat to withhold consent can enable a spouse to achieve better financial provision regardless of the merits of the case. Other serious criticisms of the present law can be found in the Law Commission's Report *The Ground for Divorce*[47] and the Government's Consultation Paper *Looking to the Future*.[48]

In its 1990 Report, the Law Commission recommended that divorce should become a 'process over time'. Irretrievable breakdown would continue to be the ground for divorce but it would be established, not by fault, but by a suggested period of twelve months for 'consideration and reflection'. During this period the couple would be expected to reflect on the implications of their divorce and on their continuing responsibilities, particularly in relation to children, and to make practical arrangements for their future apart. The Government gave very careful consideration to the Commission's proposals and its own consultation paper in 1993 builds on the Commission's recommendations.

One criticism made of the proposed process is that it would make divorce easier and thus undermine the institution of marriage. This of course depends on what is meant by easier. Usually it means more quickly. At present, divorces are typically achieved in about six months by alleging fault such as intolerable behaviour or adultery. Sometimes the process can take as little as three months. This however does nothing to encourage the couple to stay together, nor to help them separate without hostility or continue to meet their joint parental responsibility for their children. In the smaller number of cases where separation is used, divorce would be possible more quickly than at present but there would be an opportunity to use the time before the divorce more constructively. Under the proposed process over time no divorce could be achieved in less than twelve months.

During the proposed period of consideration and reflection the couple could seek marriage counselling with a view to saving their marriage. Divorce would not be the inevitable outcome it is seen to be under the present adversarial system. In some cases a chance to co-operate with the help of a family mediator may mean the couple decide to try again with their marriage, but even if they do not, they may come to a better understanding of what went wrong and increase their prospects of a new

---

People are recognising that a lot of marriages are in difficulty, and are trying to do something about it.

(from a submission by a parish in Manchester)

---

relationship being successful. Under the new system, family mediation would have a major role to play in helping couples who have decided to part to negotiate and resolve disputes themselves without fighting each other in court. Further, family mediators can help parents focus specifically on the needs of their children. Creating a framework or 'parenting plan' for their future care can prevent the eruption of the bitter disputes about children that have characterised so many divorces under existing law, and thus prevent some of the worst short-term effects on children. The consequent reduction in stress and conflict between parents would be likely to have a beneficial effect on their children in the longer term. Mediation would also provide a better environment than the courts in which to address painful accusations.

However, mediation is not a panacea. It will only work if both parties agree to take part. If carried out badly it may result in the weaker party being disadvantaged or pressurised to reach agreement, and at the end of the mediation one party may still insist on covering the same ground with a lawyer. One of the major fears is whether the services will be adequately funded and be available to all who want them at the time when they are required.

In their response to the Consultation Paper, the Board for Social Responsibility recognised the need to make sure that couples receive help at an early stage in their difficulties and pointed to the law 'as an important factor in shaping and influencing morality, both public and private'.[49] The Lord Chancellor, in his Foreword to the Consultation Paper, states that 'the law of divorce is crucial to the vast number of people in this country who are married, and to their children'. Nevertheless, we recognise that there is only so much that the law can do. As the Consultation Paper says:

> No statute . . . can make two people love each other, like and respect each other, help, understand and be tolerant of each other, or force them to live together in peace and harmony while they are married . . . What the law can do effectively is to provide mechanisms which will protect the spouses and their children, and adjust their living arrangements and their financial positions when things go wrong.[50]

When a marriage breaks down the couple go through a complex experience of pain, regret and sadness. We welcome proposals which would encourage couples to think deeply about the consequences of divorce, to make plans for their lives apart before obtaining a divorce and generally to work together for the best possible outcome for themselves and their children.

Child support

Family breakdown nearly always has financial implications and often exposes both the adults and the children to a period of financial insecurity and hardship. New ways need to be found to tackle the financial consequences. In 1993, the Child Support Act came into operation, establishing the Child Support Agency (CSA). Over a period this will take over from the courts the responsibility for assessing the maintenance obligations of separated (absent) parents (usually the father) for their children. The Government wished to stress (and enforce) a principle of parental responsibility for the maintenance of children which does not cease if the relationship of the parents ends. If the parent with whom the child is living is receiving benefit, he or she is required to provide information about the absent parent and to initiate a claim for maintenance. Benefit will be reduced if he or she refuses to co-operate, except in cases where to pursue maintenance will cause 'undue harm or distress'. The Child Support Agency then seeks information from the separated father and on the basis of this applies a formula – fixed by statute – which is set around the cost of Income Support for the children, and for the parent as their carer.

The Child Support Agency has been the focus of continual criticism ever since it started work, from the press, Parliament (including two investigations by the Social Security Committee), and from those it most affects, shown publicly through demonstrations and marches. The most vocal opposition has come from fathers receiving higher demands for maintenance, but some agencies working with families have been anxious that the Child Support Act has a number of serious consequences.[51]

On the other hand the Act does have many defenders. They point to its prospective benefits to lone parents who are not on Income Support or who might be enabled to come off Income Support, as well as to the potential savings in public expenditure. Many argue that it is an effective reaffirmation of parental obligations and will help to control men's behaviour in particular. Further change is going to be painful, they argue, but there will be long-term beneficial effects.

Some changes were made in early 1994 to the original scheme. These had the effect of reducing its impact on separated fathers, but a number of problems remained with the legislation. Further changes were proposed in January 1995, but despite the changes made so far in the Act, the matter continues to be controversial.

The first problem has been that the Child Support Agency has failed to achieve targets set for it on clearance times, accuracy, payments and responding to the customer. In spite of re-organisations, the Agency still has a huge backlog of cases and the early 1994 changes, involving many re-assessments, have further jammed the system. The Government now proposes to defer the taking on of cases where the parent with care is not on benefit and which pre-date April 1993. Until a date for take on is set and implemented, the parents concerned will continue to have access to the courts.

A second issue has been that the Child Support Act ignored previous court decisions on maintenance and property. Under so-called 'clean break settlements', the house, other property and lump sums of capital were ceded to the parent with care. Absent parents might then enter into new family commitments only to find their plans overtaken by fresh demands from the Child Support Agency. While maintaining – quite properly – that there is no such thing as a 'clean break' from one's children, the Government now proposes measures which will make some allowance for former clean break arrangements.

A third issue was the application of a set formula which it was argued did not take sufficient account of the needs of second families, ignored some essential expenses and sometimes produced extremely high maintenance demands. Some flexibility is now being introduced into the application of the formula, a ceiling of 30 per cent of the absent parent's net income is to be placed on the maintenance assessment and an appeal procedure for 'hard cases' is to be introduced. A useful change is that the costs of maintaining contact between parent and child will receive some consideration.

All of these – welcome – changes will benefit absent fathers and second families, but apart from a (hoped for) more efficient service, they do little for parents with care, or for the children. A number of organisations have strongly urged the introduction of a maintenance disregard in Income Support. At present the whole of any maintenance paid is deducted from the income of the parent with care, leaving her (usually the lone mother) no better off and struggling to support the children on inadequate Income Support benefits. While there is a disregard in Family Credit and Disability Working Allowance (allowing the mother to retain £15 per week of the child support), and some fresh concessions are planned in these benefits, the Government has continued its refusal to make a similar provision in Income Support. It argues that this would act as a disincentive to come off the benefit and move into work. The only new concession proposed is that from 1997, a small amount (probably £5 per week) of the maintenance will be set aside and saved for the day when the mother returns to work, providing her with a lump sum at the time of the transition.

There are a range of other proposals and the whole package will require careful study before its full impact for good or ill can be assessed. But it is clear that lone mothers and fathers on Income Support who believe it right for the sake of their children to remain out of work for the time being (see the next section) will continue to have an income which is below that required to meet the essential needs of the children, a situation that could be relieved a little through a maintenance disregard. Moreover it continues to be the case that the interests of children, who should have the highest priority, are ranked below the interests of the taxpayer and, in many of the changes being made, below the interests of the absent father.

Lone-parent families

The social security system, and Income Support in particular, is vital to the well-being of lone-parent families. Some 85 per cent of lone mothers and 53 per cent of lone fathers have needed Income Support at some time.[52] The key period is typically at the beginning of lone parenthood. At that time – and in later times of crisis – the benefit enables lone-parent families to survive as a family unit, to keep a roof over the heads of the family and to feed the children.

A large proportion of these families will need an extended period on Income Support, while children are very young, or while financial and property affairs are being sorted out: issues of child support (maintenance) and the family home, the legal process of divorce, and decisions about who is to care for the children and about contact. Where the marriage or cohabitation has broken down, many lone parents decide that for a time it is in the best interests of their children not to go out to paid work.

We believe that this is a responsible approach to parenthood. These parents may feel that they can offer most to their child if they reduce the stress on themselves and the child by not embarking on a life made more complex by having to fit work and child care together. Indeed, research has shown that children are best protected after separation or divorce by living with a well-adjusted parent. Whatever enables that particular parent to be well-adjusted, whether it be work or staying at home, will help the child. Parents are best placed to make this assessment of their children's interests – with help and professional guidance where necessary.

It is, therefore, a matter of serious concern that there is a substantial body of evidence that the low rates of Income Support do not provide sufficient income to feed, clothe and provide in other ways for the children at an adequate level. A report on this evidence made to the Board for Social Responsibility's Social Policy Committee strongly recommended an early review of Income Support rates, and of the rates paid for children in particular.[53]

Numerous surveys of lone-parent families have shown that most lone parents do not want to be dependent on benefits and want to get back into the labour market as soon as this is right for the family.[54] At this point they face many barriers to employment:

- through the way the benefit system works, including uncertainties about Family Credit (which supplements low earnings);
- the lack of a benefit to help with mortgage payments while in work;
- through the lack of and cost of child care;

155

- through the fact that child support (maintenance) is not yet a reliable source of income;
- because the lone parents may need refresher courses or skills if they are to earn a decent wage.

Some of these problems are being tackled, but in a piecemeal way. What we still lack, and urgently need, is a comprehensive package of measures which will enable lone parents to move rapidly into work – and off Income Support – as soon as they are ready to do so.

Families in poverty

We conclude this chapter with one of the most disturbing aspects of family life today: the number of households living on very low incomes. This includes those households where the wage-earners are on low pay

> *Living on a low income in a run-down neighbourhood does not make it impossible to be an affectionate, authoritative parent. But it undeniably makes it more difficult.*
>
> *(Joseph Rowntree Foundation, SPR no. 4)*

and those families which receive Income Support. It can include people at all stages of life: children, unemployed people, people with disabilities and long-term illnesses, and elderly people.

There is no doubt that the period from 1940 to 1980 was one of unprecedented improvement in the living standards of most British families. One of the 'Five Giants' that Beveridge identified in his 1942 report as standing in the way of social reconstruction was Want. His recommendations for social security were largely implemented in the spate of legislation of the 1940s that led to the introduction of Family Allowances (now Child Benefit), National Assistance, and a national insurance scheme covering the major contingencies of unemployment, widowhood, sickness and retirement. These benefits, together with a National Health Service free at the point of demand, fiscal and economic policies which ensured extraordinarily low levels of unemployment, and growth in dual-earner families, led to a major assault on want. Real Gross Domestic Product increased nearly threefold between 1945 and 1980; real disposable income nearly doubled; average working hours fell; and most social security benefits more than doubled in real terms. If a statistical series existed that traced poverty consistently over those 40 years, it would show that while there was always a minority of families living on low incomes due to unemployment, low wages, disablement, or family disruption, in general the proportion in poverty had fallen.

Since 1979 there has been an unprecedentedly sharp increase in income inequality and in poverty. Whilst average incomes have continued to rise (by 36 per cent between 1979 and 1991/92), income inequalities have increased. More children now live in families with low relative incomes and the least well-off families are poorer than the least well-off families were in 1979.[55]

In setting out the evidence it is necessary to define one's terms carefully since there are a range of ways of defining poverty.

Poverty as social exclusion

In our view, poverty should be understood in relative terms, as a deprivation of normal patterns of living in our society. Poverty is a form of social exclusion. It is potentially harmful for the health and well-being of the individuals and families involved, and eventually for society as a whole. As *Faith in the City* pointed out in 1985, 'Poverty is not only about shortage of money. It is about rights and relationships; about how people are treated and how they regard themselves; about powerlessness, exclusion, and loss of dignity.'[56]

It is worth reminding ourselves of the kind of income we are talking about when we talk of people living on Income Support. The amount payable in May 1994 for a couple with two children under 11 was £120 per week, plus their housing costs. That is to pay for all normal requirements. One study of the living standards of families on Income Support described their situation as follows:

> The picture which emerges from this detailed study of family lives is one of constant restriction in almost every aspect of people's activities . . . The lives of these families, and perhaps most seriously the lives of the children in them, are marked by the unrelieved struggle to manage with dreary diets and drab clothing. They also suffer what amounts to cultural imprisonment in their homes in our society in which getting out with money to spend on recreation and leisure is normal at every other income level . . .[57]

Poverty as low income

Poverty is commonly measured indirectly by using income as an indicator of a standard of living. For many years the traditional indirect measure of poverty was *Statistics on Low Income Families* which were derived annually from the Family Expenditure Survey and which related family incomes to the scale rates of supplementary benefits. This series was abandoned by the Government after 1985. It has been replaced by a new statistical series, also based on the Family Expenditure Survey, called *Households Below Average Income* (HBAI). The latest report, published in 1994, covers the two years 1991/92 compared with 1979.[58] It shows the following:

- While average contemporary incomes rose by 36 per cent between 1979 and 1991/92, the income (after housing costs) of the bottom 10 per cent fell by 17 per cent (or 9 per cent if the self-employed are excluded).

- The proportion of individuals living in families with incomes (all after housing costs) below 50 per cent of the contemporary average – a widely accepted definition of income poverty – increased from 5 per cent in 1979 to 14 per cent in 1991/92. The proportion of couples with children living below this threshold increased from 8 per cent to 24 per cent and the proportion of lone parents from 19 per cent to 59 per cent.

- This increase in the proportions with low incomes has particularly affected children. Thus the proportion of children living in families with incomes below 50 per cent of the average has increased from 10 per cent to 32 per cent or from 1.4 million to 4.1 million children.

It is likely that since 1991/92 these poverty levels will have become worse. Unemployment, and particularly long-term unemployment, went on increasing until early 1994, the number of families with children dependent on Income Support increased in 1993 and 1994 and average earnings moved further away from benefits increased in line with prices.

Poverty as minimal living standards

Another way of representing the reality of poverty is by exploring what people on low incomes can afford. The Family Budget Unit drew up a low-cost budget based on evidence of how much is needed to sustain a modern minimum living standard.[59] This revealed that the benefits paid to families dependent on Income Support were too low even to be able to afford this minimal living standard. They were particularly inadequate for families with children. The Family Budget Unit's estimate of the minimum costs of a child was 61 per cent higher than Child Benefit and 41 per cent higher than the scales of Income Support for a child.[60] This work contributes to a body of evidence that it is particularly families with children on Income Support who are bearing the brunt of the poverty that Britain has been experiencing.[61]

In the absence of a statistical series covering poverty over the last 15 years, the administrative statistics of the Department of Social Security can provide us with a substitute insight into trends. These show the number of children dependent on Supplementary Benefit/Income Support because their parents were sick, disabled, unemployed or lone parents or on Family Income Supplement/Family Credit because their parents had low earnings. The total number of children on these benefits has fluctuated over the period but the trend has been inexorably upwards. Between 1979 and 1993 the number of children living in families dependent on these benefits increased from 1.14 million to 4.2 million or from 8 per cent of all children to 33 per cent of all children.

A social policy for families

In this chapter, we have discussed a series of policy areas as they affect families and indicated some directions which we believe policy should take. We need now to look at some broader issues of family policy and the principles which underlie them.

First, we want to emphasise again that families and society depend on one another. The family has the prime responsibility for the care and upbringing of children and for the care of its own sick, disabled and frail members. In the main, families shoulder these responsibilities willingly and lovingly, and in so doing they make a major contribution to the well-being of the whole of society. But there is reciprocal responsibility on the part of society to give the family practical support through the collective arrangements already discussed. Moreover, society should refrain from making more and more extra demands on the family, often beyond its capacity to bear. We have been through a period when support for the family has been weakened while more demands were made of parents. This was implicitly acknowledged by Norman Lamont, Chancellor of the Exchequer in 1991 when he spoke of the 'widespread view in the House and in the country that more should be done to help families with children'.[62]

Second, we have to consider what the policy response should be to the fact that the family in the UK, now more than ever, takes many forms: single parents, divorced and separated parents, cohabiting unions, step-families as well as the two-parent, married couple who marry once only and stay together. Should a 'family policy' operated by Government seek to favour one family form rather than another? Should it go further and seek to disadvantage other family forms – by reducing benefits, for example – to discourage the formation of such families in the future? Such a policy implies sacrificing today's children in order that tomorrow's children will be born only into favoured family forms. We do not find this acceptable.

Family policy has to deal with families as they are today. There is a strong case for policies which teach young people about the responsibilities of parenthood and policies which have the effect of preventing family breakdown, either by reducing unnecessary stress (caused by job insecurity or homelessness, for example) or by offering help in times of stress, through a range of family and marriage support services. But once a new family is formed, the principal task of a family policy is to support the new unit to enable it to carry out its caring role.

Third, we are aware that many people and families in our society are faced with the threat of poverty, either for long periods, or for a series of short periods. Inequality has increased so much that the standard of living of a large minority is now falling further and further behind the majority. It has been well documented in the recent report (1995) from the Joseph Rowntree Foundation.[63] We see this as a very serious development, both for the individuals and families who are suffering from this disadvantage and for society as a whole. We seek a society which:

- rejects social division and aims to promote social cohesion;
- seeks greater equality in life chances for all its people, particularly for children and young people;
- seeks a balance between personal responsibility and family autonomy on the one hand, and, on the other, a sense of community and solidarity with one another.

Such a society is best suited to the well-being of families and is one to which families can make a worthwhile contribution.

Chapter 8

Resources for families
in Church and community

Churches need to develop their own policy for family work . . . and be sensitive to the needs of the local community, looking for what God is already doing there and co-operating with that.
(*from a submission by Scripture Union*)

The last chapter looked at some of the resources that public policy can and should offer. This chapter and the next have a more local, personal feel. They examine the kinds of support that families may need at different times and in differing circumstances. They comment in particular on what the Church can do, both on its own or in partnership with others.

It is good to be reminded once again that as members of families all of us are the subject-matter of this report. This is an important point to make in these chapters when, because of the limitations of language, we may seem to fall into an attitude of 'them' being helped by 'us'. The truth is far different, for, in talking and learning about families, we are talking and learning about ourselves, and in trying to give to and receive from the families of others, we are all growing and changing.

All families need help from outside themselves at some stage or other. Some may need help from professional agencies, and though in this chapter we will not be commenting in any detail on the policies and practice of such agencies, their contribution should not be overlooked. Families may benefit from voluntary and local initiatives. More generally, families do best when they are part of a wider community, which means having access to neighbourliness in the street in which they live, the companionship of long-standing friends, and a sense of rootedness that comes from belonging to an extended family.

The Church's involvement with families is as old as itself. It has traditionally had a privileged and intimate contact with them on key occasions in the family life cycle, most obviously in the celebration of the rites of passage associated with birth, marriage and death. Often its role is simply to 'be there' and to be a listening ear. But it is also involved in welfare rights advice, counselling, family therapy, family centres, self-help groups, community development and efforts to create new resources. We want to encourage such activity and promote new ways of working, and we identify examples of initiatives which are being taken, often at very local level.

Prayer

Any account of the Church's work with families must begin with the most fundamental strand of all – prayer. Many people, when asked how the Church helps them most in their family life, say quite simply that the rhythm of worship and the offering of private and corporate prayer are their main sources of strength. They recognise themselves and their own joys and struggles at a profound level in the biblical narrative. They are held by its patterns of familiarity and freshness. They pray for others and for themselves. The experience of God in stillness and silence, in colour and symbol, sacrament and story, supports and challenges them and overflows into their lives in families.

Studies like *Children in the Way*[1] and *How Faith Grows*[2] have shown how people respond to different expressions of worship and spirituality at different points in the development of their faith. For over five million adults and about 1.6 million children, coming together with others on a Sunday in one of the Christian churches of Great Britain provides the framework for their daily life, and many more seek out contact with a church at turning-points in their life, or to make a private commitment public.[3] Rites of passage touch the lives of people who are not necessarily frequent church-goers. Packed churches at Christmas, Harvest and Mothering Sunday, at moments of community grief and celebration, show how deep is the need to give pattern to existence, to place the personal journey in a wider religious context, to celebrate or to grieve with others.[4]

As one of our submissions commented:

> *Churches are communities in which significant life events are marked, cele-brated, ritualised and endowed with symbolism. This is particularly helpful in assisting people to manage changes in their lives, providing as it does community recognition and support for the people concerned, and a framework within which individual meanings can be fashioned.*
>
> *(from a submission by the Tavistock Institute of Marital Studies)*

We are also aware of countless small groups seeking new ways of connecting different stages of the life cycle with the life of faith. Two examples among many: in one city a group of all ages which meets monthly set aside a day to explore and pray about the theme 'Living our

Dying'; in another, a church holds an annual service for anyone who has been bereaved during that year. Events such as these do not figure in formal prayer books but they are important ways of meeting human need for reflection and community. Indeed we would like to see closer connections between the everyday questions, tensions and ups and downs of family life and the Sunday worship of local congregations. How far are the concerns of today's families expressed in the intercessions, for example?

Two developments seem to us particularly important. First, we are glad to see the growing interest in the *home* as a place of faith. As *How Faith Grows* puts it: 'It is in the home that our faith is first formed, and for most people it is in the context of the family that faith grows.'[5] The home is a place where faith can be nurtured and where there are many chances to celebrate God's transforming love. Anglicans have often been slow to see this, but we are beginning now to learn from Orthodox and Jewish rituals.

The second is the greater readiness to open up the life of the Church to everyone, especially children. The invitation which *Children in the Way* offers is perhaps beginning to be accepted.

> Imagine a church congregation in which men and women, girls and boys, young and old, share together to worship God, to learn from one another about their faith, to pray together about their mutual concerns and joys, to serve those in need and to reach out with the Gospel to those in the community who are outside the Church. Whenever possible, the members are not separated into groups according to age or sex but are together. At times, of course, there are activities for parents and very young children, a club for lively junior age children, a group for adolescents and study sessions for adults. But the first instinct of this Church is to say 'What can we *all* do?'[6]

We must however also bear witness to those submissions which spoke eloquently of the effect of some 'family' services. Look around most church congregations and it is clear that this is not the nuclear family at prayer. People's domestic arrangements may be very different. Yet sometimes the language and symbolism of liturgy seem to imply otherwise.

The Liturgical Commission, in *Patterns for Worship*, looks at the strengths and weaknesses of so-called 'family' services.[7] It comments that some feel the family service: 'focuses so strongly on the nuclear family that it makes those in other styles of households, the single, bereaved, divorced and elderly, feel less part of the church family'. But the Liturgical Commission also recognises that in some places the 'family service is the main sign of hope for the Church, reflecting creative energy and the kind of God-centred worship that is resulting in a considerable growth of new Christians.' The report moves on to the following reflection:

> We would want to interpret 'family' in its widest sense. All are daughters or sons; some are sisters, brothers, parents, cousins, grandparents. Some are part of a nuclear family of parents and children, or a single parent family, or a kinship family including grandparents or aunts, or a reconstituted family where parents bring children from previous relationships. Others, with no marriage or blood relationship are part of an intentional family or household, deliberately committed to one another for caring and mutual support, and sometimes for a specific purpose such as being a mission house for the local church. And some families may be mixtures of these different types.
>
> The church family needs to acknowledge and value all of these, and to embrace also those who live alone, or without such immediate family relationships. The church worship should acknowledge the presence and gifts of children, and be open to inter-generational learning and experience of worship; it should not be focused exclusively on the needs of the traditional English middle-class nuclear family. And, as the *Children in the Way* report argues, 'family' is not the only model for the church, and can sometimes damage people by appearing to exclude them.

We welcome the Liturgical Commission's careful advice.

Support for couples

At several points in this report we have emphasised that, despite the high level of divorce and the increasing numbers of families which are not created around a married partnership, marriage remains very popular. Most people are married for some part of their lives. Most people who embark on marriage have high expectations of what it can offer and what they can give and receive within it.

Here we will reflect on the following questions. How can local churches:

- help people prepare for their marriage?
- help couples grow?
- help couples facing difficulties?
- help couples and their children during a divorce?

Preparing for marriage

Two-thirds of all first marriages take place in church. The Church therefore has an important opportunity to help couples prepare for the commitment they are about to make and to understand more about their relationship and its place within the context of the families from which they both come.

Practice varies from church to church about how couples are prepared for marriage. In some churches the minister meets the couple once, perhaps twice. In others, couples are offered a combination of a meeting with the minister who is to conduct the service and some group sessions, sometimes with lay couples from the congregation. We were pleased to hear that a growing number of churches are doing this work on an ecumenical basis.

Even when a couple are both marrying for the first time, each will bring to their relationship a great deal of emotional 'baggage' from the past. The nature of this baggage will depend on the age of the couple and on their own particular stage in the life cycle. Marriage however is always experienced as a major emotional event and this can bring back memories of earlier experiences that have some similarity with the present and make people think about the patterns of family life they have known. Couples need the chance to bring these early past experiences to mind, and to do so in front of their partner. Then each may become more aware of their partner's story with its troubles and its joys, its moments of growth and its pain. Couples also need the chance to understand something about the different family customs and rules that operate in each of their two families so as to help them to understand where points of tension are likely to arise.

The second major source of emotional baggage lies in the couple's previous relationships. Most couples will have had previous experiences of creating and, by definition, leaving a partnership before making their choice of each other. What have they learnt about themselves through these experiences and what have they learned about creating and sustaining an intimate relationship? Sometimes there appears to be a major piece of unfinished business relating to a previous partnership. The person may feel guilty about the way he or she has behaved or about the way the previous relationship has ended. Sometimes the person was looking for something in the previous relationship that he or she failed to find but still longs for, such as the experience of being cared for and protected from having to take responsibility. It may be that such a longing is quite unrealistic and just as it made the previous partnership unworkable so it is likely seriously to impede the forthcoming marriage.

It is important to raise these issues in marriage preparation if the couple are to embark on marriage in a healthy, positive way. The task is to help each partner to engage with the real person of the other, not with some romantic wished-for fiction. Sometimes this work may involve helping a couple to face up to the fact that this marriage is founded more on the needs and hopes of others than on what may realistically be

> *God's purpose is to grow persons. . . the insights offered by the Christian tradition give us a picture of 'persons in community'.*
>
> *(from a submission by a man in Wales)*

expected from the relationship. Courage is needed to help couples to see that there are choices to be made about the relationship that is right for them at this stage. Marriage is the exclusive commitment to one other person for life. It is not, as has been observed elsewhere in this report, the only means of living out an intimate relationship with another person. Very occasionally marriage preparation can help a couple to review whether they should wait rather than make the commitment of marriage at this stage. This obviously requires great sensitivity, but to help a couple to make this difficult decision may spare them the trauma of a divorce later on.

How do we know that marriage preparation has any effect on supporting and sustaining marriages? It is clearly unproductive to put time and skill into work that does not help the couple live out their marriage more successfully. There has been some limited research into marriage preparation, but more needs to be done and conclusions must therefore be tentative.[8] There are however indications that timing, length, content and follow-up are all aspects of good marriage preparation. To be effective, marriage preparation should:

- be undertaken as soon as possible after the couple comes to the church to book their wedding;
- last long enough for the important issues concerning both the past and future to be adequately tackled;
- focus on the marriage as a new stage;
- offer couples the opportunity to discuss the changes that they will face in the early stages of their marriage;

- enable the couple to expand their ability to communicate with each other, solve problems and face areas of conflict;

- give the couple a good experience of discussing their relationship with someone else so that they feel able to ask for help in the future if they need it;

- include some follow up opportunity for the couple six months or a year into their marriage.

The Church of England has taken the task of marriage preparation increasingly seriously since the advent of the Family Life and Marriage Education network (FLAME). This developed in 1989 from the earlier work of the House of Bishops' Marriage Education Panel.[9] Since then, FLAME has established itself in almost every diocese in England and has made a point of encouraging more and better marriage preparation. It has focused on helping parishes to develop courses in marriage preparation for groups of couples rather than for couples on their own. One example comes from a rural diocese:

> *In our diocese, the Family Life workers organised a training day for those running marriage preparation courses. It examined an engaged couple's fears, needs, expectations, and attitudes to married life. It covered aspects of domestic situations where tensions could arise. Priorities within relationships, how finances could be handled, how the household responsibilities could be shared, and what partners value were all discussed. These issues were carefully presented in the form of questionnaires, quizzes, brainstorms and role plays, all designed to provoke discussion between couples. The positive aspects of marriage were promoted on the course.*
>
> *We were shown ways in which we could enable couples to develop each other's best qualities, and with love and encouragement, help each other sustain life-long relationships. Finally in order to enable us to set up marriage preparation courses in our parishes led by lay people, we worked on structures, presentation, timetables and practical details of planning a course.*
>
> *(from a submission by Exeter Diocese FLAME group)*

Marriage preparation can be offered by a range of people, both lay and ordained, but the work requires training in the issues which need to be tackled and the methods which should be employed. We welcome the work of FLAME and urge that greater resources be devoted to its energetic and effective work across the country. We also encourage the development of ecumenical approaches to marriage preparation. Most of the denominations developed family networks which worked together closely during the United Nations International Year of the Family in 1994, and these networks could form the pattern for much closer co-operation in the future.

Both RELATE, the national counselling body for marriage and relationships, and the Catholic Marriage Advisory Council see part of their function as contributing to preparing couples for marriage. Some parishes have made links with RELATE counsellors who work alongside clergy and lay people in providing marriage preparation in groups, as well as helping in the training of those who will undertake marriage preparation with individual couples.

All that we have said about preparation for marriage does not detract from the significance of the wedding ceremony itself. Weddings are important not just for the couples but also for their families and friends and the Church clearly has a crucial role in the conduct of marriage services, and in endowing these occasions with the right blend of solemnity and joy.

Helping couples grow

The Church can also do much to support the growth of the couple's relationship and encourage them to live out their marriage vows. The local church should contribute as far as it can to an atmosphere that enables couples experiencing difficulties to seek help at an early stage, difficult though that may be for them. Few other organisations are involved in supporting couples to help their relationships flourish. The Church has therefore a particular opportunity and responsibility to take initiatives in this work.

One of the best-known developments has been the work of the marriage enrichment and marriage encounter movements. The general goal of marriage enrichment based on the Christian concept of life-long marriage is to enable partners to create a climate which will increase

> *It is vital that the Church in its life and teaching emphasises that relationships need working at and are not to be set aside at the first hurdle.*
> *(from a submission by the Order of Christian Unity)*

self-awareness, awareness of the needs and strengths of the other and the needs and potential of the marriage. Most marriage enrichment programmes follow the same basic method and programme. Couples enrol for a weekend or short course where they can take stock and review their marriage away from the ordinary stresses of everyday life.

Many couples feel that their relationship enters new depths of understanding after taking part in one of these courses. Submissions to the Working Party on this topic included comments such as 'After the weekend it was like starting anew' and 'It deepened my love and respect for him'. Some local groups have produced their own courses. For example, the Mothers' Union in the Worcester Diocese held two weekends in 1994. The Family Life Officers in Exeter Diocese had a 'Marriage MOT – Moving On Together' weekend. Afterwards a couple wrote:

> *It was a welcome break to shed our home responsibilities and be together as a couple, having time to talk and share – no telephone, no errands! We could be ourselves again and get our marriage into a new focus. It was an opportunity to build up our relationship and affirm our loving care for each other. When we arrived we were a little apprehensive. What should we be asked? What would be revealed? Would we be lectured at? However, we were soon able to relax as we started out on a humorous exercise that put everyone at ease.*
>
> *In fact the whole weekend was led most sensitively, without undue pressure and in a constructive and non-threatening manner. We gained many new insights about our partner and realised that some of our assumptions about each other were way out of date. Parts of the weekend were deeply moving, when we were able to say things which had been deeply felt but never expressed before. I began to feel even more confident about my relationship with my wife, in fact I felt quite excited about tackling certain things in a new way. We made an action plan for now and the future, and it felt good.*

Sometimes only one person in the partnership is aware of wanting to build the relationship and to improve things in certain areas, knowing there is no possibility of the other partner wanting to take part. The Family Caring Trust in their 'Married Listening' course allow for the fact that only one of the partnership may be on the course. Audio tapes of typical dilemmas that occur within marriages, and a workbook, offer resources for use in groups, with or without a leader, or for a couple, or a partner to use on their own. It stresses the importance of listening and developing attentiveness to the needs of the other.

In some places the anniversary of the couple's wedding has been turned into a means of supporting marriage through celebration. In the Chester and Chelmsford Dioceses and elsewhere, couples have arranged their own services to celebrate their wedding anniversary, sometimes renewing their marriage vows. In one Urban Priority Area parish, a couple asked the priest if he would conduct a service to celebrate their 40th wedding anniversary, after they had been through a difficult period which had almost resulted in the ending of their marriage. The blessing of their wedding rings held particular meaning for this couple. A different idea came from FLAME in Liverpool who used the Cathedral one Valentine's Day and made it the centrepiece of a huge celebration of marriage for all who wanted to participate.

We also heard of the support often needed by the many couples where partners are from different denominations. Those couples can suffer intensely because of Christian divisions, but they also have special opportunities to contribute to Christian unity. The Association of Interchurch Families offers a support network for such families, usually where one partner is Roman Catholic and the other a Christian of another denomination.

Couples in conflict

There is now a wide spectrum of approaches to helping couples who are experiencing marriage problems. Some of these are offered by professional therapists and counsellors working within specialised clinics or attached to statutory agencies. Others are provided by volunteer groups who have received different levels of training and continuing support. Much of the relationship counselling is offered by RELATE, which provides a high quality service across the country, in both rural and urban areas.

Some local church-based agencies offer relationship counselling, usually on a short-term basis. These may be staffed by professional counsellors who happen to be members of the congregation. The church may be in a position to use a counselling agency on a free or low-fee basis for couples unable to pay for private counselling and where no public provision exists. Many Christian counselling centres, operating inter-denominationally, offer marital and other forms of counselling. Examples of these include Network in Bristol and the Cogwheel Trust in Cambridge. So long as volunteer agencies adhere to a rigorous selection policy, high standards of training and the supervision of their volunteers, the Church and other volunteer groups can do much to increase counselling services to couples experiencing difficulties.

Perhaps even more important are the new initiatives being taken at diocesan and parish level to increase the confidence and competence of parish visitors and befrienders in the area of relationship difficulties.

These are usually developed within the wider context of helping members of a congregation to become more able to understand and listen to people who are encountering difficulties in family relationships in general. For example, the London Diocese advertised a recent course as follows, under the heading 'Putting the Family on the Agenda':

> Family life and church life are both often so busy and demanding that we have little time to talk to each other about what it means to be a Christian in a family, about the stresses and strains endured by families today and about how we might best help when people are struggling with enormous life changes, like leaving work to look after our family, or looking after elderly parents or becoming separated from marriage partners of long standing. This course offers a space to reflect, look and listen.

Some couples will not want the formality of ringing for an appointment, fixing a date and attending hourly sessions. They may seek help through chance conversations at a community centre, a playgroup or social events. Such approaches need to be respected and special efforts made to meet people on their own ground and in ways appropriate to them.

Couples who are contemplating or going through divorce

Because of the high value accorded to marriage in the Christian community, it can be very difficult for couples who are approaching divorce to speak about their fears and their pain. Yet there are numerous informal opportunities for members of congregations to offer a lifeline to families facing this crisis. An important aspect of becoming helpfully involved is to avoid taking sides or becoming viewed by one partner or by the children as really the other person's friend. Alternatively within a congregation, it may be possible for several people to 'hold' a family between them, each being a little closer in to different family members.

Sometimes it is useful to get professional help for a family and to encourage them to take the perhaps difficult step of contacting a counsellor. Each diocese has an adviser in pastoral care and counselling, or the equivalent in post, although we note that some of these services are still quite embryonic. Part of that person's task is to make known the resources for counselling and pastoral care in the area and to assist with making referrals where appropriate. He or she may be able to give advice to individuals who are trying to support a family approaching divorce. Divorce counselling is now offered by RELATE on an individual basis, to couples and in groups.

The decision to divorce is part of a process that begins much earlier with one of the partners beginning to consider divorce as a means of resolving his or her dissatisfaction with the marriage. It is rare for both partners to be equally committed to divorce as a solution to their problems, and much of the pain and the difficulty lies in this imbalance between them. It may be extremely distressing for friends and others who are trying to support the family as they witness the efforts of one partner to 'save' the marriage as the other moves further towards divorce. Trying to remain a calm, dependable presence, able to listen and absorb the suffering, alongside each of the family members in turn, without acting on one's own anxious need to give advice, take sides or bring about some premature end to the struggle, is a hard but worthwhile piece of compassionate Christian care.

The purpose of any kind of help for families who are divorcing is to try to limit the damaging effects of the experience while creating some hope of new life for the future. Some indicators which predict a poor outlook for the family's future are:

- a belief on the couple's part that their problems lie solely in their current relationship and will not therefore reappear in a future one;
- a belief that the 'cause' of their problems is the other person's behaviour;
- a denial of the extent of the losses that will be involved;
- making decisions based on a desire to take revenge on the partner;
- an inability to accept that whilst the marriage is going to end, the couple's joint parenting responsibilities will continue.

Anyone involved with families going through a divorce needs to help them avoid these pitfalls as far as possible. Enabling partners to discover ways of helping each other remain involved and active as parents, especially the non-resident parent, is particularly important for the welfare of the children (an issue discussed in Chapter 3). A child's self-esteem can best be protected by living with a well-adjusted parent and having good conflict-free contact with the other parent. Anything that can be done to reduce the child's experience of disruption and loss must be of value both in the present and in strengthening his or her capacity to form satisfying and lasting relationships in the future.

The following things, even if undertaken at very modest levels, will be of great help to the family during this period of upheaval and change. It will greatly assist the family if they can be helped to

- tell their children a coherent story of what has happened and why;
- maintain relationships with both 'sides' of the wider family;
- grieve for what is lost and cannot be restored;
- hold on to and treasure what was good and of value in their past relationship;
- approach the future realistically in terms of the inevitable changes in life style, social life and financial provision.

Clergy, Readers, Pastoral Assistants and many others in parishes could increase their ability to help couples at an early stage in their difficulties, and bridge the gap that often exists between limited high-quality professional services and no available help at all. Increasing the training and skill of clergy and other church workers in relationship work was a recommendation that was accorded a high priority by several respondents. We believe that this should indeed be a priority in planning the mission of the parish within and outside its own congregations. Enabling people to see that nearly all marriages go through tough times is far more helpful than proclaiming standards of behaviour and qualities of experience that may seem light years away from how people feel their own relationships actually are.

As the General Synod debate on clergy marriage breakdown in 1993 made clear, there are particular difficulties to be faced by clergy and other Christians who hold a high profile in the Christian community.[10] The growth in the number of clergy marriages which are breaking down means that dioceses need to review the counselling and support services for clergy and their partners. Every diocese should be able to offer high quality marital counselling at as early a stage as possible in a couple's difficulties. Ease of access, strict confidentiality and appropriate financial provision must be essential aspects of the service. Referral agencies and individual counsellors should be available through the diocesan adviser in pastoral care and counselling. Broken Rites offers support for divorced clergy wives through a network of local groups, and this service, together with that of the Clergy Visitor, offered to the wives of separating couples, should be well publicised.

Mediation

Divorce, like marriage, is a family affair. Its effects reach out to touch the whole network of family and friends. The highest incidence of divorce occurs in families with young children and the second highest at the point when children are leaving home. This points to the rather obvious conclusion that the arrival and departure of children has a disruptive effect on the whole family, and that help is sometimes needed so that the couple can get used to the change. It underlines the value of good preventative work with families at these points, before the drastic solution of divorce is contemplated.

As Chapter 7 noted, an important development in helping families who have made the decision to separate or divorce has been the growth of conciliation and mediation services. In-court and out-of-court conciliation services began in Bristol in the late 1970s and many similar schemes, both independent and court-based, have been set up in other areas of the country. Mediation services are designed for couples who prefer to work out their family problems for themselves, but who may need some help in order to achieve this. It offers them an opportunity to look at options and come to an agreement on the important decisions, for example on the arrangements for the care of their children and for their home and finances. Where the couple reach an agreement through mediation, they are still likely to need the help of a solicitor to draw up a consent order. An example of a service run by the Church is Merton Family Links, which is part of Wel-Care in the Diocese of Southwark, providing mediation services and counselling for separated or divorced couples.

Mediation reduces the cost of divorce, both financially and emotionally and, where there are children, creates the basis on which a continuing parental relationship can be constructed. Over the years, its effectiveness has been clearly established. A research project on work carried out by National Family Mediation produced clear evidence that the mediation of all issues has a high rate of success in reducing bitterness between parents and helping them to focus on their children.[11] Among many quotations from clients expressing their approval for the mediation they have experienced, one woman said: 'It gave me peace of mind where I'd been afraid and it freed me to concentrate on the children and on looking after myself.'

However the take-up of mediation remains small. We urge dioceses to consider undertaking further work in this area, in partnership with other social agencies. Whatever can be done to encourage more couples contemplating divorce to make use of mediation services is likely to be a highly effective way of helping families at this time of stress.

The difficulty that the non-residential parent experiences in maintaining a relationship with his/her children has been well documented. Most often the non-residential parent is the father, and the organisation Families

Need Fathers offers fathers help and advice in tackling some of the problems that they face. It is estimated that half of the visiting parents lose contact within two years of the divorce. This is partly due to the difficulty of continuing to sustain something approaching a normal relationship when it is conducted in an atmosphere of an outing, and outside the normal experiences of everyday living. Contact is made more difficult because the residential parent's home is usually an uncomfortable place to visit, either because of the memories it holds or because of the presence of a new partner.[12] To help overcome this difficulty, a number of voluntary groups, including church groups, have established contact centres, which provide neutral territory for parents and children to meet in a relaxed and 'homely' atmosphere.

The first contact centre was set up in 1976 through the United Reformed Church. From there has sprung up a network of places where parents can make contact with their children after divorce. In 1994 there were 120 centres in the UK, nearly half run in church halls or church centres. Most of the centres are members of the National Network of Access and Child Contact Centres which sets out the basic requirements for the buildings, the training needs of volunteers, and suggestions for getting funding.

We received descriptions of several contact centres, including the following:

The Mansfield Centre came into being because local churches became aware of the acute need for such a facility in the neighbourhood. Premises and volunteers are provided by St John's Church with an organiser acting as a central referral point. The Centre is open every Saturday 2.00 – 5.00pm with three volunteers on duty each week.

There are a few families who use the Centre over a long period because they cannot make alternative arrangements, but the majority of families only attend for short periods of time. The Centre is used mainly during the time when a Welfare Report is being prepared in order that families may become accustomed to renewed contact, or to help them sort out previous difficulties with contact – the aim being to help families move on to make their own arrangements.

Parents who even refuse to speak to each other on the first visit gradually begin to accept that although their relationship has broken down the children still need both of them. By meeting on neutral ground the parent with custody feels safe to leave the children knowing the access will be supervised. The children renew their relationship with the other parent and after a few weeks most couples move on to meet elsewhere on a regular basis.

One young father said recently 'This will be our last visit. We have agreed that I can now see my son at my parents' house. Thank you for just being here. If we hadn't been able to come where no one interfered I would have lost contact with my son. Now we will be able to see each other regularly.'

Contact Centres are child centred and aim to keep children and parents in contact with each other. This father's experience is what we are all about.

(from a submission by a church in Mansfield)

We also heard from a user of the Neutral Ground contact centre in Abbey Wood, South London:

I feel I must praise those kind volunteers who give up their mornings and afternoons to help families with problems. Please let the church know that their Centre is most welcome, appreciated and a wonderful, practical view of the Christian Spirit. In my own particular case the Centre provided a bridge between a situation where my daughter had not seen her father and one where she could do so supervised . . . Thank you.

The phrase 'broken family' conveys a finality and a hopelessness which may be a part, but only a part, of the total experience of living through divorce. But it can also be a turning point for the individuals involved and be a liberation from a violent and destructive marriage. Sometimes being helpful is simply a matter of not getting in the way of the healing and new growth that is part of God's promise to us all. Churches often want to be supportive of people suffering from the pain, self-doubt and depression that usually accompany the ending of a marriage, but may not be too sure how to be more useful. Some churches run Surviving Divorce workshops or set up support groups of people who have experienced divorce. One such group from Shropshire wrote:

Please acknowledge that the separation or divorce has happened, and does happen to people in congregations. Please don't ignore us, even if you don't know what to say. Most of us felt very much alone at the time of the divorce and would value companionship, people for the children to talk to, together with the opportunity to spend time at weekends with other families. We would like to be asked to coffee, or just to natter and to have someone to contact in emergencies or to go with us to the DSS. We may need someone to show us how to do the practical things round the house the partner used to do. We value help in sorting out the finances, or someone to come round when the children are ill. Meeting people who have gone through similar experiences helps us feel that we are not condemned or judged as failures. Some of us would still want to be asked to do things in the church.

Chapter 9

Support for parents and children

Perhaps the greatest role the local church can have is to be vulnerable, take risks, look for the good in families and rejoice in it, and look for the broken-ness too, bringing healing, hope and the good news of God's grace into the hurting places.

(from a submission by a parish in East Anglia)

In this chapter we continue to look at the resources which Church and community can offer families. We look at:

- learning about parenting;
- support for families with children;
- child protection;
- helping children become adults.

We also look briefly at bereavement, families who are separated in different ways, black families and stepfamilies. Finally we consider how the Church can encourage the development of wider families.

Learning about parenting

Chapter 6 looked at some of the issues that are brought into sharp focus by becoming a parent. This section considers some of the practical help that can be given.

We recognise and share the considerable concern that exists in relation to the care of children. The last few years have seen a growth in the belief that parents should be better prepared and supported in their exception-ally important task of bringing up children. Over the last few years, educa-tional opportunities have gradually increased, allowing parents to improve their parenting skills.

There has been much public discussion about the place of training for personal relationships in schools. 1994 saw the launch of *Education for Parenthood,* a pack published by The Children's Society which aims to encourage 15 to 18-year-olds to think about the responsibilities of parent-hood.[1] It is designed for use in schools and youth groups, to encourage discussion about the way relationships work, the roles of men and women, their responsibilities as parents, and the rights and needs of children. We welcome the discussion that is taking place about how best to educate children in the sphere of human relationships, in social and spiritual values and in preparing them for responsible parenthood.

Much learning about parenting is informal, gained from friends and neighbours, and transmitted by mothers and fathers to daughters and sons. There has, however, been a growing recognition that the models of parenting gained from one's own experience of being parented may not be enough to cope with the radically altered context that parents face today. Many parents value and benefit from more organised learning experiences and there has been a tremendous growth in parenting courses. Some focus on parenting skills; others on the sharing of experience, knowledge and resources; some are designed more for helping parents with young children; others are more relevant for families with adolescents. Most combine educational and self-help elements with building up a supportive group of parents who can continue to support each other after the course has ended.

Several models of parenting courses have been developed by organisations such as Exploring Parenthood, Parent Network, the Family Caring Trust, the Church Pastoral Aid Society and Scripture Union. Diocesan children's officers, FLAME groups and the Mothers' Union across the country have done pioneering work in this area and are putting much effort into training leaders from parent groups who will go on to run parenting skills courses themselves. Most Christian denominations have developed courses for local churches[2] and the Department of Health has actively encouraged such initiatives.

A rural church wrote about their experience of material produced by the Family Caring Trust:

A couple of years ago, we were looking for ways in which our parish churches could serve our community better. We discovered that many young parents were isolated and lacking in confidence and were concerned to bring up their children well. So, encouraged by FLAME, we started a parenting skills course.

The course had the full support of the local primary schools, the health visitor and the school nurse. After some suspicion that it might be 'all religious', some brave (and perhaps desperate) young mothers joined. Right from the start it was a resounding success. Although based on Christian values, it was not 'all religious', but used much common sense and psychological research . . .

> *All have found it helpful and enjoyable, and several have felt that it has literally transformed their lives. Here is something that is so simple yet so important, and to my surprise actually works. This course has brought Christ's practical love into many families, changed people's perception of the Church and even brought some families into it.*
>
> *(from a submission from Devon)*

Some churches have experimented with combining a course in parenting skills with other forms of support. We were told of an imaginative project set up by a church in the London Diocese to address the issues of isolation, anxiety and lack of confidence amongst parents. Members of this church felt that these were often most intensely experienced on Sundays – the family day of the week. They have therefore opened a Sunday centre one Sunday in the month, where parents are offered a meal and crèche facilities whilst they have an opportunity to meet each other in a parenting skills group.

Helpful as these approaches to parenting obviously are, we feel it important to sound some soft notes of caution. Parenting courses tend to tackle a limited range of practical topics which can be very helpful to parents on a day-to-day basis. However, broader issues, such as the shaping of gender or racial identity, are not usually tackled although it is these that are likely to have long-term consequences for the child's ability to form and sustain a satisfying adult partnership.

No course, however good or well run, is the right way for every parent to learn more about parenting. For many, the idea of joining a group, will not feel helpful or acceptable. We suspect, too, that these courses appeal mainly to middle-class parents, although we also note the efforts being made by some organisations and some dioceses to develop work in Urban Priority Areas, often with funding from the Church Urban Fund. It is crucial that any interventions either by professionals or volunteers are perceived as increasing, not undermining, the confidence of parents. Thus, we believe any kind of pressure on parents to participate in parenting courses, on young parents or lone parents for example, would be counter-productive and unacceptable. Moreover, it is essential for us all to recognise that no one kind of intervention will solve all the difficulties that parents face. Whilst building up the confidence and competence of parents has its place, it is equally important to create and maintain attitudes which demonstrate that the upbringing of children is of central significance to the well-being of society. Parenting should be recognised as being as important as any career.

Support for families with children

The Church has a special role in creating a supportive community which is life-giving and sustaining to family life at this early stage. The sacrament of Baptism provides the Church with an early opportunity for pastoral involvement, as do the traditional ministries of welcome, teaching and pastoral care, enabling the worship of God to be created and expressed fully by all its members, young and old together. For this to be effective, church buildings need to be made as welcoming as possible, putting in toilets and heating where none exist, and creating a family-friendly environment. Initiatives such as ramps, to make churches more accessible for people with disabilities, can also benefit parents with young children.

Several of our respondents pointed out that the Church itself is sometimes a negative influence on families. Local churches can expect their members to spend so much time on church premises or at evening meetings, 'keeping things going', that they are taken away from their proper commitments at home. There can be a real tension between the local church and the family, and churches need to be aware of the conflict of interests which their demands can create.

The tradition of godparents as extended kin is centuries old and is a particularly good way of creating a wider family for both parents and child. Generations of children have grown up knowing that they are specially loved and cherished by their godparents, and have valued the commitment of the relationship well into adult life. We see much scope for the development of this tradition. We note that it is not uncommon for vulnerable families, who may have few if any links with the Church, to approach the Church for Baptism for a child, with a request for a large

> *I have always been glad to have godparents. They live at the other end of the country now, but I know that they are always there for me.*
>
> *(from a submission by a man in Essex)*

number of godparents. Neither they nor the godparents may be able to put into words exactly what they are asking for in Baptism; their hopes might not conform to even the most liberal theological interpretation of what Baptism is about. Instinctively however they may feel that the Church will help them to belong to a community that is more dependable and reliable than they feel their own family to be. They may also be reaching out to create for themselves a new kind of extended family in choosing people to be godparents whom they perceive as strengthening and protecting. Such requests may pose a considerable challenge to the local church, yet they invite us to respond creatively. It is only by beginning with the request as it is presented that people can ever hope to be helpful to families in a way which is both relevant and acceptable. Some churches have experimented with using expanded thanksgiving services instead of Baptism and others with linking church members as godparents with the new family.

The involvement of godparents in Baptism, both as a ceremony and as a means of creating a family of affiliation, has been highlighted by the Family Covenant Association. This proposes a secular naming ceremony by which those who do not wish Baptism for their children could mark the birth of a child in a dignified and celebratory way. As well as putting forward ideas for the ceremony itself, it includes suggestions for how parents might safeguard the well-being of the child in the event of their deaths or the breakdown of their relationship. A suggested form for a will is included, as well as a form of commitment on behalf of the secular counterpart of godparents, to provide a family support network for both the child and the family.

Families with young children need a network of supportive relationships. Opportunities to meet and come together for mutual support and self-help are provided by a large number of voluntary organisations such as the National Birthday Trust, the Pre-school Playgroups Association, and many church-based groups. Sometimes, especially with first babies, what the parents need most is support from other parents with young children of a similar age. Parent and Toddler groups come into their own at this point. They help to supply what may be lacking because of the absence of the extended family network when sisters and cousins living near each other were able to compare notes about their children and support each other through the weariness and worries, sharing child-minding and encouraging each other. Now that happens less and parents rely more on friends they make at the ante-natal class or clinic. Many simple neighbourly initiatives in bringing together parents and their babies for an hour or so each week can be fostered by individuals seeing a need and responding to it. For a woman who leaves work to have her baby, the companionship of a regular meeting place amid the loneliness of a new and changing routine is rewarding. It is harder still when the father is the one who stays at home to look after the baby. This may be a particularly isolated role and it is important that Parent and Toddler clubs, and other resources, make themselves welcoming, natural places for fathers to attend.

Often a club started primarily for parents and young children to meet for a couple of hours a week leads on to other things. One such club, run by a group of parents in a lively but struggling church, sent this report of their Caterpillar Club:

> *Thursday is the most exciting day of the week in our church. Twenty or thirty prams and buggies are crowded in the church entrance. Inside, a group of church parents with their babies put toys out in the Hall, arrange the coffee and milk facilities in the kitchen, check the lavatories are clean and the towels within easy reach, wheel out the children's library, housing a mixture of children's books from Christian and secular publishers, and organise the materials for the craft table for the toddlers. All is set for a noisy two hours, which includes a story, a song and a prayer and a lot of talking and sharing together. Church events are publicised, and everyone whatever their sex, age, and marital or baptismal status is welcome and valued there.*
>
> *We recruit most people from baptisms, but some parents come because they hear about us. Friendships grow there, and we started a babysitting circle as well. Badminton nights and quiz nights for both parents followed next, then family cycle rides and communal outings, even a mass camping holiday. Some people who had been shy of entering the church building have grown in confidence, some now join in Sunday worship from time to time, and the children are happy in the church because they know it is a place where they are safe and have a good time.*
>
> *(from a submission from the East Midlands)*

The Caterpillar Club is in a fairly small market town, but new parents in rural areas also have problems finding support. In the Diocese of St Edmundsbury and Ipswich, the Family Life officer takes a caravan from village to village, parks it on the green and opens up a toy library from the van. Parents come to exchange toys and to meet each other. Sometimes the health visitor holds a session in the caravan afterwards.

Encouraging families with young children to keep in touch with grand-parents and others in the extended family network can sometimes be done informally by observant and sensitive friends. Making concerted efforts to build a sense of solidarity between the generations in families is particularly worthwhile at this stage of family life when the couple are learning to be parents. Often the support that is on offer through the numerous counselling centres attached to churches, will enable a family unit to re-create relationships with their wider family and develop more links within their neighbouring community.

Accurate accessible information about local resources is also helpful to families. Public libraries and Councils for Voluntary Service index local organisations, leisure clubs and self-help groups. Social Services departments provide details of registered daycare facilities. Many of these groups are also advertised in the telephone directories, the local papers and in the local directories of voluntary organisations. The details however change rapidly. If local churches checked that these lists were up to date, that would be a real service to local families and it would also mean that at least one person in the church would know what was available when a need arose.

Innumerable voluntary initiatives, many of which are supported by church-based groups or by the major child-care agencies, exist to support families with young children. The Children's Society, Barnardo's, NCH Action for Children, and the Catholic children's agencies are all active in the community, running family centres, playgroups and specialist projects for families with special needs. Other agencies such as Newpin and Homestart have gained a special position for delivering high-quality services. Some organisations such as Exploring Parenthood and Parent Network specialise in offering support, advice and counselling for parents through workshops run by professionals from different disciplines working in partnership with parents.

A variety of telephone helplines have also developed over the last few years. Parentline offers a confidential telephone listening service for parents under stress with local helplines. In some areas, Parents Anonymous groups also offer confidential telephone advice. ChildLine was set up in response to the growing awareness of the needs of children to have a confidential 24-hour telephone counselling resource when they are in trouble or in danger. Taking children seriously as they tell their stories about abuse, as they talk about their wishes when their parents are divorcing, or as they try to come to terms with separation from their birth family and subsequent adoption is a major development in good practice and must also be part of what the Church tries to develop in its own response to children in need.

Child protection

Churches ought to be safe places for children. Every church has a duty of care for the children in its community. To this end, we believe that there should be greater awareness of the kinds of child abuse described in Chapter 2, and a greater readiness to accept that children need protection. The Children Act and the Home Office Code of Practice *Safe from Harm*[3] have alerted all voluntary organisations to the responsibilities they have to the children in their care. Good procedures advocated in the Code of Practice have a vital role to play in limiting opportunities for abuse and avoiding wrongful allegations being made.

There is also an urgent need for a wide variety of support services for families, in order to make it less likely that a family experiencing stress be violent or abusive to a child. Thus, a society which does not invest the necessary time and resources in supportive services for families at both the individual, community and state level of provision is itself implicated in abusing its children.

Complex links exist between sexuality and spirituality. The local church may therefore provide both the opportunity and the alibi for the perpetration of sexually abusive behaviour. Effective safeguards need to be in place which prevent such occurrences during church gatherings. The Church should be meticulous in following good practice in ensuring that volunteers and staff are appropriately selected, trained and monitored and that males and females work together with groups of children and young people. We welcome the House of Bishops' policy on child abuse and the work undertaken by other denominations and Christian voluntary organisations.[4] We also welcome the emphasis on developing partnerships with social services, the police and probation services which will be of benefit if allegations of abuse are made against clergy, paid employees or volunteers.

The Church can also be helpful in supporting not only families under stress but also those where there is suspected child abuse. Parents and older children are now almost always encouraged to attend Child Protection Conferences, which are convened by the Social Services department when there is special concern about the care of the child. Such meetings bring together the family and the professionals concerned with child protection and give them the opportunity to exchange information and plan together. Parents and older children may bring with them a supporter of their choice who could be a minister or a friend from their church. This person may be able to play an important part in supporting the family and in helping them to hear, understand and act on the recommendations of the case conference. Often he or she can reduce the anxiety and stress involved, and encourage the family to use the support that the local authority may be offering them.

It is also important that clergy and church leaders are aware of the needs of adults in their congregations who were abused as children and we urge all dioceses to address this issue. The Church should be a safe place where adult survivors of sexual abuse can begin to come to terms with their experiences, perhaps for the first time.

Helping children become adults

Much of society's concern about family life is focused on the way in which young people are perceived as being delinquent, promiscuous and beyond their parents' control. Many of the submissions we received commented on these anxieties and on the experiences of people trying to parent their adolescent children successfully. Respondents spoke of the immense peer-group pressure on teenagers to have sex, smoke, drink and take drugs. They felt that children are often expected to cope with the adult world before they are really mature and emotionally ready.

Recent debate has focused on what educational approaches might better enable young people to prepare themselves for the challenges of adult life and, conversely, what destructive imagery and influences in our social life could be reduced or eliminated altogether. A major area of debate has been the content of education for personal relationships in general, and sex education in particular, within the school setting. A great deal of controversy has arisen over whether it is part of good sex education to teach young people about contraception and safer sex or whether this simply encourages them to be promiscuous. Equally controversial is the continuing debate about the extent to which television and video material encourages violence. Negative aspects of our contemporary social life which make it harder for people to form constructive, loving relationships include the increase in pornographic books and video material, much of which is easily accessible to young people and even children.

A number of services offer support and counselling specifically to young people. Much of this work is co-ordinated by Youth Access in Leicester. Likewise the work of the YMCA and YWCA provides a national network of resources for young people. Counselling and pastoral care for young people and their families must focus on the crucial issues of helping young people move into a new relationship with their parents and find their way into a world which often has few jobs or prospects to offer.

The Church of England has a long tradition of involvement with young people and their families at this critical point in their development. The range of activities which comprise the Church's youth work, usually under the general direction of diocesan Boards of Education, continues to offer

> *Our experience is that people, young and old, are interested in God but that modern city life, modern church life and modern life are not creating the space to deepen that interest. We need to help people make time for worship and the enjoyment of each other.*
>
> *(from a submission by the Mothers' Union, London Diocese)*

an important contribution. In addition, there have been many interesting developments fostered by Christian groups of all kinds. For example, the Footprints Theatre Company from Nottingham is one of several professional groups of young Christians which tour youth clubs, schools and other centres, and explore, through theatre, problematic issues facing young people such as drugs, AIDS and sexual identity. New ways of working with young people in schools are being pioneered by Scripture Union amongst others. For example, long-term work in comprehensive schools in the Oxford area has enabled young people having difficulties with their parents to explore family and relationship issues. In all of this there is a growing determination to try to reach young people who feel excluded from the Church.

We received reports of a number of drop-in centres run by parishes from church premises or based on coffee shops or cafes. The Lozells project in Birmingham, for example, has become a drop-in centre for people, mainly from the Asian community, especially girls and young women. The project is run by the Scripture Union and through long-term bridge-building and friendship, it has been possible to talk through differences in customs, family patterns and understanding of family roles. Giving young people time within a secure and accepting environment away from their home is a most useful service. This is illustrated in this story by a staff member at the Potter's House in Nottingham, a Christian outreach centre based on a coffee shop:

> *Julie was a lively 16-year-old, one of a group who came regularly to Potter's at the end of most college days.*
>
> *We knew that she had difficulties at home. Like most others of her age*

she had rejected many of her parents' values and was beginning to live her own life in her own way. She stayed out late, sometimes not returning home until the next morning, went to parties and pubs. There were the inevitable conflicts with her parents and when they came to a head Julie walked out.

At first her parents were relieved and thought she would turn up in a day or two, suitably repentant – but she wasn't and didn't. Friends took her in and she slept on floors, in spare beds and the odd sofa. She stopped attending college and spent much of her day in Potter's. She was determined not to go home, particularly until the long-lasting conflicts with her mother were sorted out. Her friends and college staff were concerned about her and with Julie's permission we contacted the college. Her parents also contacted us. Little by little we were able to encourage Julie to get back in touch with her parents.

Eventually Julie did go back home. Overall she came through the experience relatively unharmed. We haven't seen so much of her since then, but when she does come in she is warm and responsive to the staff. Whilst it was all going on her parents had the comfort of knowing that there were caring adults keeping a watchful eye on her. Julie, likewise, felt she had a safe place to go to, a group of adults who had her interests at heart and who would listen to her without taking sides.

Families and bereavement

Death is as much a part of life as birth or marriage, and death, at its best, is also a family affair. Families enable children, youngsters and young adults to learn about the processes of dying and death which might otherwise pass them by, and the Church has an important role to play in assisting in this. The number of weddings which take place in churches remains remarkably high, and the level of church involvement in funerals is even higher. The solemnity of funerals is an important aspect of the natural processes of grieving, and the pastoral care which follows bereavement can often help yet further.

The Board for Social Responsibility's report, *Ageing*, sets out the Church's views on the processes of ageing and dying, of caring within families, and of caring for carers. We do not intend repeating them here, apart from one quotation:

> A Christian approach to ageing emphasises the confidence that, even in situations of extreme difficulty, there is hope and the possibility of growth and change. The human spirit can stay alive through the most painful and constricting of situations. This hope is no glib optimism; rather a knowledge that suffering has been transformed through Christ's death and

187

resurrection. This Christian understanding of resurrection changes utterly our attitude to loss and finally to death.[5]

Of course not all deaths happen to elderly people, and death is most devastating when it is unexpected and unprepared for. Disasters in which many people die, such as the football tragedies at Heysel and Hillsborough, touch the public consciousness and demand some ceremony of public mourning. People still tend to look to the Church in these circumstances, and the Church is usually able to respond with dignity and imagination. Such ceremonies may help to soften the sense of shock and outrage, but grieving within families lasts longer.

Every year several thousand children go through the traumatic experience of a parent dying. Much more is known now about the needs of such children and the ways in which they can be helped slowly to make some kind of sense of what has happened.[6]

The death of a child is a particularly distressing form of bereavement. It is the end of hope and of the symbol of hope for the future. The death of a child is so 'untimely' that it is proper to ask how such an intolerable event can ever be borne by those who are most personally affected by it. We know that it cannot and that all parents bereaved of children will carry the open wounds of that experience within them until they die. The experience is that of 'Rachel weeping for her children and refusing to be comforted because they were no more'.

Bereavement may occur even before a child is conceived, in the sense that people may live with the secret grief and pain of longing in vain for a child of their own. There is also bereavement involved in miscarriage or abortion. The unwanted miscarriage may not be so far removed in experience from the apparently chosen abortion, in that many women who have an abortion experience a sense of loss and grief even when they feel that they have made the right choice. Only by acknowledging the major psychological and emotional event represented by an abortion can we satisfactorily address a woman's need for sensitive and compassionate care, a need which may be manifested immediately after the event or many years later.

Major advances have been made in the care of those who experience a neonatal death in the family. Pioneering work by hospital chaplaincies and hospital staff has identified the importance of encouraging parents to mourn for the death of their stillborn or prematurely born child. Services, burials and other rituals conducted for the child are now part of the pastoral care that every parent may rightly expect. Good follow-up care of bereaved parents is often offered by a chaplain or a social worker as well as by two national organisations, the Foundation for the Study of Infant Deaths and the Still Birth and Neonatal Death Society (SANDS). Both offer befriending for individual parents and couples, and support through membership of local groups. A third organisation, Compassionate Friends, was founded for the specialised care of parents bereaved of a child of any age. Cruse also offers help and support to all bereaved people, not only those bereaved of a partner.

Even with this greater understanding of the needs of bereaved parents, there is still some way to go in recognising the impact of such deaths on the family as a whole. The effects of a child's death on the parents' relationship is often profound, with high levels of separation and divorce following such a death, particularly when the child has died in hospital. The levels fall for children cared for in hospices or at home, with a similar reduction in levels of parental depression and anxiety. The reaction of the family to a child's death will depend upon the particular role and place of the child in the family. Grandparents are often deeply affected. Brothers and sisters often feel acute guilt and confusion. Their needs may be overlooked by outsiders who may see the children as supports in their parents' grief rather than as needing their own grief to be recognised. This will be exacerbated if the parents remain so disabled by their loss that they are unable to care for the other children appropriately or they conceive another child in the vain attempt to replace the child who has died.

A different kind of bereavement is experienced by those families who lose children through adoption. Years ago young women gave up babies for adoption and were told to forget them and get on with their lives. We know now that many mothers carried on longing to know what became of their children and whether they are still alive and happy. Today, children are more likely to be adopted after coming into the care system and many families suffer great pain at the loss of a child, grandchild or other young relative, even when they recognise that they are not able to care for the child themselves.

Families separated by mobility and migration

In Chapters 1 and 7 we described some of the pressures that are placed on families as a result of the demands of economic life. The changes that have taken place in working practices over the last 20 years mean that those families who have one or more members in paid employment may now be working away from home in full or part-time work. Family life may have to be sustained across the absences of weeks or months (for those working on an oil rig , for example, or in a company office abroad) or just through a very long working day.[7] Family relationships of all kinds are difficult to sustain under the combined pressures. It may even be that absence in itself is less difficult to handle than compulsive overwork.

Whilst many families now face different degrees of separation from one another because of the need for wage earners to be a mobile part of the work force, this is highlighted most obviously in those families who migrate. There are many different combinations in these separation experiences. Perhaps the most straightforward is the corporate family where wife and children accompany the husband across the world when he is relocated by his company. Such families often need a good deal of social support over a short period of time. Church congregations have an important part to play in welcoming, befriending, and, where there are several in the neighbourhood, networking between families sharing this experience. Some simple, neighbourly assistance at this point can make a real difference.

Some families come from a traumatic past to an uncertain and long-term future in a country far from home. Some come by choice or through the encouragement and invitation of employers here – as was the case with many who came from the Caribbean in the 1950s and 1960s and took up work as hospital, transport and factory workers. Others such as the Vietnamese 'boat' people of the 1970s and the Bosnian people of the 1990s may be refugees fleeing from severe political and economic oppression. Often these families are severely fragmented, having left behind crucial family members who may be hoping to follow later. For example, amongst the small number of families who have been allowed in to Britain from Bosnia, many have the experience of watching their troubled country nightly on the news, while their hopes of seeing parents or grand-parents again remain uncertain. Whilst some family members remain behind, the parts of the family which have arrived are beginning the process of joining their new community. The greater the success that they have in this process the greater the difficulty there may be in eventually absorbing the members left behind.

Many families are separated by British immigration law. Many asylum seekers only manage to escape to Britain without their families. Few wait less than six months to hear if they can remain here; some wait up to two years or longer. If they are granted refugee status, they can apply for their families to join them straight away. However, only a tiny proportion are granted this, and those who are granted 'exceptional leave to remain' have no right to apply for family reunion for four years – even if they are children who are unaccompanied here by their parents and who comply with the international standards defining who is a refugee. Unfortunately for many, 'family' means only parents (in the case of children), spouse or children, and other relatives – grandparents, aunt or nephew – who may have been part of the family unit before flight to exile, must always remain behind.

There are also many other cases of families who are divided – people who have moved to Britain quite legally but who wish their children to join them later. Family members then have to undergo blood tests and long bureaucratic delays, sometimes of several years, before visas are granted to the children. There are also those who have residence in Britain and who marry abroad. Children may be conceived but permission for the wife and children to move to Britain may not be granted for many years. A recent publication by the Churches Commission for Racial Justice, *Breaking up the Family*[8], draws attention to the destructive effect of the application of the immigration laws on some black and minority ethnic families, and argues for an amnesty for families that meet certain quite stringent criteria.[9]

The commitment and success with which the Church can mobilise help for these families at the local level is often impressive. The Church may be one of the few organisations able to be sufficiently flexible and available in its response and we heard of many encouraging examples.

Christian Care is based at a local Baptist Church. This group offers a combined service of befriending, using interpreters, advice and practical assistance in helping families when they are re-housed to find the basic necessities for their home. The group runs a furniture warehouse and because of its close connections and good liaison with the local authorities in the area, it can offer an immediate response. The group assigns a visitor to each family it takes on, who may remain in regular contact for as much as a year, helping the family to re-settle.

(from a submission from south London)

But the adjustment to a new culture is a long process. It affects family members in different ways depending on the stage they have reached in the life cycle, and it goes on affecting them throughout their lives. There may be a problematic reversal of influence and authority in the family whereby children learn English more quickly than their parents and become the parents' interpreters. This then leaves the children having to mediate between their experience of two cultures – at school and at home – which are effectively insulated from one another. The Church can offer specific support and help to these families in many different ways. As is often the case, the most effective ways of being helpful are often the simplest. Being interested, being available, having time to visit in order to learn and enjoy the different customs and food that a family shares – all of these simple activities can greatly lessen a family's sense of isolation, and increase its faltering confidence and sense of belonging in its strange new home.

Black and white families together

Over 40 per cent of black people in this country were born here and many thousands have had their roots in British society for generations. Whether black families are long established or newly arrived, they are likely to have to contend with the racism that is present in our society.[10] But, shamefully, racism is also found in our churches. The lack of welcome to African Caribbean, African and Asian families during the 1950s and since is well documented. Even now, those black majority churches which developed out of this rejection are often treated as tenants rather than partners when they share 'our' Church buildings. We believe that part of the Church's contribution to changing racist attitudes could be a greater demonstration of commitment to a real ecumenical partnership with black majority Churches.

Where black and white families worship together the Church needs continually to question how far its language, music and symbols represent all its members and their cultures. Black children attending church need to feel at home in a place which values their cultural heritage. Churches cannot demonstrate that they hold every member of Christ's Body in equal regard unless they make this tangible in their church services and buildings, showing humble and joyful acceptance of all that families from all ethnic groups (whether long established or newly arrived) can offer. Renewal, mission and ministry are as much undertaken by receiving from others as by giving to them.

The Church in its social life can provide opportunities for families from different cultural groups to come together and share their food and music. But even when such activities are frequent and successful, this can still leave a Church profoundly (even though politely) split, with different ethnic groups still deeply divided. Only a real transformation, a real effort to redistribute power and influence in the structures and leadership of the

Church will provide that deep sense of whole-hearted acceptance which is the hallmark of the followers of Christ, and the means by which all will find healing and grace.

It would be misleading however to focus only on division and racism. Churches of all denominations are beginning to live out a life of greater sharing. A Black Anglican Celebration for the Decade of Evangelism in July 1994 celebrated the gifts that some 27,000 black Anglicans contribute to the life of the Church of England. A survey carried out for the conference showed that black people are worshipping in every diocese and participating at all levels of the Church. It also showed that black Anglicans bring a higher proportion of children to church.[11] As the 'trumpet call' at the end of the conference stated:

> Let our gifts and calling be recognised and affirmed, our partnership in the life of the Church of England be evident and welcome. We seek to walk confidently in Christ, one in him with all of every ethnic group, tribe and tongue, who name his name . . . We are ready to play our part in reclaiming our rich biblical inheritance for both black people and white people. We are ready to encourage the Church to live the Christian faith authentically and therefore to confront our society in areas of racial injustices.[12]

Families separated by imprisonment

The separation of families is an inevitable consequence of imprisonment – partner from partner, parent from children, brother or sister from siblings.

At the beginning of 1995, approximately 50,000 people were in prison in England and Wales. Increasing use of custody, and particularly long-term imprisonment, will result in more families experiencing the adverse effects of separation. The National Prison Survey 1991 showed that 19 per cent of those in custody reported that they were married prior to imprisonment and 31 per cent said they were cohabiting. Almost half of female prisoners (47 per cent) and one-third of all prisoners had dependent children living with them prior to imprisonment.[13]

The survey also showed that the longer prisoners had been in prison, the more likely it was that their marital status had changed. Only 12 per cent of those under six months in to their sentence reported such a change, compared with one half of those who had served over four years. Nine out of ten of these changes appeared to involve the loss of a marriage/cohabitation relationship.

193

The Church's involvement in prisons is partly through the professional work of many of its members as probation officers and prison staff. It also provides an important service to prisoners through the work of its prison chaplains. Most of the larger dioceses have a contact person for prison affairs whose task is to link prison chaplains in the diocese, and be a resource for parishes on all issues of criminal justice. Many prison chaplains are in a position to encourage joint work with prisoners and their families and also to foster work with prisoners' families by parishes.

We were told of a number of such projects being undertaken by parishes with prisoners and their families, both in the prison itself and in the community. Many of them had been initiated by the Mothers' Union. For example the Mothers' Union in the London Diocese started a crèche for babies of prisoners in Holloway Prison, providing the toys and some baby clothes themselves. The prisoners were so pleased with this arrangement that they asked to start a branch of the Mothers' Union in the prison. Times of prayer have become particularly important; groups of four people at a time now undertake to pray for someone else in the prison in special need.

In the Wakefield Diocese, a new baby unit is being built at New Hall women's prison. The Mothers' Union is celebrating its centenary by raising money to buy small items for the women in the unit. Mothers' Union members are knitting clothes for babies in the unit and collecting toiletries for them. Five day-visit chalets are also in the prison building plan and the Mothers' Union is involved in equipping these units which are used by women preparing to live outside with their families again.

Ripon and Wakefield Mothers' Union members run a crèche at Armley prison in Leeds. Appreciation of this service has been expressed by officers, prisoners and their partners as well as by the children who are looked after. The Manchester Diocese has received a grant from the Church Urban Fund to run a support group for partners of prisoners.

Stepfamilies

Although there are several ways of becoming a stepfamily – after the death of a partner, divorce, cohabitation breakdown or lone parenthood – the changes and challenges to be faced are often similar. Becoming a stepfamily involves a total reorganisation of the family system. There are few patterns and guidelines for living in this complex group of new relationships.

Over a third of all marriages are remarriages for one or both partners, and many of the partners in remarriages bring with them children of a previous relationship. Where the previous marriage ended with the death of a partner, the second marriage ceremony may evoke painful memories of the first. Couples where one or both has divorced may ask for a church wedding, in the hope that it may help to create a lasting relationship 'this time around'. They may find it difficult to articulate their hopes and fears for this new relationship beyond expressing a belief that being married in church may make a difference. Clergy who are approached in this way are able to offer help to a family who are unlikely to get it from anyone else, perhaps through special preparation for the marriage which addresses the particular issues that the couple and their children face.[14]

Stepfamily weddings often challenge traditional family rituals, roles and responsibilities but they are also an important celebration of renewed commitment to family life, whether it is a parent remarrying or the marriage of a child in the stepfamily. We are conscious that the question of the further marriage of divorced people in church is another issue about which Christians feel strongly. The current position in the Church of England, where the practice varies from diocese to diocese and priest to priest, is confusing and unhelpful. It can be particularly difficult to understand for the many partners for whom it is their first marriage. We welcome the fact that the House of Bishops is looking again at this very sensitive issue. In the attention they will no doubt give to all aspects of this question, we hope that they will look carefully at the opportunities remarriage offers to new families.

Our earlier review of marriage preparation applies equally to preparation for remarriage. It will be of even greater importance for couples to understand the nature of their earlier relationships and what caused them to end. Special attention will need to be paid to the predicaments of any children involved; children will be helped if their parents are able to tell a coherent account of what has happened, since this will make sense of the uncertainty and loss which they are likely to be experiencing. Where a previous partner has died there will still be a need to acknowledge the grief that the children will feel and to be aware that they may feel ambivalent about learning to live with a new parent.

A relatively new area of interest and concern to secular counsellors and therapists is forgiveness, and it is one where the Church has a great deal to teach. For couples beginning a new relationship after divorce or other kinds of breakdown, the Church's sacramental resources of confession and absolution may be very helpful. Even where it does not seem appropriate to offer the sacrament of reconciliation in a formal way, the priest's knowledge of the healing and restorative love of God can be used to help the couple's growth and their ability to forgive and let go.

The Church may be able to help stepfamilies to get to know each other and find mutual support from families 'like us'. Good pastoral care of family members in stepfamilies will include being able to listen to the widower, now remarried, who is having to discover how to relate to his first wife's relations. It will include recognising the distress of the grandparent who is facing the threatened loss of a much-loved daughter-in-law and the prospect of seeing his or her grandchildren less often. It will include listening to the anxieties of a young woman, who has acquired the role of stepmother to teenage children simultaneously with that of wife to her husband. The temptation to play a game of 'let's pretend' that this is really a family just like any other family may be very strong, and may be shared by several family members. This may in turn lead to the wish to exclude the children's other birth parent and deny him or her contact. Helping the family to recognise that being a stepfamily is different, but can and often does work out well, is an important part of offering the resurrection hope of new life, based on a realistic recognition of what stepfamily life is all about.

There are events which are particular to stepfamilies which often cause a great deal of stress, for example the remarriage of a former partner or the birth of a child within the new relationship. Children too are faced with challenges, especially when they relate to two different households, and when both are coming to terms with the separation in different ways. Professional help may be beneficial, and the families may welcome support in the practical and emotional re-negotiations that have to happen with former partners.

Churches can be helpful only in so far as their members are able to approach stepfamilies free of the comparative yardstick of what is 'real', 'normal' or 'ideal', particularly since this may reinforce a stepfamily's own need to pretend to be other than what it is. Members of congregations who can be fully accepting, generous and open-minded in their response may find many opportunities to offer pastoral care, to stimulate self-help and to foster opportunities for stepfamilies to meet for mutual help and support.

A good resource for stepfamilies is the National Stepfamily Association which offers practical help, support, information and advice to all members of stepfamilies. It also publishes two newsletters, one mainly for adult family members called *Stepfamily*, and *Stepladder* for children. In one issue of *Stepfamily*, this stepmother offered the following example of step-family life which succinctly expresses some of the difficulties:

> When my husband Chris's two children descend on us for the school holidays, it's like an invasion. There just isn't enough room with my three here as well, and that's the biggest problem. My kids don't like having to share their rooms and I can understand that. I mean, why should Beth and Grace have to see a pile of clothes in the middle of their floor after they've cleaned the room up that morning? And why should Toby have to take his car collection off the shelf in his room and hide it so that Chris's boy doesn't break one of them, like he did the last time? His kids don't seem to have any rules in their home. They don't help with the housework, they lie in bed for half the day, and they don't sit down to eat meals – instead they just grab things from the fridge without asking and take off. They don't seem to understand the small courtesies like knocking before you open a closed door. By the time they leave, I feel like a nervous wreck! I can't help thinking that Chris's ex-wife gets a kick out of letting her kids loose on us. I'm sure she knows how much it disrupts our home.

Wider families

Most people are part of a family. Being bold in asserting this truth helps us towards an inclusive concern for people, whatever kind of family they find themselves in or choose to create.

Chapters 5 and 6 offered some theological reflection on singleness. Many people who live alone maintain valuable family contacts, but others feel lonely and isolated. The Church needs to find ways of helping them to know that they belong fully. One such response is the formation of an organisation called 'Singularly Significant' by an alliance of evangelical Christians. It seeks to reflect the diversity of single adults, old and young, never married and previously married. Its main aim is to encourage evangelical churches to meet the growing needs of single people within the Church, and to this end it produces a pack containing tapes and study notes as well as a regular free bulletin. In a survey on singleness conducted in 300 churches by Singularly Significant, loneliness was the difficulty that was most commonly cited as affecting single people. It may be particularly acute for men and women who have been married but must now learn to be single again.

The Church has an important role to play in the lives of single people, and should be able to provide them with an obviously hospitable environment. It may however be held back by its adherence to an exclusive view of the family, which is expressed not only through its teaching but also in its style of family worship and its emphasis on family social events. One pastor commented that the local church should be a community which minimises the effort which single people often feel they have to make in managing the social and emotional side of their lives creatively: 'We must make it easy for people to come to things on their own. It's easy to feel conspicuous coming by yourself.'

The Church needs to integrate single people into its social, spiritual and liturgical life in a full and equal way, creating with their help a new community of adoption and grace, out of the diversity of expressions of family to be found within its membership. House-groups and fellowship groups will, in some churches, offer good opportunities for welcome, mutual care and the building up of warm supportive relationships. Many single people will look to the Church to offer them a place for meeting other like-minded people, with a view to finding friendship, and in some cases forming a committed partnership or marriage or network of friends. A variety of groups run Christian introduction agencies on a national basis as well as organising locally based events, holidays and outings where Christians can meet and develop relationships. Such initiatives answer a real need, but at the same time they should avoid suggesting that singleness, for some people, is anything other than a full and integrated expression of being a person.

Many single people are elderly or very elderly people living alone. Most elderly people live in their own homes but sometimes they live with relatives, often with a single daughter or son. Because of our increased life expectancy many of those who care for very elderly

---

Religion is for some older people one of the most enduring features of their inner world, sustaining them through the difficulties that can be experienced in later life. The Church can help reduce social isolation of older people by providing activities and visiting schemes, both formal and informal.

(from a submission by the Centre for Policy on Ageing)

---

people are themselves well into their seventies and beginning to be in need of support themselves. The Church can campaign for adequate resources to meet the growing needs of elderly people and create a supportive environment in which elderly people and their carers can flourish. This will include continuing faithfully and vigorously many of the activities that it has developed over generations of service and care. Clubs, visiting schemes, befriending and regular opportunities for experiencing the warmth of belonging to a caring community is what the 'family' of the Church can at its best, offer both to its own members and to the parish community. It has the power to encourage families of affiliation as well as birth families. This is a particularly important way of supporting those people who no longer retain a strong sense of membership to birth families or kinship networks. As one of our respondents commented, the Church is the only voluntary body which operates at a local level in every corner of the land; its network covers the whole community. Thus many people who feel themselves otherwise to be outside the family can, in the family of the Church become full insiders again.

The Church is itself a family of affiliation. As such, it can encourage the formation of other such families in several ways:

- For elderly people, this may involve simply making sure that they have a regular, dependable link with a member of the congregation.

- For the carers of elderly people and those with the life-long task of caring for family members who are mentally or physically disabled, it may mean provision of respite care by another family. Often such arrangements lead to the development of special relationships of a lasting nature.

- For people who have lost touch with or been abandoned by their blood families, such as those with AIDS, those who have been in prison, discharged psychiatric patients or homeless young people, it will mean making sure they are welcomed and included.

Many Churches and voluntary groups are already active in these ways. For example, they provide adult foster care for ex-offenders or mentally ill people; they run 'adopt-a-granny' schemes connecting elderly people to families with young people, creating mutual benefit; there are many different kinds of 'buddying' arrangements linking people with AIDS to friends who can be relied on for the rest of the life of the person with AIDS – a powerful example of the creation of a family of affiliation. Countless young people in inner cities are benefitting from over-night hospitality offered by families through night-stop schemes, giving these young people a glimpse of care and welcome. All these ways of establishing alternative forms of relationship have been found to make a real difference to everyone involved.

Conclusion

In a decade when there is such emphasis on what is going wrong, and such preoccupation with divisions in Church and society, it is easy not to notice the acts of ordinary loving kindness and commitment which go on daily. It is easy to ignore the resources which churches of all denominations put into the care of people of all faiths and none. In the previous two chapters we have drawn on our thousand or so submissions – many of them both moving and modest – to describe some of the ways in which members of families can be supported by Church and community. It is inevitably an incomplete account. For every example which we have had space for here, a dozen others could have been quoted. Most readers will be able to add from their own experience. We honour these signs of hope.

PART FOUR

In conclusion

Chapter 10

Conclusions and recommendations

While family life today is much in need of support, so it is in many respects proving to be remarkably resilient. Over 60 per cent of marriages survive, and there is much to celebrate in the often unobtrusive victories which families achieve against all the odds.

(from a submission by RELATE)

This report was commissioned in a spirit of inquiry, concern and hope. *Inquiry* – to get behind the newspaper headlines and offer a fuller picture of what is happening to families as a resource for the Churches. *Concern* – that the speed and scale of changes at the end of the twentieth century are leading to new difficulties for families, the individuals within them, and for society in general. *Hope* – that we could offer a Christian vision for families and suggest ways in which they could be better supported by the Church and the wider community.

At the first meeting of the Working Party the Bishop of Sherwood commented that we had been given an 'impossible task'. Our final report was certain to be controversial, he said, because people hold such different views and with such conviction. Our work over the last two years suggests that he was right. Discussion about families always draws on people's own experience and often provokes passionate disagreement. It touches on our deepest longings, hopes and fears for ourselves and our families for the kind of society we wish to build.

Our consultation exercise showed that there is lively debate within the Church of England about what is best for families. This is sometimes expressed as a tension between honouring traditional ways and exploring the new possibilities offered by the present. Sometimes it becomes a disagreement between those who expect the Church to make authoritative statements about how people ought to behave, and those who insist we must start with people where they are. We hope that those who might stand firmly on one side or the other of this divide will look for common ground. Action to support families is needed now; ideological or theological differences, important as they are, must not prevent Church and society from addressing the issues and priorities which we identify in this report.

Finding this common ground is vital. The Church has to hold in tension the need both to offer guidance and to care for people in the complexity of their own lives. There is no escaping either calling. While Christians affirm the continuing validity of many of the forms and customs of the past, they must also remain open to new developments that make for human flourishing. Christians must be ready to let the light of the Gospel shine on contemporary society in order to discover what a Christian vision of life in families might mean, and then to seek the grace of God's transforming love to live it out. They must also be rooted in the world as it is with all its uncertainties and ambiguities, and be ready to learn from the world, where God is at work.

Christians are called to discern where the Holy Spirit is leading. We must care passionately about the quality of relationships, and how love, caring, faithfulness, commitment and trust can be encouraged. We must also be concerned about the structures within which these relationships are lived out, and the values of the wider society. Finally, we must address the context in which families live and the social and economic policies which sustain or undermine family life.

Changing families

This report has described some of the changes facing families at the end of the twentieth century. We see much that is positive and many signs of hope: the changing role of women, the possibility for fathers to be more involved in the care of their children, greater awareness of the needs and contribution of people with disabilities. It is something to celebrate that more of us are living longer and that more children will know their grand-parents and great-grandparents. But the signs of hope bring with them new challenges which are here to stay: pressures on women struggling to combine child care with work outside the home; pressures on men learning new roles at work and at home; pressures to find ways of caring for frail older people. Unemployment, poverty, racial violence and in-adequate housing all make family life much more difficult than it should be. Because these issues are not just about personal morality, but about technological, social and economic change across the world, solutions are far from simple.

Our work has highlighted the diverse ways in which people experience family life. Several kinds of family structure are now common in the United Kingdom and across Europe and most people move in and out of different family situations during the course of their lives. Elderly people and single people, living alone or with others, are part of families. Many of the phenomena which cause anxiety now – such as cohabitation, births outside marriage, lone-parent families, repartnering and reconstituted families – were common in earlier centuries, even if the causes and consequences were different.

Historical perspectives suggest that there have always been families which have not worked well. Domestic violence and abuse of young and old people, betrayal, cruelty, depression and isolation – all these scar people's lives. Previously these things were largely hidden; they are now coming increasingly into the open.

The fact that some families are unhappy or destructive does not mean that we should give up on them. Experiences within families may be positive or negative and often a mixture of the two. For most people, however, families are the places where they have their deepest experiences of love, intimacy, commitment and interdependence. Families are the fundamental unit of society, where children are born and raised, values handed on from one generation to the next and where people go on learning throughout life.

Christian perspectives

We believe that families are an essential part of the way in which God shows love and care for all people. Families exist to receive and respond to God's love, to live out that love between their members and to pass on that love to others.

Families offer a crucial context for human growth. But they are also marred by human frailty and sin. They need God's redeeming grace and the continuing blessing of forgiveness, healing and fresh starts.

God creates people to live in community: with one another in families, and in families which are rooted in society. Individuals find their true identity through their relations with God, with fellow human beings and with the rest of creation. It is, however, essential to recognise the reality of sin. Frequently, the Church has concentrated on sexual sin, yet the recognition that sin affects both what individuals do and the way family systems work, makes sin much wider than that. Sin is present wherever there is unfaithfulness, neglect, exploitation, abuse, greed, injustice, selfishness or disloyalty.

The Ten Commandments challenge these kinds of sinful behaviour, by offering standards for behaviour which will enable people to be what God intends them to be. Their stress is on right relations with God which will

205

result in care for our families, neighbours, societies and all of creation. They are not simply lists of 'do's and don'ts', but point to the underlying values which make possible that human flourishing which is God's intention for all people. We are reminded again and again of the inter-dependence of families. Families are not just private groups, dedicated to their own well-being or the development of the individuals within them. They are also embedded in the wider community and are ways of creating healthy societies under God.

The biblical tradition speaks of the importance of *relationships* – with God and with one another. We reaffirm this biblical emphasis. Relationships are good in so far as they express qualities of love, faithful-ness, commitment and mutual responsibility. Equally, relationships which are casual, promiscuous, adulterous or exploitative have no place in promoting human well-being and cannot therefore be acceptable in whatever kind of family structure they are expressed or experienced. Christians therefore need to encourage and support patterns of life which are conducive to human nurture and flourishing.

We believe, therefore, that steps need to be taken to show that the Church's ministry exists for all people living in all kinds of families. We believe in particular that, while continuing to affirm the centrality of marriage, the Church of England should make it plain that the love of God is lived out in a variety of relationships. We were disturbed to hear from people who had felt unwelcome in congregations because they were cohabiting or divorced, gay or lesbian. We were disturbed to hear that some children are refused Baptism by clergy because their parents are unmarried.

Challenges to a changing society

As we have looked at contemporary culture, we have found much to celebrate. But nine aspects concern us particularly:

- We believe that undue emphasis on individual fulfilment impoverishes relationships and a wider sense of community. Christians have a strong doctrine of the human person, unique, created and loved by God. But our trinitarian faith implies that, made as we are in the image of the Trinity, we are also persons-in-community, who belong to one another. Families can only thrive if they seek the common good.

- The contemporary emphasis on individual independence can mean that our proper dependence on others goes unrecognised and

206

unacknowledged. People who are weak, ill, very old or very young are often marginalised or stigmatised. We all have recurring times in our lives when we are dependent on others. Families enable us to give and receive in a spirit of interdependence and mutuality.

- Words like duty, self-sacrifice, loyalty, faithfulness and responsibility have become unpopular. They need to be reclaimed. For it is only in attending to other people's needs as well as to our own that we can grow into the fullness of the image of God. This is a calling to all men and women, to younger and older people and to the strong and weak alike.

- Families are increasingly exposed to a culture and an advertising industry which offers them rosy images of instant happiness and sexual fulfilment. We believe that families cannot bear the weight of the expectations placed on them by these fantasies.

- We view with deep concern the fact that there is such a marked and increasing inequality of income and opportunity between different sections and families of our society.

- Families are not primarily units of consumption, but places where relationships are forged over time. We deplore the imbalance between work and family life, where some have no paid work to do at all and others (by choice or necessity) are so overworked that they have little time to spend with their families.

- The gospels show Jesus giving a special place to children and commending the pattern of the child-like to us all. Two thousand years later, in a world of sophisticated communications and technology, we are still unable to prevent children suffering through poverty, home-lessness, abuse and the effects of conflict and divorce between their parents. Given the problems of our society it becomes more important than ever that adults are supported and enabled by child-centred social and economic policies to be 'good enough' parents to their children.

- The commandment to honour one's father and mother teaches us the importance of respecting those who are elderly. We need to honour older people and be aware of their needs and contributions.

- The reordering of relations between men and women has had a profound effect on family life, bringing the good fruits of justice and freedom for many. One of the difficulties in contemporary relationships between the sexes however is the likelihood that women's expectations have changed more rapidly than men's. Men have often been left unsupported in discovering a response to these changes which will enable them in turn to achieve new confidence and freedom for themselves.

Opportunities for churches

The Church can be confident in the power of the Gospel to liberate and nourish family life. But it must also be penitent. Often in the past the Church has upheld too narrow a view of family life. It has spoken about families in ways which are sentimental or excluding or which do not connect with people's lives as they are really experienced. The idea of mutual, equal relationships between men and women in marriage, family and society is rooted in the Christian Gospel. But the Christian tradition has often failed to uphold this essential equality. The differences between the sexes have been allowed to become a basis for inequality and oppression.

The Church has often failed to respect the integrity of people's struggles and has left them feeling excluded. Many of the people who wrote to us had sought welcome and haven in the Church in times of darkness but had instead encountered disapproval and sometimes downright rejection.

We have observed that many a church discussion about families turns swiftly to the subject of marriage and sexuality. Such discussions about family life sometimes give the impression that Christians are only interested in the ordering of sexual relationships. They often seem to care more about the legal status of a relationship than in the qualities of that relationship or the flourishing of the people within it. Marriage and sexuality are crucial to the lives of most people, but they should not be emphasised to the exclusion of all other aspects. Just as important is the role of families in caring for their members throughout the life cycle – in particular, children and older people and those with disabilities – and in giving opportunities for companionship and security, joy and fun. Important also is the encouragement of what makes families work well – and how housing, social security and fiscal policies can make or destroy these possibilities for families.

Churches are deeply involved in the lives of families in this country. The ministry of the Church touches people throughout their life cycles. Half of all weddings take place in church, many parents still bring their children for Baptism and a high proportion of funerals involve contact with a minister and a Christian congregation. The submissions we received showed how much people appreciate friendly, sensitive welcome and support at times of change in family life.

As well as the formal rites of passage, the Church has much to offer families in their daily lives. Chapters 8 and 9 give examples of some of the thousands of community-based projects which exist. This is often pioneering work. The Church has buildings and facilities in every part of the land and we would want to see these resources used creatively and made as welcoming to families as possible. Parent-and-toddler groups, luncheon clubs for elderly people, family centres, drop-in centres for unemployed people, contact centres for children and separated parents – these facilities may not hit the headlines but they make a great difference to many thousands of people in their everyday lives.

We end by honouring the commitment and love shown by vast numbers of families today. Up and down the country, in quiet, often invisible ways, members of families offer each other loving, faithful care. Taking seriously what can go wrong should not blind us to the everyday goodness and happiness of millions of family relationships across the country.

We do not believe that family life is disintegrating. The evidence we have received shows that most people care deeply for their children, their partners, their parents and those whom they regard as belonging to their family. But we do believe that many families are under new and severe pressures and that action is needed to relieve them. The practical challenge to Church and society today is how to be loving and neighbourly in the increasingly complex world of contemporary family and household life and how to be a source of hope and community in a world of alienation and anonymity.

This report has discussed a number of areas where action is needed. We list some of them below.

Main recommendations to the Church

Our consultation with churches suggested that people welcomed the chance to come together to discuss family issues. The submissions showed a striking range of views about family life and a real willingness to look for common ground. Our prime recommendation to the Church, therefore, is that all churches continue to encourage reflection on the family and use this report as a basis for discussion and action. There will never be a 'final word' on family life, but we offer this report as a contribution to the Church's ministry and mission, in the hope that it will offer vision and encouragement for all those who read it.

We are aware that for recommendations to be effective, they need to be taken up by those with the power to implement them. We have not specifically targeted our recommendations to such individuals or groups, because we would wish all those in the churches to examine the recommendations and to ask in what way they themselves might build on them. The task ahead is as much one for people in the pew as it is for clergy, synods, boards and bishops.

1. The Church needs to recognise and value the different ways in which people live in families at the end of the twentieth century. *We recommend that the life of local churches be ordered in ways which help everyone feel welcome, whatever their family circumstances.*

2. Many members of families know that they are profoundly supported by the worship of the Christian community. *We recommend further reflection on how the language and symbolism of worship can reflect both diversity and continuity in family life. We welcome the work of the Liturgical Commission in this area.*

3. Church buildings are a vital context for the Church's work with families. *We recommend continuing effort to make churches family-friendly, available and easily accessible.*

4. We recognise the importance of neighbourhoods for the well-being of families. *We recommend that local churches create strong partnerships with the community around them, working in co-operation with other groups.*

5. We welcome the greater participation and empowerment of black members of the Church of England. *We urge local churches to review their worship, leadership and organisation so that black members are encouraged to contribute fully.*

6. This report draws attention to the multi-cultural nature of British society, and the racism which many black families still experience in white-led churches. *We urge congregations to undertake training in racism awareness among their own members.*

7. We note the way in which, as *Issues in Human Sexuality* commented, a great many gay and lesbian people 'grow steadily in fidelity and in mutual caring, understanding and support (and) whose partnerships are a blessing to the world around them'. *We welcome continuing discussion of issues relating to gay and lesbian people and urge that this take place in a spirit of openness and generosity.*

8. Much discussion in local churches focuses on what appears to be going wrong in families. *We suggest that attention also needs to be given to what helps families work well.*

9. The Church has always exercised pastoral care to its members. *We recommend that when it offers pastoral care to families, the Church move its focus from the individual to the family group as a whole, in order to understand and respond to the interrelated needs of individuals within their family relationships.*

10. Preparing couples for marriage, and helping them understand the depth and costliness of their commitment to each other is a crucial task for the Church. *We recommend that where possible marriage preparation be undertaken as a partnership between clergy and lay people, and that ecumenical co-operation in this area be explored further.*

11. The Church can do much to create an atmosphere which encourages couples with difficulties to seek help at an early stage. *We recommend that clergy and lay people interested in this area be encouraged to develop their skills through further training. All clergy should know where to refer couples for professional help.*

12. We welcome the energetic and effective work of the Family Life and Marriage Education network (FLAME). *We urge that, even in a time of financial constraint, financial support continue to be given by dioceses to this work.*

13. Church-based voluntary agencies such as the Mothers' Union, The Children's Society, the Church Army, the Girls' Friendly Society, and organisations in other denominations do substantial work with families. *We urge continuing support for such organisations.*

14. Local churches are well placed to act as points of information about statutory and voluntary services for families. *We recommend that there be at least one person in each church who keeps up-to-date information about sources of local help.*

15. We note the particular need to support men in adapting to new roles and opportunities within families and in the workplace. *We urge the Church to encourage discussion amongst men of the new challenges and opportunities, and to reach out to men who have up to now been under-represented as active members of congregations.*

16. The Church of England has long experience in running social and community work projects and much recent work has been made possible by the Church Urban Fund. Many dioceses run specialised projects with lone-parent families, families experiencing stress and couples offering themselves as adoptive parents. *We recommend that ways be found – where possible in partnership with other groups and other denominations – to maintain this crucial work at the core of the Church's witness and mission.*

17. Elderly people are vitally important members of families. *We recommend that local churches acknowledge and use the experience of older people and address the needs of their carers.*

18. The Church has been slow to understand and challenge violence in families. *We recommend that greater awareness of the prevalence of domestic violence, child abuse and elder abuse be developed and that the inequalities in relationships between the sexes which foster violence be addressed.*

19. We welcome the greater determination in church congregations to prevent child abuse. *We recommend that all dioceses and parishes adopt policies on the recruitment and training of people working with children in line with the Home Office's Code of Practice, Safe from Harm.*

20. We note the pressure on clergy marriages, and welcome the help that is currently available. *We recommend continuing reflection on how clergy marriages can best be supported.*

21. The issues raised in this report are clearly important for lay and ministerial training. *We recommend that this report be studied by all those in training for ordination and lay ministry in theological colleges and courses.*

Main recommendations to the Nation

We were asked in our terms of reference to make recommendations to the Nation. We were aware of doing this in the context of a wide and continuing debate about family issues. In particular we commend the Family Agenda for Action developed out of the International Year of the Family 1994.

It is not possible for a report of this nature to make specific, costed proposals, but we do wish to identify some key areas and positive principles related to public policy which need addressing if families are to thrive.

1. We recognise with grave concern the plight of families living in poverty. We recommend that Government, as a matter of urgency, review the following areas of policy:

    * *the adequacy of social security support for families and for young people;*

    * *the arrangements for responding to family homelessness and homelessness among young people;*

    * *the arrangements for responding to long-term unemployment;*

    * *the availability of support services in disadvantaged areas.*

2. We are concerned that families are placed under great stress when they are suffering from housing problems and homelessness. *We recommend that housing policies be developed which ensure that all families have access to safe and affordable accommodation.*

3. We note the importance of pre-school education. *We recommend that a comprehensive policy for pre-school children be developed, which gives parents access to child care so they can choose whether or not to work, and which provides appropriately for children's social, educational and developmental needs.*

4. Education is vital for the future of our society. *We recommend that all children have access to schools which provide education of high quality; that the role of parents as equal partners in the development of their children's education continue to be developed; and that a greater emphasis be placed on educational experiences which are supportive of family life.*

5. Many families struggle to balance the demands of the home and the work-place. *We would like to see 'family-friendly' policies adopted by employers and the state, so that the tasks of parenting and caring are given greater support and value. Employment practices need to be developed which*

recognise the needs of some parents and carers for flexible working. We further recommend that employment protection, maternity/paternity leave arrangements and allowances be upgraded.

6. We would like to see a greater appreciation within society of the importance of parenting. *We recommend that courses in parenting skills be made more widely available to give parents, particularly fathers, more confidence in their roles.*

7. We welcome the growing awareness of the problems that can exist within families and the more serious response to instances of child abuse, domestic violence and elder abuse. *We recommend that the network of services which provides support for families be extended and improved and that local authorities be enabled to implement the provisions of the Children Act 1989 for the support of families before crisis point is reached.*

8. We share the widespread concern about the high levels of family breakdown. The distress that this causes for all the individuals involved, especially children, and the cost to society is plain to see. *We recommend that the network of high-quality family counselling services – such as marriage counselling and child psychological services be extended and that funding for the agencies providing such services be placed on a more secure basis.*

9. We recognise the need for clear and constructive divorce procedures which allow partners to make appropriate arrangements for their future, particularly for their children. *We support the General Synod in welcoming the Lord Chancellor's Department's proposals on Mediation and Divorce Law reform. We endorse its concern that mediation services be adequately and securely funded.*

10. Carers need to be affirmed and supported. Caring for a dependent relative can be very rewarding but the personal cost is often high. Caring may disrupt careers, detract from other relationships and lead people into poverty and social isolation. *We recommend that carers be given adequate financial and emotional support and help not only from professionals, but from the wider community.*

11. It is a matter of grave concern to us that the incidence of early sexual activity by young people is increasing. *We recommend support for the efforts being made by parents, schools, churches and other bodies to help young people towards a mature understanding of sexuality and relationships and urge increased co-operation between these groups.*

12. We recognise that families can thrive only where there is a stable and sympathetic framework for relationships both within families and between families and society generally. *We recommend that Government, both national and local, continue to develop a more co-ordinated approach to the needs of families in all aspects of policy development.*

References

The term 'GS' in the references refers to General Synod reports only available from Church House Bookshop, Great Smith Street, London SW1P 3BN.

Introduction

1 Board for Social Responsibility, *Marriage and the Family in Britain Today*, Church Information Office 1974.

2 *The Family in Contemporary Society*, SPCK 1958.

3 Board for Social Responsibility, *Personal Origins*, Church House Publishing 1985.

4 Board for Social Responsibility, *Not Just for the Poor*, Church House Publishing 1987.

5 Board for Social Responsibility, *The International Year of Shelter for the Homeless*, GS 783, 1987.

6 Board for Social Responsibility, *All That is Unseen*, GS 781, 1987.

7 Board for Social Responsibility, *Ageing*, Church House Publishing 1990; *Happy Birthday Anyway!* Church House Publishing 1990.

8 Board for Social Responsibility, *Divorce Law Reform: The Government's Proposals*, GS 1095, 1994.

9 The General Synod debate on sexual morality took place in November 1987.

10 Board for Social Responsibility, *Child Abuse and Neglect*, GS Misc. 297, 1988.

11 The General Synod debate on the effect of violence on children took place in February 1990.

12 Board for Social Responsibility, *Community Care and Mental Health*, GS Misc. 386, 1992.

13 Board for Social Responsibility, *Abortion and the Church: What are the Issues?* GS Misc. 408, 1993.

14 The General Synod debate on clergy marriage breakdown took place in July 1993.

15 The General Synod debate on the further marriage of divorced people in church took place in November 1994.

16 *Children in the Way*, National Society/Church House Publishing 1988.

17 *All God's Children?* National Society/Church House Publishing 1991.

18 Church of England House of Bishops, *Issues in Human Sexuality*, Church House Publishing 1991.

19 Data from *Family Spending: a report on the 1990 Family Expenditure Survey*, HMSO 1991

20 From a speech by Herman Ouseley, Commission for Racial Equality, 28 March 1994.

Chapter 1: The cultural context

1 A survey published in *The Independent*, 22 January 1995.

2 Quoted in D. Sherwin Bailey, *The Man–Woman Relation in Christian Thought*, Longmans 1959. This study discusses the teaching of the Early Fathers fully.

3 Augustine, *Confessions*, Book VI, chapter 12.

4 Augustine, *City of God*, Book XIX, chapter 14.

5 Aquinas, *Summa Theologicae*, Blackfriars edition, 36.91 and 28.15.

6 J.I. Packer, *A Quest for Godliness*, Hodder 1990.

7 R. Baxter, *Reformed Pastor*, 1656.

8 L. Stone, *The Road to Divorce: England 1530–1987*, Oxford University Press 1990. There is also some discussion of the history of marriage in *An Honourable Estate*, Church House Publishing 1988, and David Atkinson, *To Have and to Hold*, Collins 1979.

9 M. Anderson, *Today's Families in Historical Context*, paper to Church of England/Joseph Rowntree Foundation seminar, 4 February 1994.

10 Quoted in J.L. Morgan, *A Sociological Analysis of Some Developments in the Moral Theology of the Church of England*, Ph.D thesis, 1976.

11 Morgan, *A Sociological Analysis*.

12 Morgan, *A Sociological Analysis*.

13 *The Family in Contemporary Society*, SPCK 1958.

14 *Transforming Families and Communities*, Anglican Consultative Council 1988.

15 Church of England House of Bishops, *Issues in Human Sexuality*, Church House Publishing 1991.

16 *Life in Christ: Morals, Communion and the Church*, Church House Publishing and Catholic Truth Society 1994.

17 For details of some of these reports, see the Further Reading list.

18 For a discussion of this work, see, for example, P. Hall and I. Howes, *The Church in Social Work*, Routledge and Kegan Paul 1965.

19 Pope John Paul II, *Veritatis Splendor*, Catholic Truth Society 1993.

Chapter 2: Families today

1 J. Olsen, *Is Human Fecundity Declining?* Scandinavian Journal of Work, Environment and Health, vol. 20 Helsinki 1994, pp 72–7; R. M. Sharpe and N.E. Skakkebaek, *The Lancet*, vol. 341 1993, pp 1392–1395.

2 See, for example, K. Kiernan and V. Estaugh, *Cohabitation, Extra-marital Childbearing and Social Policy*, Family Policy Studies Centre 1993; S. McRae, *Cohabiting Mothers: Changing Marriage and Motherhood?* Policy Studies Institute 1993; J. Haskey, 'Patterns of marriage, divorce, and cohabitation in the different countries of Europe', *Population Trends 69*, OPCS 1992.

3 Kiernan and Estaugh, *Cohabitation*

4 D. Dormor, *The Relationship Revolution*, One Plus One 1994.

5   *Social Trends*, HMSO 1993; J. Haskey, 'Pre-marital cohabitation and the probability of subsequent divorce: analyses using new data from the General Household Survey', *Population Trends 68*, OPCS 1992; Marriage and Divorce Statistics, HMSO 1993.

6   J. Haskey, 'Estimated numbers of one-parent families and their prevalence in Great Britain in 1991', *Population Trends 78*, OPCS 1994; General Household Survey, 1993; J.C. Brown, *Why Don't They Go to Work? Mothers on Benefit*, HMSO 1989.

7   J.R. Bradshaw and J. Millar, *Lone Parent Families in the UK*, DSS Research Report no. 6, HMSO 1991.

8   Bradshaw and Millar, *Lone Parent Families.*

9   J. Haskey, 'Stepfamilies and Stepchildren in Great Britain', *Population Trends 76*, 1994.

10   Chart 2.5 *Social Trends*, HMSO 1995.

11   F. McGlone and N. Cronin, *A Crisis in Care? The Future of Family and State Care for Older People in the European Union*, Family Policy Studies Centre 1994.

12   H. Kirk and P. Leather, *Age File: The Facts*, Anchor Housing Trust 1991.

13   J. Ermisch, 'Analysing the dynamics of lone parenthood: socioeconomic influences on entry and exit rates', E. Duskin (ed.), *Lone Parent Families: The Economic Challenge*, Paris, OECD 1990.

14   R. Jowell, et al. (eds) *British Social Attitudes: The 8th Report*, 1991.

15   J. Dominian, P. Mansfield, D. Dormor, F. McAllister, *Marital Breakdown and the Health of the Nation*, One Plus One 1991. This reviews the research on the impact of divorce on men and women.

16   B.J. Elliott and M.P.M. Richards, 'Children and divorce: educational performance and behaviour before and after parental separation', *International Journal of Law and the Family 5*, 1991, pp 258–276; L. Burghes, *Lone Parenthood and Family Disruption: The Outcomes for Children*, Family Policy Studies Centre 1994.

17   M. Cockett and J. Tripp, *The Exeter Family Study: Family Breakdown and Its Impact on Children*, University of Exeter Press 1994.

18   Burghes, *Lone Parenthood.*

19   For a review of the literature relating to domestic violence, see, for example, L.J.F. Smith, *Domestic Violence: An Overview of the Literature*, Home Office Research Study No. 107, 1989.

20   L.J.F. Smith, *Domestic Violence.*

21   Family Homes and Domestic Violence Bill. The Bill is the result of recommendations made in the Law Commission Report, *Domestic Violence and Occupation of the Family Home*, Law Commission no. 207, 1992.

22   See, for example, A.A. Baker, 'Granny battering', 5 (8) *Modern Geriatrics 20*, 1975; G.R. Burston, 'Granny-battering', *British Medical Journal*, 592, 1975.

23   In 1990 the Age Concern Institute of Gerontology was commissioned by the Department of Health to undertake an exploratory study. C. McCreadie, *Elder Abuse: An Exploratory Study*, 1991; Social Services Inspectorate, London Region Survey, *Confronting Elder Abuse*, 1992; Department of Health, *No Longer Afraid*, HMSO 1993.

24   Definition agreed by Action on Elder Abuse, c/o Age Concern.

25   A. Homer and C. Gilleard, 'Abuse of elderly people by their carers', *British Medical Journal* 301, 1990.

26   Law Commission, *Mental Incapacity*, Law Com. no. 231, 1995.

27   J. Scott et al., 'The family way' in R. Jowell et al. (eds), *International Social Attitudes: The 10th BSA Report*, Dartmouth 1993.

28   S. Ashford, 'Family matters' in R. Jowell and S. Witherspoon, *British Social Attitudes: The 1987 Report*, Gower 1987.

29   Commission of the European Communities, *The Europeans and the Family*, Eurobarometer 1993.

Chapter 3: Windows on the family

1   M. Roche, *Rethinking Citizenship*, Polity 1992.

2   D. Morgan, *The Family, Politics and Social Theory*, Routledge and Kegan Paul 1985.

3   H.R. Schaffer, *Studies in Mother–Infant Interaction*, Academic Press 1977.

4   J. Bowlby, *Attachment and Loss*, vols 1–3, Hogarth Press 1969, 1973, 1980; C.M. Parkes and J. Stevenson-Hinde, *The Place of Attachment in Human Behaviour*, Tavistock 1982.

5   D. W. Winnicott, *The Child, the Family and the Outside World*, Penguin 1994; D. W. Winnicott, *The Maturational Processes and the Facilitating Environment*, Hogarth Press 1965.

Chapter 4: What are families?

1   From a draft policy document on family learning, prepared by the National Institute of Adult Continuing Education, 1994.

Chapter 6: Where we are now: exploring the tensions

1   C. Clulow and J. Mattinson, *Marriage Inside Out: Understanding Problems of Intimacy*, Penguin 1989.

2   E. De'Ath, G. Pugh and C. Smith , *Confident Parents, Confident Children*, National Children's Bureau 1994.

3   This is discussed by M. Tanner in *Christian Feminism: a Challenge to the Churches*, Loughborough University and Colleges Anglican Chaplaincy Annual Lecture, 1986.

4   *The Independent on Sunday*, 23 October 1994.

5   J. Brannen and P. Moss, *Managing Mothers: Dual Earner Families After Maternity Leave*, Unwin Hyman 1991.

6   De'Ath, Pugh and Smith, *Confident Parents*.

7   See R. McCloughry's account in *Men and Masculinity*, Hodder and Stoughton 1992.

8   See, for example, Board for Social Responsibility, *Personal Origins*, Church House Publishing 1985.

9   *Choices in Childlessness*, British Council of Churches 1982.

10   N. Pfeffer and A. Woollett, *The Experience of Infertility*, Virago 1983.

11   An Evangelical Alliance survey in 1992 found that about 35 per cent of adults in churches are single.

12   A. M. Johnson and others, *Sexual Attitudes and Lifestyles*, Blackwell 1994.

13   Church of England House of Bishops, *Issues in Human Sexuality*, Church House Publishing 1991.

14   P. Mansfield, 'Understanding Changing Families' in *Priests and People*, Aug-Sept 1994.

15   K. Kiernan and V. Estaugh, *Cohabitation, Extra-marital Childbearing and Social Policy*, Family Policy Studies Centre 1993.

16   R. Jowell et al (eds), *British Social Attitudes: The 7th Report*, Gower 1990.

17   S. McRae, *Cohabiting Mothers: Changing Marriage and Motherhood?* Policy Studies Institute 1993.

18   J. Haskey, 'Pre-marital cohabitation and the probabilities of subsequent divorce', *Population Trends 68*, OPCS 1992.

19   J.R. Bradshaw and J. Millar, *Lone Parent Families in the UK*, HMSO 1991, put the figure at 24 per cent for 1989.

20   L. Le Tissier, 'The pastoral relationship between church and co-habitees', *Theology*, Nov/Dec 1993, SPCK.

21   *Issues in Human Sexuality.*

22   S. Golombok, A. Spencer and M. Rutter, 'Children in lesbian and single-parent households', *Journal of Child Psychology and Psychiatry*, vol. 24, 1983; F.L. Tasker and S. Golombok, 'Children raised by lesbian mothers', *Family Law*, vol. 21, 1993. C.J. Patterson, 'Children of lesbian and gay parents', *Journal of Child Development*, vol. 63 1992, reviews the American research.

Chapter 7: Families and social policy

1   *The General Household Survey*, HMSO 1992.

2   J. C. Brown, *Escaping from Dependence: Part-time Workers and the Self-employed: The Role of Social Security*, IPPR 1994.

3   A. Bryson, 'The 80s: decade of poverty', *Low Pay Unit New Review*, December 1989/January 1990; NACAB, *Hard Labour: Citizens Advice Bureaux Experience on Low Pay and Poor Working Conditions*, NACAB 1990; NACAB, *Job Insecurity: CAB Evidence on Employment Problems in the Recession*, NACAB 1993.

4   *Parents at Work: UK Employer Initiatives*, Wainwright Trust 1994, gives many examples of this.

5   *Employment Gazette Monthly Statistics*

6   *Employment Gazette*, April 1993.

7   Department of Employment Claimant Count, April 1993.

8   *Labour Force Survey*, September 1993; and *Employment of People with Disabilities*, Policy Studies Institute Seminar, December 1990.

9   P. Gregg and J. Wadsworth, *More Work in Fewer Households*, National Institute of Economic and Social Research 1994.

10   A. Dilnot, 'Social security and labour market policy' in E. McLaughlin (ed.), *Understanding Unemployment: New Perspectives on Active Labour Market Policies,* Routledge 1992.

11   M. White, *The Restart Effect,* Policy Studies Institute 1993.

12   *Joseph Rowntree Foundation Inquiry into Income and Wealth,* Joseph Rowntree Foundation 1995.

13   M. Evans, D. Piachaud and H. Sutherland, *Effects of the 1986 Social Security Act on Family Incomes,* The Welfare State Programme, London School of Economics 1994.

14   National Association of Citizens Advice Bureaux, *Severe Hardship: CAB evidence on young people and benefits,* NACAB 1992; I. McLagan, *Four Years Severe Hardship,* COYPSS/Youthaid/Barnardo's 1993; J. Greve, *Homelessness in Britain,* Joseph Rowntree Foundation 1991.

15   J.C. Brown, *Child Benefit Options for the 1990s,* Child Poverty Action Group 1990.

16   *Faith in the Countryside: Report of the Archbishops' Commission on Rural Areas,* Churchman Publishing 1990.

17   Table 8.12, *Social Trends,* HMSO 1994.

18   Greve, *Homelessness.*

19   Table 10.26, *Social Trends,* HMSO 1995.

20   A. Katz, 'The Family is fine . . . but under pressure', *Sainsbury's Magazine,* May 1994.

21   S. Holtermann and K. Clarke, *Parents, Employment Rights and Child Care,* Equal Opportunities Commission 1992; Table 3.1, *Social Trends,* HMSO 1995.

22   *General Household Survey 1991,* HMSO 1992.

23   K. Sylva and J. Wiltshire: *The Impact of Early Learning on Children's Later Development,* a review prepared for the RSA Inquiry 'Start Right', 1993.

24   G. Pugh, *Second Times Educational Supplement/Greenwich lecture,* November 1992.

25   F. Smith, *To Be or Not to Be a Working Mother – Equal Opportunities in the Workplace,* paper presented to the British Geographers Annual Conference, 1994.

26   Scottish Office Education Department, *Taking Account of the Views of Pupils, Parents and Teachers,* research for pilot project, 1992.

27   *Manual of Practice Guidance for Guardians ad Litem and Reporting Officers,* prepared for the Department of Health by Judith Timms, 1992.

28   G. Farrell and K. Pease, *Once Bitten, Twice Bitten: Repeat Victimisation and Its Implications for Crime Prevention,* Police Research Group, Crime Prevention Unit Series Paper no. 46, Home Office Police Department 1993.

29   M. G. Maxfield, *Fear of Crime in England and Wales,* Home Office Research Study 78, HMSO 1984.

30   *Social Focus on Children,* HMSO 1994; *Information on the Criminal Justice System in England and Wales Digest 2,* Home Office Research and Statistics Department 1993.

31   D. Farrington and D. West, 'The Cambridge study in delinquent development: a long term follow up of 411 London males' in G. Kaiser and H. Kerner (eds) *Criminality: Personality, Behaviour and Life History,* Springer Verlag 1990.

32   D. Utting, J. Bright and C. Henricson, *Crime and the Family: Improving Child-rearing and Preventing Delinquency,* Family Policy Studies Centre 1993.

33   *Information on the Criminal Justice System in England and Wales Digest 2.*

34   Sir Douglas Black et al., *The Black Report: Inequalities in Health,* DHSS 1980.

35   M. Whitehead, *The Health Divide,* Penguin 1992.

36   *Tackling Health Inequalities: An Agenda for Action,* King's Fund 1995.

37   *The Health of the Nation: a Consultative Document for Health in England,* HMSO 1991.

38   B. Dobson, A. Beardsworth, T. Keil and R. Walker, *Diet, Choice and Poverty,* Family Policy Studies Centre 1994.

39   Brown, *Escaping from Dependence.*

40   For a wider discussion of these issues, see *Leave Arrangements for Workers with Children,* European Commission Network on Child Care, V/773/94-EN, 1994.

41   R. Hancock, C. Jarvis, A. Tinker and J. Askham, *After Care: Summary Findings from a Study of the Long-term Effects of Being a Carer,* Age Concern Institute of Gerontology 1994.

42   Mental health and care in the community was discussed by General Synod in 1992.

43   Figure estimated by the Carers National Association from a survey carried out by Sandwell Metropolitan Borough Council, 1988; see also J. Aldridge and S. Becker, *My Child, my Carer,* Loughborough University, 1993.

44   *Putting Asunder: A Divorce Law for Contemporary Society,* report of a group appointed by the Archbishop of Canterbury, SPCK 1966.

45   Law Commission, *The Field of Choice.* Law Com. no. 6, 1966.

46   Law Commission, *The Ground for Divorce,* Law Com. no. 192, 1990.

47   *The Ground for Divorce.*

48   *Looking to the Future,* Lord Chancellor's Department 1993.

49   *Divorce Law Reform: The Government's Proposals,* response by the Board for Social Responsibility, General Synod of the Church of England, GS 1095, 1994.

50   *Looking to the Future.*

51   See for example P. Daniel and E. Burgess, *The Child Support Act: The Voice of Low Income Parents with Care,* Welcare 1994; NACAB, *Child Support: One Year On,* NACAB 1994; *Losing Support,* (a report from the five main childcare charities), The Children's Society 1994.

52   J.R. Bradshaw and J. Millar, *Lone Parent Families,* HMSO 1991.

53   J.C. Brown, *Children on Income Support,* Social Policy Committee of the Board for Social Responsibility, 1994.

54   Bradshaw and Millar, *Lone Parent Families.*

55   *Joseph Rowntree Foundation Inquiry into Income and Wealth.*

56   *Faith in the City,* Church House Publishing 1985.

57   J.R. Bradshaw and H. Holmes, *Living on the Edge,* Tyneside Child Poverty Action Group 1989.

58   Department of Social Security, *Households Below Average Income 1979 to 1991/92,* HMSO 1994.

59   Family Budget Unit, 'Household budgets and living standards', *Findings 31,* Joseph Rowntree Foundation 1992.

60   N. Oldfield and A.C.S. Yu, *The Cost of a Child*, Child Poverty Action Group 1993.

61   Brown, *Children on Income Support*.

62   *Hansard* 19 March 1991, col. 179.

63   *Joseph Rowntree Foundation Inquiry into Income and Wealth*.

Chapter 8: Resources for families in Church and community

1   *Children in the Way*, National Society/Church House Publishing 1991.

2   *How Faith Grows*, Church Housing Publishing 1991.

3   P. Brierley and V. Hiscock (eds.), *UK Christian Handbook*, Christian Research Association 1994/5.

4   H. Ward and J. Wild (eds.), *Human Rites: Worship Resources for an Age of Change*, to be published by Mowbray, November 1995. This collection of worship material includes liturgies devised by Christians to mark occasions in the lives of families: for example, thanksgivings and namings for babies; marriage services and blessings that recognise previous marriages and include the participation of children; services of healing and remembrance around miscarriage, abortion, death of young children; endings of relationships; retirement.

5   *How Faith Grows*.

6   *Children in the Way*.

7   Liturgical Commission, *Patterns for Worship*, GS 898, 1989

8   The results of the USA research are summarised by D.D. O'Leary and D.A. Smith in a review article entitled 'Marital Interaction' *Annual Review of Psychology*, vol. 42, 1991. Other useful books on marriage preparation include P. Chambers, *Made in Heaven?* SPCK 1988.

9   Two other bodies were also encouraging marriage education work in the 1980s: the Family Life Education Advisory Group (FLEAG) and the Family Life Ecumenical Educational Project (FLEEP).

10   See for example M. Kirk and T. Leary, *Holy Matrimony? An Exploration of Marriage and Ministry*, Lynx Communications 1994.

11   J. Walker, *Mediation: the Making and Remaking of Cooperative Relationships*, University of Newcastle 1994.

12   J. Walker, in *Parenting After Separation*, a paper to the Joseph Rowntree Foundation on 26 November 1993, summarises some recent research on this subject.

Chapter 9: Support for parents and children

1   *Education for Parenthood*, The Children's Society 1994.

2   A list of material about parenting education is available from FLAME (see list of addresses) and from the Board of Mission, Church House, Great Smith Street, London SW1P 3NZ.

3   *Safe From Harm*, Home Office 1993.

4   Church of England House of Bishops, *Policy on Child Abuse in the Church*, 1995.

    Publications from the denominations include:

> *Safeguarding Children and Young People,* Methodist Church Division of Education and Youth 1994.
>
> *Safe to Grow,* Baptist Union of Great Britain 1994.
>
> *Child Abuse: Pastoral and Procedural Guidelines,* A report from a Working Party to the Catholic Bishops' Conference of England and Wales on cases of sexual abuse of children involving priests, Religious and other church workers 1994.
>
> *Good Practice,* United Reformed Church 1994. A pack for local churches to help safeguard the welfare of children and young people.
>
> *Taking Care: A Church Response to Children, Adults and Abuse,* H. Armstrong (ed.), National Children's Bureau 1991. This gives information about child abuse, guidance about practical steps churches may want to take to protect children, to support families and to support adults who were abused as children or adults involved in an abusive situation.

5   Board for Social Responsibility, *Ageing,* Church House Publishing 1990.

6   W. Duffy, *Children and Bereavement,* Church House Publishing 1995.

7   See, for example, P. Semper, *Weekly Long-distance Commuting: Its Effects on Family and Community Life,* Jubilee Centre 1989.

8   *Breaking up the Family,* Churches Commission for Racial Justice 1994.

9   The criteria in question are that people should be allowed to stay in this country if they have lived in the UK for over five years and are *either* the parent of at least one child born here who has lived here for two years, *or* are self-sufficient in terms of income and housing.

10 *One Race: a study pack on racial violence,* has been prepared by the Council of Churches for Britain and Ireland and is available from Inter-Church House, 35-41 Lower Marsh, London SE1 7RL.

11 *How We Stand: A Report on Black Anglican Membership of the Church of England in the 1990s,* General Synod of the Church of England 1994.

12 *Roots and Wings,* Committee on Black Anglican Concerns, General Synod of the Church of England 1994.

13 R. Walmsley, B.E. Howard and S. White, *The National Prison Survey 1991: Main Findings,* Home Office Research Study no. 128, HMSO.

14 Two useful publications are K. Cox, *Another Step: Weddings in Stepfamilies,* Stepfamily Publications 1995; *Step Carefully: Preparation for Marriages where there are Children of a Previous Relationship,* published by the Methodist Church Division of Education and Youth on behalf of an ecumenical group, 1995.

Questionnaire

WHAT IS THE FUTURE OF THE FAMILY?

Consultation paper for church groups

1. Introduction The Church of England Board for Social Responsibility is undertaking a study on 'the family'. As part of our work we are keen to gather views from as many people as possible. This leaflet describes what we are doing and asks some questions to which we hope you'll respond. It also includes ideas for groups who want to look at the issue in more depth.

The BSR study began in autumn 1992 and will go on until 1994. A group of ten people is meeting regularly and will publish its findings. It will also report to the General Synod of the Church of England in order to encourage further discussion and action.

2. Why is the Church of England doing this work?

Because families are changing in all kinds of ways.

We know that...

- There are more very old people in our population, particularly older women.

- More than ever before, children are growing up in a country enriched by different faiths and different cultures.

- The roles of men and women are changing. More women have economic independence and go out to work.

- Many families live in poor housing and struggle to make ends meet.

- The divorce rate in the United Kingdom is one of the highest in Europe.

- More people are choosing to live together and have children without marrying.

- Many children spend part of their childhood living in a one-parent family. And there are growing numbers of stepfamilies.

- Many people spend part of their life living alone, with relatives living many miles away. Some have no relatives.

We also know that.....

- Marriage is still very popular. Over 8 out of 10 people marry at some point in their lives.

- Parents nearly always love their children very much and want the best for them.

- Families can be places where children and adults suffer emotional and physical damage.

225

3. What is the working party going to do?

We are going to:

*   Reflect on how the insights of faith, Scripture and our Christian tradition help us understand what is happening to families today.

*   See what the social sciences can tell us about these changes.

*   Try to find out what would encourage stable, faithful and committed relationships.

*   Make recommendations for action in public policy and in the life of the Church.

The full terms of reference are available from the address below.

4. We would like to know what you think!

Please fill in the next page (or write on a separate sheet if you want more space) and return it to **Alison Webster, Board for Social Responsibility, Church House, Gt Smith Street, London SW1P 3NZ.**

You might like to start by thinking about the different stages of your own life and the different families you know. You might also like to meet with other people from your church and then write down what you all think. Ideas for getting going on this are on the green sheet.

We need your comments by 31st October 1993 preferably, or by December 31st 1993 at the latest. Thank you for helping us.

5. Other resources

1994 is the International Year of the Family. A leaflet about how churches can get involved in this is available from Family Life Education Ecumenical Project, C/o FCFC, 27 Tavistock Square, London WC1H 9HH.

If you want to read more about families in Britain today you could send for fact sheets from:

Family Policy Studies Centre
231 Baker Street
London NW1 6XE   Tel: 071-486 8211

FPSC's current fact sheets cover.... the Family Today: continuity and change, Ageing Population, One Parent Families, Family Finances, Young People, Children, Children under Five. They cost between £2 and £3.

Some organisations with publications and training material on family issues are

FLAME (Family Life and Marriage Education)
11 Mundy Street, Heanor
Derbyshire DE7 7EB   Tel: 0773-761579

Mothers' Union
Mary Sumner House, 24 Tufton Street
London SW1P 3RD   Tel: 071-222 5533

The Children's Society
Edward Rudolf House, Margery Street
London WC1X 0JL   Tel: 071-837 4299

Barnardo's
Tanners Lane, Barkingside
Essex IG6 1QG   Tel: 081-550 8822

NCH (National Children's Home)
85 Highbury Park, London N5 1UD   Tel: 071-226 2033

Stepfamily
72 Willesden Lane, London NW6 7TA   Tel: 071-372 0844

Relate (Marriage Guidance)
Herbert Gray College, Little Church Street,
Rugby, CV21 3AP   Tel: 0788 57324

Response Form

General Synod Board for Social Responsibility

Some questions about families.....

What are the most hopeful things you see happening in families today?

What worries you about families today?

What in your own experience are the things that make relationships work well? What damages them? Would you be prepared to let us have, in confidence, your own family story? (If so, please enclose it with this form.)

How can the Church at local and national levels respond to changing family patterns? How can it support families?

How can the Government (especially in its education, health, housing and social security policies) support families?

In which ways have you found Christian teaching and belief about the family helpful or unhelpful?

Name _____

Address _____

Appendix B

Evidence received

1.   Meetings with Government and political parties

Policy Unit, No. 10 Downing Street
Rt. Hon. Virginia Bottomley MP, Secretary of State for Health
Rt. Hon. Peter Lilley MP, Secretary of State for Social Security
Ms Joan Lestor MP, Shadow spokesperson for children and the family
    until October 1994
Policy Unit, Liberal Democrats.

2.   Other consultations

Networks of the General Synod's Board of Education, June 1993
Joint seminar with Joseph Rowntree Foundation (and kindly funded by
    the Foundation) on the social history of the family, February 1994
A group of moral theologians, April 1994
Member Churches of the Council of Churches in Britain and Ireland
Bishops of the Church of England
Theological Colleges and Courses in the Church of England

3.   A consultation document designed for voluntary bodies was distributed
widely; the following sent in submissions or material:

Access and Child Contact
Anglican Marriage Encounter
Barnardo's
Bishops' Advisory Group for Urban Priority Areas, General Synod
Bristol Council for Voluntary Service
Board for Social Responsibility's Race and Community Relations
    Committee
Working Party, Catholic response to the UN International Year of the
    Family
Churches' Social Responsibility Commission, New Zealand
Counsel and Care
Carers National Association
Centre for Policy on Ageing
Centre for Family Research, University of Cambridge
Childwatch
Christian Research Association
Christian Action Research and Education

Committee for Black Anglican Concerns, General Synod
Congregational Federation
Conservative Christian Fellowship
Coventry and Warwickshire Family Mediation Service
Diocese of Gloucester Board for Social Responsibility
Epoch
Exploring Parenthood
Family Service Units
Family College, Reading
Family and Youth Concern
Jubilee Centre
Lesbian and Gay Christian Movement
Manchester Diocesan Board of Education
Mencap
Methodist Church, Sheffield District
Mill Grove
Mothers' Union Young Families' Committee
National Viewers and Listeners' Association
National Council for One Parent Families
National Family Trust
One Parent Families, York
Order of Christian Unity
Parent Network
Pastoral and Family Education Department, Mothers' Union,
    London Diocese
RELATE
Religious Society of Friends
Runnymede Trust
Scripture Union
SHAC
Shelter
Tavistock Institute of Marital Studies
Thomas Coram Foundation for Children
UK Band of Hope
Women's National Commission

4.   Individuals and church groups

Over a thousand submissions from individuals, parishes and church groups
were received and were carefully considered by the Working Party. To
respect their privacy we have not listed them by name, but we are grateful
to them all.

Appendix C

Further reading and study material

This is a brief selection of books and study material on the family. Other more specific empirical studies and statistical sources are noted in the references.

The Baptist Union of Great Britain, *Belonging*, 1994 (study material).

Stephen C. Barton, *Discipleship and Family Ties in Mark and Matthew*, Cambridge University Press 1994.

Brigitte Berger and Peter Berger, *The War over the Family*, Hutchinson 1983.

Anne Borrowdale, *Reconstructing Family Values*, SPCK 1994.

Paul Brett, *Love Your Neighbour*, Darton Longman and Todd 1992.

Louie Burghes, *One Parent Families: Policy Options For the 1990s*, Family Policy Studies Centre 1993.

Louie Burghes, *Lone Parenthood and Family Disruption: The Outcomes for Children*, Family Policy Studies Centre 1994.

Judith Chernaik (ed.), *Reflecting Families: An Anthology of Poetry*, BBC Educational Developments 1995.

John Cleese and Robin Skynner, *Families and How to Survive Them*, Methuen 1983.

John Cleese and Robin Skynner, *Life and How to Survive It*, Methuen 1994.

Children and the Churches – Unfinished Business, Council of Churches in Britain and Ireland 1995.

Rodney Clapp, *Families at the Crossroads: Beyond Traditional and Modern Options*, Inter-Varsity Press 1993.

The Board of Social Responsibility of the Church of Scotland, *The Future of the Family*, Saint Andrew Press 1992.

Churches Together in Marriage: Pastoral Care of Interchurch Families, Churches Together in England/CYTUN 1994.

L. William Countryman, *Dirt, Greed and Sex: Sexual Ethics in the New Testament and their Implications for Today*, SCM Press 1989.

Jack Dominian, *Passionate and Compassionate Love*, Darton Longman and Todd, 1991.

Faith Robertson Elliot, *The Family: Change or Continuity*, Macmillan 1986.

Tony Gough, *Couples Arguing; Couples in Counselling; Couples Growing; Couples Parting*, 4 vols, Darton Longman and Todd, 1987-1992.

Margaret Grimer, *Making Families Work: A New Search for Christian Family Values*, Geoffrey Chapman 1994.

A. E. Harvey, *Promise or Pretence? A Christian's Guide to Sexual Morals*, SCM Press 1994.

Stanley Hauerwas, *A Community of Character: Toward a Constructive Christian Social Ethic*, University of Notre Dame Press 1981.

Paul Henderson and Jo Hasler, *Working in Communities*, The Children's Society 1995.

Patricia Hewitt, *About Time: the Revolution in Work and Family Life*, IPPR/Rivers Oram Press, 1993.

Penelope Leach, *Children First*, Penguin 1994.

Patricia Morgan, *Farewell to the Family*, Institute of Economic Affairs 1995.

Oliver O'Donovan, *Begotten or Made?* Oxford University Press 1984.

On the Way: Towards an Integrated Approach to Christian Initiation, Church House Publishing 1995.

Chris Powell (ed.), *Families of God*, Scripture Union 1994 (study material).

Gillian Pugh, Erica De'Ath and Celia Smith, *Confident Parents, Confident Children*, National Children's Bureau 1994.

Jonathan Sacks, *Faith in the Future*, Darton Longman and Todd 1995.

Alan Storkey, *The Meanings of Love*, Inter-Varsity Press 1994.

David Utting, *Family and Parenthood: Supporting Families, Preventing Breakdown*, Joseph Rowntree Foundation 1995.

Sue Walrond-Skinner, *The Fulcrum and The Fire*, Darton Longman and Todd 1993.

Hannah Ward and Jennifer Wild (eds), *Human Rites: Worship Resources for an Age of Change*, to be published by Mowbray, November 1995.

John H. Westerhoff III, *Living the Faith Community*, Harper and Row 1985.

John H. Westerhoff III, *Bringing up Children in the Christian Faith*, Winston Press 1980.

Christopher J. H. Wright, *God's People in God's Land: Family, Land, and Property in the Old Testament*, Paternoster Press 1990.

Appendix D

Getting help

Listed below are some of the main agencies which can help families. We cannot list all the groups. Wherever you live, the local Citizens Advice Bureau or Council for Voluntary Service will have lists of local helping agencies, and can usually point you in the right direction. Their phone numbers are in the telephone directory.

Alcohol and drugs

Adfam
5th Floor
Epworth House
25 City Road
London EC1Y 1AA
Tel: 0171 638 3700
(To support the families and friends of
   drug users)

Alcoholics Anonymous
Box 1, Stonebow House
Stonebow
York YO1 2NJ
(local phone numbers)

Alcohol Concern
Waterbridge House
32-36 Loman Street
London SE1 OEE
Tel: 0171 928 7377

Hope UK (formerly UK Band of Hope Union)
25f Copperfield Street
London SE1 0EN
Tel: 0171 928 0848 (24 hours)

Standing Conference on Drug Abuse
Waterbridge House
32-36 Loman Street
London SE1 0EE
Tel: 0171 928 9500

Bereavement

Cruse
Cruse House
126 Sheen Road
Richmond
Surrey TW9 1UR
Tel: 0181 940 4818

Stillbirth & Neonatal
   Death Society (SANDS)
28 Portland Place
London W1N 4DE
Tel: 0171 436 5881

Compassionate Friends
53 North Street
Bristol BS3 1EN
Tel: 01179 539639

Gay Bereavement Project
Vaughan Williams Centre
Colindale Hospital
London NW9 5GH
Tel: 0181 455 8894

Child abuse

ChildLine
2nd Floor
Royal Mail Building
Studd Street
London N1 0QW
Tel: 0800 1111 (helpline)

Safety Net
14 Virginia Close
New Malden KT3 3RB

Christian Survivors of Sexual Abuse
BM – CSSA
London WC1N 3XX

National Society for the Prevention
of Cruelty to Children
42 Curtain Road
London EC2A 3NH
Tel: 0171 825 2500
(Help line 0800 800 500)

Also local Social Services departments. (See your local phone book).

Children

Children's Legal Centre
20 Compton Terrace
London N1 2UN
Tel: 0171 359 9392

National Children's Bureau
8 Wakley Street
London EC1V 7QE
Tel: 0171 843 6000

Tavistock Clinic
Department of Children and Parents
120 Belsize Lane
Hampstead
London NW3 5BA
Tel: 0171 435 7111

Christian communities

National Association of Christian
   Communities and Networks (NACCAN)
1046 Bristol Road
Birmingham B29 6LJ
Tel: 0121 472 8079

Counselling for couples (together or separately)

RELATE
Herbert Gray College
Little Church Street
Rugby
Warwickshire CV21 3AP
Tel: 01788 573241

Tavistock Institute of Marital Studies
120 Belsize Lane
London NW3 5BA
Tel: 0171 435 7111

Catholic Marriage Advisory Council (CMAC)
Clitherow House
1 Blythe Mews
Blythe Road
London W14 0NW
Tel: 0171 371 1341

Both Relate and CMAC have branches across the country.

Disability groups

Royal Association for Disability
  and Rehabilitation (RADAR)
12 City forum
250 City Road
London EC1V 8AF
Tel: 0171 250 3222

Church Action on Disability
Charisma Cottage
Drewsteignton
Exeter EX6 6QR
Tel: 01647 281259

Domestic violence

Women's refuges.
Police service (where there are specially trained police officers).
Social Services departments.

Information about families

Family Policy Studies Centre
231 Baker Street
London NW1 6XE
Tel: 0171 486 8211

One Plus One – Marriage & Partnership Research
12 New Burlington Street
London W1X 1FF
Tel: 0171 734 2020

Some organisations working with families

FLAME (Family Life and
  Marriage Education)
11 Mundy Street
Heanor
Derbyshire DE7 7EB
Tel: 01773 761579

ATD Fourth World
48 Addington Square
London SE5 7LB
Tel: 0171 703 3231

Mothers' Union
Mary Sumner House
24 Tufton Street
London SW1P 3RB
Tel: 0171 222 5533

Marriage Enrichment
c/o Westminster Pastoral Foundation
23 Kensington Square
London W8 5HN
Tel: 0171 937 6956

Marriage Encounter
39 Mayfield Avenue
Orpington
Kent BR6 OAj
Tel: 01689 820466

The Children's Society
Edward Rudolf House
Margery Street
London WC1X 0JL
Tel: 0171 837 4299

Institute of Family Therapy
43 New Cavendish Street
London W1M 7RG
Tel: 0171 935 1651

Association of Interchurch Families
Inter-Church House
35-41 Lower Marsh
London SE17RL
Tel: 0171 620 4444

Family Service Units
207 Old Marylebone Road
London NW1 5QQ
Tel: 0171 402 5175

Family Welfare Association
501-505 Kingsland Road
London E8 4AU
Tel: 0171 254 6251

CARE Trust
53 Romney St,
London SW1P 3RF
Tel: 0171 233 0455

Church Action on Poverty
Central Buildings
Oldham Street
Manchester M1 1JT
Tel: 0161 236 9321

Church Army
Independents Road
London SE3 9LG
Tel: 0181 318 1226

Lesbian and Gay Christian Movement
Oxford House
Derbyshire Street
London E2 6HG
Tel: 0171 739 1249
Helpline: 0171 739 1249

Network of Access and Child Contact Centres
St Andrew's with Castlegate Church
Goldsmith Street
Nottingham NG1 5JT
Tel: 0115 948 4557

Barnardo's
Tanners Lane
Barkingside
Ilford
Essex IG6 1QG
Tel: 0181 551 8822

NCH Action for Children
85 Highbury Park
London N5 1UD
Tel: 0171 226 2033

Families Need Fathers
134 Curtain Road
London EC2A 3AR
Tel: 0171 613 5060

Girls Friendly Society
126 Queen's Gate
London SW7 5LQ
Tel: 0171 589 9628

Fostering and adoption

British Agencies for Adoption and Fostering (BAAF)
Skyline House
200 Union Street
London SE 0LY
Tel: 0171 593 2000

HIV and AIDS

The Terrence Higgins Trust
52-54 Gray's Inn Road
London WC1X 8JU
Tel: 0171 831 0330

ACET
PO Box 3693
London SW15 2BQ

Cara
The Basement
178 Lancaster Road
London N11 1QU
Tel: 0171 792 8299

International

International Anglican Family Network
The Palace
Wells
Somerset BA5 2PD
Tel: 01749 679660

Loneliness and depression

The Samaritans
(see your local phone book).

Lone parents

National Council for
 One Parent Families
255 Kentish Town Road
London NW5 2LX
Tel: 0171 267 1361

Broken Rites
30 Steavenson Street
Bowburn
Durham DH6 5BA
Tel: 0191 377 0205

Gingerbread
35 Wellington Street
London WC2E 7BN
Tel: 0171 270 0953

(for divorced and separated clergy wives, with or without children)

Mediation and conciliation

Solicitors' Family Law Association
PO Box 302
Orpington
Kent BR6 8QX
Tel: 01689 850227

National Family Mediation
9 Tavistock Place
London WC1H 9SN
Tel: 0171 383 5993

Older people

Age Concern
1268 London Road
London SW16 4ER
Tel: 0181 679 8000

Tel: 01279 444964
Christian Council on Ageing
20 West Way
Rickmansworth
Herts WD3 2EN
Tel: 01923 774998

Grandparents' Federation
Moot House,
The Stow,
Harlow
Essex CM20 3AG

Action on Elder Abuse
1268 London Road
London SW16 4ER
Tel: 0181 679 8000

Singleness

Singularly Significant
Evangelical Alliance
Whitefield House
186 Kennington Park Road
London SE11 4BT
Tel: 0171 582 6221

Stepfamilies

National Stepfamily Association
Chapel House
18 Hatton Place
London EC1N 8JH
Tel: 0171 209 2460
Helpline: 0171 209 2464

Support for carers

Carers National Association
20-25 Glasshouse Yard
London EC1A 4JS
Tel: 0171 490 8818

National Schizophrenia Fellowship
28 Castle Street
Kingston-upon-Thames
KT1 1SS
Tel: 0181 547 3937

Alzheimer's Disease Society
Gordon House
10 Greencoat Place
London SW1P 1PH
Tel: 0171 306 0606

MIND (National Association for
  Mental Health)
Granta House
15-19 Broadway
London E15 4BQ
Tel: 0181 519 2122

Support for parents

Parent Network
44-46 Caversham Road
London NW5 2DS
Tel: 0171 485 8535

Exploring Parenthood
Latimer Education Centre
194 Freston Road
London W10 6TT
Tel: 0181 960 1678

Parentline
Endway House
The Endway
Hadleigh
Essex SS7 2AN
Tel: 01702 559900

Family Caring Trust
44 Rathfriland Road
Newry
Co Down BT34 1LD
Tel: 01693 64174

Young people

Youth Access
Magazine Business Centre
11 Newarke Street
Leicester LE1 5SS
Tel: 01533 2558763

National Youth Agency
17-23 Albion Street
Leicester LE1 6GD
Tel: 0116 2856789